Mastering Business Intelligence with MicroStrategy

Build world-class enterprise Business Intelligence solutions with MicroStrategy 10

Dmitry Anoshin
Himani Rana
Ning Ma

PUBLISHING

BIRMINGHAM - MUMBAI

Mastering Business Intelligence with MicroStrategy

First published: July 2016

Production reference: 1250716

Published by Packt Publishing Ltd.
Livery Place
35 Livery Street
Birmingham
B3 2PB, UK.
ISBN 978-1-78588-440-5

www.packtpub.com

Credits

Authors

Dmitry Anoshin

Himani Rana

Ning Ma

Reviewer

Felipe Vilela

Commissioning Editor

Veena Pagare

Acquisition Editor

Reshma Raman

Content Development Editor

Riddhi Tuljapurkar

Technical Editor

Pranav Kukreti

Copy Editor

Safis Editing

Project Coordinator

Devanshi Doshi

Proofreader

Safis Editing

Indexer

Tejal Daruwale Soni

Graphics

Abhinash Sahu

Production Coordinator

Melwyn Dsa

About the Authors

Dmitry Anoshin is a data-centric technologist and a recognized expert in building and implementing business/digital analytics solutions. He has a successful track record when it comes to implementing business and digital intelligence projects in numerous industries, including retail, finance, marketing, and e-commerce. Dmitry possesses in-depth knowledge of digital/Business Intelligence, ETL, data warehousing, and big data technologies. He has extensive experience in the data integration process and is proficient at using various data warehousing methodologies. Dmitry constantly exceeds project expectations when he works for financial, machine tool, and retail industries. He has completed a number of multinational full BI/DI solution life cycle implementation projects. With expertise in data modeling, Dmitry also has a background and business experience in multiple relation databases, OLAP systems, and NoSQL databases. He has a technical blog at `http://techbusinessintelligence.blogspot.ru/` and publishes his presentations at `http://www.slideshare.net/dimoobraznii`. In addition, he has written books for Packt Publishing, SAP Lumira Essentials and Learning Hunk. In addition, he reviewed the following books for Packt Publishing: SAP BusinessObjects Reporting Cookbook, Creating Universes with SAP BusinessObjects, and Learning SAP BusinessObjects Dashboards.

For my beautiful wife Svetlana, for my son Vasily, who is a champion of everything, and my daughter Anna, who is a little princess. Thank you for support. I love you!

Himani Rana is a senior data scientist and has been working as database developer and MicroStrategy specialist for multinational companies since 2007. She is currently pursuing her PhD in data mining and big data. She completed her master's in data mining and vehicular ad hoc networks. She has to her credit the following publication: `http://ieeexplore.ieee.org/xpl/articleDetails.jsp?arnumber=6557928`. Himani possesses in-depth knowledge of Business Intelligence and big data technologies. She specializes in insurance and financial data analysis because of her Chartered Insurance Professional (CIP) designation. In addition, she was a committee member and reviewer of *Information Systems, Technology and Management* (`http://www.springer.com/gp/book/9783642291654`) and 2011 Third International Conference on Advanced Computing (ICoAC) (`http://ieeexplore.ieee.org/xpl/mostRecentIssue.jsp?punumber=6156880`).

I would like to thank four pillars of my life: my father (V.K. Rana), my mother (Usha Rana), my husband (Rahul Jaswal) and my daughter (Samaira Jaswal), for their love and support. Also, I would like to thank everyone who helped me in completing this work.

Ning Ma is an experienced data analyst working in an insurance company. He is experienced with statistical modeling, creating executive dashboards, fraud detection, text mining and teaching. He is also knowledgeable about implementing predictive analysis in MicroStrategy. He enjoys helping business users discovering knowledge from data, by visualizing data patterns and testing hypotheses. He is passionate about producing easy-to-use data products to support business decision making. Prior to his current position, he worked in China doing IT and investment jobs. He did his computer science and economics undergraduate studies in Beijing, economics and finance graduate studies in Canada, and did research on quantitative finance in Canada. In his free time, he loves reading, electronic arts, and all kinds of outdoor activities.

I would like to express my sincere appreciation to Karen Kramer, who opened the door of MicroStrategy for me, and funded my advanced training programs. I am deeply in debt to Charlene Harris and Heather Morrison for teaching me applied MicroStrategy skills. I am also grateful to Neil Mehta for assembling the team together. I thank Dmitry Anoshin for being a great team leader, and a whip. I also thank Himani Jaswal for her help, Riddhi Tuljapurkar and Pranav Kukreti for giving me comments and for their amazing patience.

About the Reviewer

Felipe Vilela has worked for many years with system development, and then started working with BI/DW mainly using MicroStrategy. He worked with many companies in Brazil and the United States, implementing MicroStrategy projects, customizing and administrating the tool. He taught BI/DW and MicroStrategy to many companies using the company's courses and MicroStrategy's official courses. He also has a blog (www.vilelamstr.com) and is a guru in the MicroStrategy official community, Guru. He was one of the developers of MicroStrategy's official app for MicroStrategy World 2016 Miami and he has the MicroStrategy's MCEP certification.

First, I would like to thank God, who is my father and savior; my wife, who I love so much; my family, who are always there for me; and my friends.

www.PacktPub.com

eBooks, discount offers, and more

Did you know that Packt offers eBook versions of every book published, with PDF and ePub files available? You can upgrade to the eBook version at www.PacktPub.com and as a print book customer, you are entitled to a discount on the eBook copy. Get in touch with us at customercare@packtpub.com for more details.

At www.PacktPub.com, you can also read a collection of free technical articles, sign up for a range of free newsletters and receive exclusive discounts and offers on Packt books and eBooks.

https://www2.packtpub.com/books/subscription/packtlib

Do you need instant solutions to your IT questions? PacktLib is Packt's online digital book library. Here, you can search, access, and read Packt's entire library of books.

Why subscribe?

- Fully searchable across every book published by Packt
- Copy and paste, print, and bookmark content
- On demand and accessible via a web browser

Table of Contents

Preface

According to Forrester and Gartner, MicroStrategy is one of the leaders in the Enterprise Business Intelligence (BI) market. MicroStrategy constantly improves their BI product in order to meet the requirements of all sizes of businesses, from small businesses or startups and to worldwide international companies.

MicroStrategy 10 is an absolutely new product and has lots of new capabilities. It allows companies to quickly analyze their data and find business insights. It has rich functionality for all kinds of users, such as powerful desktop clients, in-memory technologies, and great visualizations capabilities. In addition, it supports modern trends of machine learning and data science because it can be integrated with analytical vendors such as SAS and IBM, and open source technologies, such as R and Python. Moreover, it allows us to use extended visualization libraries such as D3.js and others in order to create dashboards with the best user experience ever. In addition, MicroStrategy is a leader in mobile analytics, and offers the best solutions for mobile devices. Finally, MicroStrategy 10 was designed specifically for working with big data and big data technologies.

This book will be focusing on providing an extensive guide to plan how to design and develop complex BI architecture for real-world scenarios using MicroStrategy 10, best practices, and collected experience working with BI, predictive analytics, MicroStrategy, and big data.

What this book covers

Chapter 1, *Getting Started with MicroStrategy*, will talk about how to download and install MicroStrategy Analytics Enterprise as well as create a MicroStrategy repository. Moreover, the reader will learn about the various components of MicroStrategy as well as learn MicroStrategy architecture. In addition, the reader will meet the analytics project life cycle. Finally, the reader will learn about real-world business scenarios and deploy data marts in local databases.

Chapter 2, *Setting Up an Analytics Semantic Layer and Public Objects*, covers schema design; schema objects such as attributes, hierarchies, facts, and displays; and the parent-child relationship between these attributes. It will also cover public objects such as metrics, prompts, and filters, which are important in creating reports.

Chapter 3, *Building Advanced Reports and Documents*, explains the design of reports, documents, and interactive dashboards. It discusses advanced techniques such as creating banding and other custom groups using year-to-date or month-to-date transformations, and creating virtual attributes using consolidations.

Chapter 4, *Advanced Visualization Techniques*, covers graphical techniques of presenting data for analysis using maps, graphs, and advanced charts. Also, we will discuss integrating third-party ESRI map tools with MicroStrategy to create geo-based reports.

Chapter 5, *Customization of MicroStrategy*, will provide information about the MicroStrategy SDK and how to use it in order to customize the web interface or change functionalities. Despite the fact that MicroStrategy has rich functionality, it is possible to customize MicroStrategy in order to meet taught business requirements. In addition, the reader will learn how to create custom widgets and visualizations.

Chapter 6, *Predictive Analysis with MicroStrategy*, will explain native analytical functions as well as how to connect to open source data mining products in order to solve real-world business tasks. MicroStrategy maximizes the impact of BI solutions with powerful predictive analytics. MicroStrategy provides an extensive library of native analytical functions and scoring algorithms, along with an SDK to integrate with third-party and open source statistical and data mining products.

Chapter 7, *Accelerating Your Business with Mobile Analytics*, will talk about MicroStrategy mobile architecture as well as the development process, which involves visual design and deployment. In addition, the reader will learn how to deploy a mobile server. Mobile applications are ubiquitous in today's world. Mobilizing reports and analytics enables a superior level of information sharing and collaboration within an organization.

Chapter 8, *Data Discovery with MicroStrategy Desktop*, will cover how to download and install Desktop and explains the business cases that can be solved with this powerful tool. MicroStrategy Desktop is a powerful self-service data discovery tool. Moreover, the reader will learn about data discovery and Desktop capabilities, such as connecting various data sources and building interactive dashboards.

Chapter 9, *MicroStrategy System Administration*, will learn about administrator tools and duties. Moreover, the reader will learn about common errors with MicroStrategy Server and their solutions. Usually, Enterprise BI has complex architecture, a lot of users, and high load. As a result, MicroStrategy offers rich functionality, which helps us to handle the complexity of BI architecture and make our analytics solution reliable with a higher performance.

Chapter 10, *Design and Implementation of the Security Model*, will include information on the best practices of the design, deployment, and documentation of a complex security model, which can handle 1,000+ users using various capabilities of MicroStrategy. Usually, big companies have many departments and employees with various levels of access to corporate data and the enterprise data warehouse. In addition, the reader will meet various authentications methods that are supported by MicroStrategy.

Chapter 11, *Big Data Analytics with MicroStrategy*, explains big data and its relevance. Also, it will cover Hadoop and its distributions and, finally, show you how to connect to the Hadoop database and integrate MicroStrategy with Hadoop. Moreover, the reader will learn how to connect MicroStrategy to Splunk.

Chapter 12, *MicroStrategy Troubleshooting*, cover the best way of shooting any issues with the MicroStrategy platform using logs and many other things.

What you need for this book

For this book is good to have laptop or desktop. Moreover, you should have access to the Internet in order to download software. In addition, this book requires deploying a virtual machine with Linux. It is good to have some Linux knowledge. Finally, it is good to have at least 8 GB of RAM.

Who this book is for

This book is intended for Business Intelligence, data warehouse workers, ETL developers, managers, and analysts who use MicroStrategy in their daily work, and for business users who desire to make the best use of their enterprise information asset.

We highly recommend this book to anyone who is just starting out in BI, who has experience with other analytics platforms and BI fundamentals, or just wants to understand the entire BI implementation from start to finish in a complete, detailed and comprehensive fashion. In addition, it is a good knowledge base for decision makers to determine the value of using BI within their company. Hands-on practical examples, real-world scenarios, and best practices make this book an essential guide for mastering MicroStrategy 10.

Conventions

In this book, you will find a number of text styles that distinguish between different kinds of information. Here are some examples of these styles and an explanation of their meaning.

Code words in text, database table names, folder names, filenames, file extensions, pathnames, dummy URLs, user input, and Twitter handles are shown as follows: "Let's download distributive `10.2.0008.0052_10.2_GA_Linux.tar` and put it on the virtual machine with Linux `10.2.0008.0052_10.2_GA_Linux.tar`."

A block of code is set as follows:

```
<%--Adding panel around the new report bean for the second report --%>
<br><br> <web:panel name="report2Panel" language="1" useImage="true">
```

Any command-line input or output is written as follows:

```
$ pip install packagename
```

New terms and **important words** are shown in bold. Words that you see on the screen, for example, in menus or dialog boxes, appear in the text like this: "Select the **Internet Protocol Version 4 (TCP/IPv4)** entry and then click the **Properties** button."

Warnings or important notes appear in a box like this.

Tips and tricks appear like this.

Reader feedback

Feedback from our readers is always welcome. Let us know what you think about this book—what you liked or disliked. Reader feedback is important for us as it helps us develop titles that you will really get the most out of.

To send us general feedback, simply e-mail `feedback@packtpub.com`, and mention the book's title in the subject of your message.

If there is a topic that you have expertise in and you are interested in either writing or contributing to a book, see our author guide at `www.packtpub.com/authors`.

Customer support

Now that you are the proud owner of a Packt book, we have a number of things to help you to get the most from your purchase.

Downloading the color images of this book

We also provide you with a PDF file that has color images of the screenshots/diagrams used in this book. The color images will help you better understand the changes in the output. You can download this file from `https://www.packtpub.com/sites/default/files/downloads/MasteringBusinessIntelligencewithMicroStrategy_ColorImages.pdf`.

Errata

Although we have taken every care to ensure the accuracy of our content, mistakes do happen. If you find a mistake in one of our books-maybe a mistake in the text or the code-we would be grateful if you could report this to us. By doing so, you can save other readers from frustration and help us improve subsequent versions of this book. If you find any errata, please report them by visiting `http://www.packtpub.com/submit-errata`, selecting your book, clicking on the **Errata Submission Form** link, and entering the details of your errata. Once your errata are verified, your submission will be accepted and the errata will be uploaded to our website or added to any list of existing errata under the Errata section of that title.

To view the previously submitted errata, go to `https://www.packtpub.com/books/content/support` and enter the name of the book in the search field. The required information will appear under the **Errata** section.

Piracy

Piracy of copyrighted material on the Internet is an ongoing problem across all media. At Packt, we take the protection of our copyright and licenses very seriously. If you come across any illegal copies of our works in any form on the Internet, please provide us with the location address or website name immediately so that we can pursue a remedy.

Please contact us at `copyright@packtpub.com` with a link to the suspected pirated material.

We appreciate your help in protecting our authors and our ability to bring you valuable content.

Questions

If you have a problem with any aspect of this book, you can contact us at `questions@packtpub.com`, and we will do our best to address the problem.

1
Getting Started with MicroStrategy

The modern market for **Business Intelligence (BI)** tools is full of various products with different advantages and disadvantages. For example, some of them are easy to deploy but hard to maintain. Another has strong data discovery capabilities but restricted data governance and struggles with complex enterprise data models. MicroStrategy 10 is one of the leading platforms on the market, can handle all data analytics demands, and offers a powerful solution. It combines self-service BI, data discovery and preparation, and big data exploration, bringing the vision of a single-vendor solution within reach of BI and analytics leaders. It combines data discovery and enterprise BI in a single platform, allowing organizations to invest in a single vendor that provides both agile self-service BI and traditional reporting, with integration between the two.

This chapter will cover:

- BI best practices
- BI maturity model
- MicroStrategy 10 new features
- Deploying MicroStrategy 10 on top of Linux
- Deploying business case

Modern BI

According to a Gartner survey conducted among 2,800 CIOs of top companies, BI and analytics remain the number one investment priority. MicroStrategy has done a great job since 1991. MicroStrategy is a leader in Enterprise BI and can handle the modern demand for BI and analytics.

MicroStrategy 10 can easily handle modern hot topics such as big data analytics, predictive analytics, and mobile analytics. It is easily scalable and secure.

The main roles of BI are to discover new opportunities, improve processes, help to make the right decisions at the right time and reduce operational costs. As a result, BI tools should improve business performance and help to meet organizational goals, such as higher revenue, lower costs, and decreased risks.

BI market

Nowadays, we see lots of BI tools. Sometimes, we have to ask "What is the best BI tool?" In order to find the answer, we can look at reports from two main analytical agencies: Gartner and Forrester. Here is the Gartner Magic Quadrant for BI & Analytics Platforms for 2015:

This quadrant shows us the leaders in the market. But do not trust this rating, because it is a kind of marketing. The best way to understand the pros and cons of any BI tool is practically; just download and install a trial version and play with it. Most tools, especially the leading ones, have common functionality or similar features. A good example is the interface of Tableau. It is so good that other companies have tried to reproduce it in their own products.

Maturity level of the organization

Every organization uses BI. The question is, just how good are they? Even if the organization does not have BI at all, it at least uses spreadsheets to consolidate numbers. This is also a kind of BI. We can observe many levels of BI maturity. Let us try to demonstrate this, based on four phases shown here:

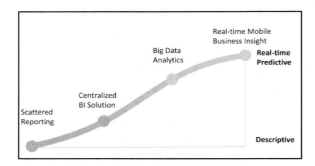

The first phase is **Scattered Reporting**, in other words, the organization doesn't have any BI solution and even doesn't try one. Various departments grab data from transaction systems and try to figure out what's going on. We see this situation especially in startups or small companies. It is the most inefficient way to measure business and make decisions.

 If you are at the beginning of your analytics journey, then we highly recommend you meet **Lean Analytics** methodology.

The next phase is **Centralized BI Solution**. It is the most common approach nowadays, when organizations build corporate data warehouses, integrate data from internal sources and systems, deploy a BI solution, and try to force everyone to use a *single point of truth*. It is a long journey to leave this phase, and sometimes it is an endless process because business constantly changes.

The third phase is **Big Data Analytics**. Despite the fact that the term **big data** is almost gone, we still use it, because it is a very popular phrase that means lots of unstructured data such as social data, open source data, and so on. In other words, organizations try to enrich their internal data in order to find more insights. As a result, companies are forced to use new technologies such as Hadoop or NoSQL datastores. In addition, companies start to use machine learning technologies and try to make them part of their BI framework.

The last phase is **Real-time Mobile Business Insight**. This phase means that finally organizations can focus on the speed of delivery of business insights, their mobility, and predictive capabilities.

Of course, this maturity model is not standard, we just tried to structure BI maturity levels based on our experience. MicroStrategy can handle even the final phase, a real competitive advantage.

BI project life cycle

Every BI project has its own life cycle. Let us look at a common life cycle:

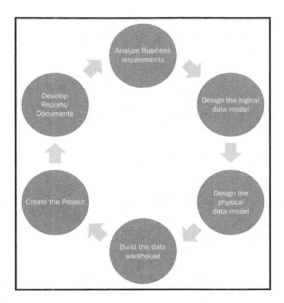

The first step is **Analyze Business requirements**, which means that we should gather the business requirements and transform them into functional and non-functional specifications, create a template for reports, and so on. The next step is **Design the logical data model**, where we build a logical data model based on business requirements, which shows the business entities and the relationships between them. The third step is **Design the physical data model**, where we transform the logical data model into a physical data model which defines the structure of the data warehouse. The fourth step is **Build the data warehouse**. In this step, we create the data warehouse, build data marts, and load data.

On the fifth step, **Create the Project**, we start to work directly in MicroStrategy, where we define schema, attributes, facts, hierarchies and so on. All this information is stored in metadata, the core of MicroStrategy, in a relation database. The sixth step is **Develop Reports/Documents** and of course dashboards. In addition, we share our insights across the organization using various channels such as email, FTP, and so on.

Meet MicroStrategy 10

MicroStrategy is a market leader in BI products. It has rich functionality in order to meet the requirements of modern businesses. In 2015, MicroStrategy provided a new release of MicroStrategy, version 10. It offers both agility and governance like no other BI product. In addition, it is easy to use and enterprise ready. At the same time, it is great for both IT and business. In other words, MicroStrategy 10 offers an analytics platform that combines an easy and empowering user experience, together with enterprise-grade performance, management, and security capabilities. It is true bimodal BI and moves seamlessly between styles:

- Data discovery and visualization
- Enterprise reporting and dashboards
- In-memory high performance BI
- Scales from departments to enterprises
- Administration and security

MicroStrategy 10 consists of three main products: **MicroStrategy Desktop**, **MicroStrategy Mobile** and **MicroStrategy Web**.

MicroStrategy Desktop lets users start discovering and visualizing data instantly. It is available for Mac and PC. It allows users to connect, prepare, discover, and visualize data. In addition, we can easily promote to a MicroStrategy Server. Moreover, MicroStrategy Desktop has a brand new HTML5 interface and includes all connection drivers. It allows us to use data blending, data preparation, and data enrichment. Finally, it has powerful advanced analytics and can be integrated with R.

To cut a long story short, we want to notice the main changes of the new BI platform. All developers keep the same functionality, the looks as well as architect the same. All changes are about web interface and Intelligence Server. Let's look closer at what MicroStrategy 10 can show us.

MicroStrategy 10 expands the analytical ecosystem by using third-party toolkits such as:

- **Data visualization libraries**: We can easily plug in and use any visualization from the expanding range of Java libraries
- **Statistical toolkits**: R, SAS, SPSS, KXEN, and others
- **Geolocation data visualization**: This uses mapping capabilities to visualize and interact with location data

MicroStrategy 10 has more than 25 new data sources that we can connect to quickly and simply. In addition, it allows us to build reports on top of other BI tools, such as SAP Business Objects, Cognos, and Oracle BI. It has a new connector to Hadoop, which uses the native connector. Moreover, it allows us to blend multiple data sources in-memory.

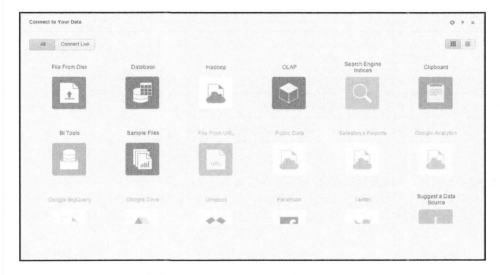

We want to notice that MicroStrategy 10 has got reach functionality for work with data such as:

- Streamlined workflows to parse and prepare data
- Multi-table in-memory support from different sources
- Automatically parse and prepare data with every refresh
- 100+ inbuilt functions to profile and clean data
- Create custom groups on the fly without coding

In terms of connection to Hadoop, most BI products use Hive or Impala ODBC drivers in order to use SQL to get data from Hadoop. However, this method is bad in terms of performance. MicroStrategy 10 queries directly against Hadoop. As a result, it is up to 50 times faster than via ODBC.

Let's look at some of the main technical changes that have significantly improved MicroStrategy. The platform is now faster than ever before, because it doesn't have a two-billion-row limit on in-memory datasets and allows us to create analytical cubes up to 16 times bigger in size. It publishes cubes dramatically faster. Moreover, MicroStrategy 10 has higher data throughput and cubes can be loaded in parallel 4 times faster with multi-threaded parallel loading. In addition, the in-memory engine allows us to create cubes 80 times larger than before, and we can access data from cubes 50% faster, by using up to 8 parallel threads. Look at the following table, where we compare in-memory cube functionality in version 9 versus version 10:

Feature	Ver. 9	Ver. 10
Data volume	100 GB	~2TB
Number of rows	2 billion	200 billion
Load rate	8 GB/hour	~200 GB/hour
Data model	Star schema	Any schema, tabular or multiple sets

In order to make the administration of MicroStrategy more effective in the new version, MicroStrategy Operation Manager was released. It gives MicroStrategy administrators powerful development tools to monitor, automate, and control systems. Operations Manager gives us:

- Centralized management in a web browser
- Enterprise Manager console within Tool
- Triggers and 24/7 alerts
- System health monitors
- Server management
- Multiple environment administration

MicroStrategy 10 education and certification

MicroStrategy 10 offers new training courses that can be conducted offline in a training center, or online at http://www.microstrategy.com/us/services/education. We believe that certification is a good thing on your journey. The following certifications now exist for version 10:

- MicroStrategy 10 Certified Associated Analyst
- MicroStrategy 10 Certified Application Designer
- MicroStrategy 10 Certified Application Developer
- MicroStrategy 10 Certified Administrator

After passing all of these exams, you will become a MicroStrategy 10 Application Engineer. More details can be found here: http://www.microstrategy.com/Strategy/media/downloads/training-events/MicroStrategy-certification-matrix_v10.pdf.

History of MicroStrategy

Let us briefly look at the history of MicroStrategy, which began in 1991:

- 1991: Released first BI product, which allowed users to create graphical views and analyses of information data
- 2000: Released MicroStrategy 7 with a web interface
- 2003: First to release a fully integrated reporting tool, combining list reports, BI-style dashboards, and interface analyses in a single module.
- 2005: Released MicroStrategy 8, including one-click actions and drag-and-drop dashboard creation
- 2009: Released MicroStrategy 9, delivering a seamless consolidated path from department to enterprise BI
- 2010: Unveiled new mobile BI capabilities for iPad and iPhone, and was featured on the iTunes Bestseller List
- 2011: Released MicroStrategy Cloud, the first SaaS offering from a major BI vendor
- 2012: Released Visual Data Discovery and groundbreaking new security platform, Usher
- 2013: Released expanded Analytics Platform and free Analytics Desktop client

- 2014: Announced availability of MicroStrategy Analytics via **Amazon Web Services** (**AWS**)
- 2015: MicroStrategy 10 was released, the first ever enterprise analytics solution for centralized and decentralized BI

Deploying MicroStrategy 10

We know only one way to master MicroStrategy, through practical exercises. Let's start by downloading and deploying MicroStrategy 10.2.

Overview of training architecture

In order to master MicroStrategy and learn about some BI considerations, we need to download the all-important software, deploy it, and connect to a network. During the preparation of the training environment, we will cover the installation of MicroStrategy on a Linux operating system. This is very good practice, because many people work with Windows and are not familiar with Linux, so this chapter will provide additional knowledge of working with Linux, as well as installing MicroStrategy and a web server. Look at the training architecture:

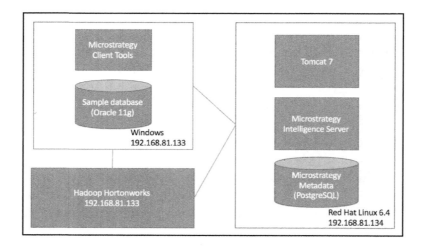

There are three main components:

1. **Red Hat Linux 6.4**: Used for deploying the web server and Intelligence Server.
2. **Windows machine**: Uses MicroStrategy Client and Oracle database.
3. **Virtual machine with Hadoop**: Ready virtual machine with Hadoop, which will connect to MicroStrategy using a brand new connection.

In the real world, we should use separate machines for every component, and sometimes several machines in order to run one component. This is called **clustering**. Let's create a virtual machine.

Creating a Red Hat Linux virtual machine

Let's create a virtual machine with Red Hat Linux, which will host our Intelligence Server:

- Go to `http://www.redhat.com/` and create an account
- Go to the software download center: `https://access.redhat.com/downloads`
- Download RHEL: `https://access.redhat.com/downloads/content/69/ver=/rhel-7/7.2/x86_64/product-software`
- Choose `Red Hat Enterprise Linux Server`
- Download `Red Hat Enterprise Linux 6.4 x86_64`
- Choose `Binary DVD`

Now we can create a virtual machine with RHEL 6.4. We have several options in order to choose the software for deploying virtual machine. In our case, we will use a VMware workstation.

Before starting to deploy a new VM, we should adjust the default settings, such as increasing RAM and HDD, and adding one more network card in order to connect the external environment with the MicroStrategy client and sample database. In addition, we should create a new network.

When the deployment of the RHEL virtual machine is complete, we should activate a subscription in order to install the required packages. Let us do this with one command in the terminal:

```
# subscription-manager register --username <username> --password <password> --auto-attach
```

Performing prerequisites for MicroStrategy 10

According to the installation and configuration guide, we should deploy all necessary packages. In order to install them, we should execute them under the root:

```
# su
# yum install compat-libstdc++-33.i686
# yum install libXp.x86_64
# yum install elfutils-devel.x86_64
# yum install libstdc++-4.4.7-3.el6.i686
# yum install krb5-libs.i686
# yum install nss-pam-ldapd.i686
# yum install ksh.x86_64
```

Moreover, we should change the parameters of the kernel:

```
# nano/etc/sysctl.conf
kernel.sem=250 32000 32 2048
kernel.shmmni = 4096
vm.max_map_count=5242880
```

Then, save and reboot.

Installing MicroStrategy 10 Intelligence Server

In order to download MicroStrategy software, we should already have an account on the MicroStrategy Resource Portal at https://resource.microstrategy.com, or we can create one using a corporate email address. Even if we do not have a license for MicroStrategy, we can obtain one for 30 days. That is enough to finish this book and learn the new features of MicroStrategy 10.

MicroStrategy 10.2 is available, and we are going to use this version in the book.

Let's download distributive `10.2.0008.0052_10.2_GA_Linux.tar` and put it on the virtual machine with Linux `10.2.0008.0052_10.2_GA_Linux.tar`.

Let's create a folder for MicroStrategy using the root user and change its rights in order to extract the archive into this folder:

```
# mkdir mstr10
# chmod 777 mstr10
```

Then we should extract the MicroStrategy distributive into our new folder. We can use the default Archive Manager.

After successful extraction, we should create four folders for MicroStrategy, in order to deploy the software and write the installation logs.

Using the root user, we can run the following commands:

```
# mkdir /mstr10/microstrategy
# mkdir /mstr10/microstrategy_home
# mkdir /mstr10/microstrategy_logs
# mkdir /mstr10/microstrategy_health_agent
```

Installation process

By default, there are three methods of installation for MicroStrategy Server:

- **GUI**: The most common approach, using a graphical interface and navigation with a mouse
- **Command line**: The approach for terminal-only machines
- **Silent installation**: Automatic installation process that does not need human participation, but it is important to think about parameters and settings

In Red Hat, we have a GUI and can use its benefits. Let's install:

```
# cd /mstr10/Installations/QueryReportingAnalysis_Linux
# ./setup.sh
user name Microstrategy
name masteringbi
```

Copy and paste your license key.

Choose the destination locations that we have already created:

- **Home directory**: /mstr10/microstrategy_home
- **Install directory**: /mstr10/microstrategy
- **Log directory**: /mstr10/microstrategy_logs
- **Health agent**: /mstr10/microstrategy_health_agent

All the other parameters we can leave as is.

Configuring Intelligence Server

After successful installation of MicroStrategy 10.2, we should set up a MicroStrategy repository and connect it to the Intelligence Server. In our case, we will use a PostgreSQL database on the RHEL virtual machine for the repository.

Installing a PostgreSQL database

Let's download and install the PostgreSQL database server:

```
# yum install postgresql-server
# service postgresql initdb
# chkconfig postgresql on
# service postgresql start
# s
# psql
```

Creating a metadata database

Let's create a new database in PostgreSQL for MicroStrategy metadata. In order to do this, we should go to the terminal and run the following:

```
# psql
# CREATE DATABASE mstrmd;
# CREATE USER mstr PASSWORD 'happy2016';
# GRANT ALL ON DATABASE mstrmd TO mstr;
```

In addition, we should register the plpgsql language in our new database:

```
# \c mstrmd
# CREATE TRUSTED LANGUAGE plpgsql;
```

By default, PostgreSQL uses IDENT-based authentication, and this will never allow you to log in with a username and password. We should change the method of authentication by modifying the pg_hba.conf file. Go to this folder:

```
# cd /var/lib/pgsql/data
# nano pg_hba.conf
```

Replace IDENT on trust and restart PostgreSQL:

```
# service postgresql restart
```

Creating a metadata data source

Using the MicroStrategy connectivity wizard, we can create a new DSN. In order to open the wizard, we should run the following commands:

```
# cd /mstr10/microstrategy_home/bin
# ./mstrconnectwiz
```

Let's choose PostgreSQL ODBC driver and fill in the form with our credentials:

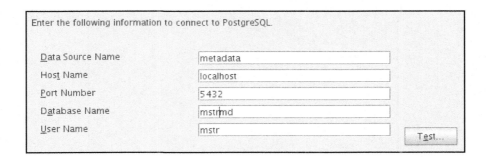

MicroStrategy has a configuration file that keeps all DSNs. We can create a new DSN directly in this file. We can look at our new DSN like this:

```
# vi /mstr10/microstrategy_home/odbc.ini
```

Here is our DSN metadata. In addition, we can configure the parameters of our connection in order to increase performance.

Creating metadata tables

In order to create metadata tables in the brand new database, we should run Configuration Wizard:

```
# cd /mstr10/microstrategy_home/bin
# ./mstrcfgwiz
```

During this process, wizard will automatically:

- Create metadata tables and history list tables
- Configure Intelligence Server

MicroStrategy metadata is a core piece of software. In other words, the number of tables in a database that contain a definition of all MicroStrategy objects.

In Configuration Wizard, we should create a new database and choose our DSN:

The next step is the configuration of Intelligence Server using fresh metadata tables. We can use `masteringbi` as a server definition. After successful configuration we can close wizard and deploy MicroStrategy Web.

Installation of MicroStrategy Web

We need a web server in order to deploy MicroStrategy Web and other components, such as Mobile Server and Operations Manager. For this book, we have chosen the Tomcat web server as our web application server.

Web application server installation

Let us install Tomcat on our RHEL server. Open the terminal and give the following commands:

1. Install Java if it is needed:

```
# yum install java-1.8.0-openjdk
# java -version
openjdk version "1.8.0_65"
```

2. Download and deploy the Tomcat server:

```
# cd /tmp
# wget
  http://www.us.apache.org/dist/tomcat/tomcat-7/v7.0.67/
  bin/apache-tomcat-7.0.67.tar.gz
# tar xzf apache-tomcat-7.0.67.tar.gz
# mv apache-tomcat-7.0.67 /usr/local/tomcat7
```

3. Run Tomcat:

```
# cd /usr/local/tomcat7
# ./bin/startup.sh
```

4. Create a Tomcat user for MicroStrategy Web:

```
# cd /usr/local/tomcat7/conf
# nano tomcat-users.xml
  <role rolename="admin"/>
  <role rolename="manager-gui"/>
  <user username="admin" password="admin" roles="admin,manager-gui"/>
```

5. Then, restart Tomcat.

In order to access Tomcat, we should go to `http://localhost:8080/`.

Deploying WAR files

Now we can deploy MicroStrategy Web and Operations Manager on a brand new Tomcat server. Let's do it:

```
# cp /mstr10/microstrategy/OperationsManager/MicroStrategyWeb.war
  /usr/local/tomcat7/webapps
# cp /mstr10/microstrategy/OperationsManager/MicroStrategyOM.war
  /usr/local/tomcat7/webapps
```

Then we need restart Tomcat:

```
# /usr/local/tomcat7/bin/shutdown.sh
# /usr/local/tomcat7/bin/startup.sh
```

After deploying, we should go to the web admin:

`http://localhost:8080/MicroStrategy/servlet/mstrWebAdmin`

Then, connect to our server. We can do this just by adding the localhost server. In properties, we should mark that it automatically connects to Intelligence Server.

Later in the book, we will create projects and they will be available here:

`http://localhost:8080/MicroStrategy/servlet/mstrWeb`

In addition, we can go to Operations Manager in order to configure it:

`http://localhost:8080/MicroStrategyOM/servlet/mstrOM`

 If you change the war filename, you will have to use a different URL. For example, `mstr.war` the URL will be `http://localhost:8080/mstr`.

The Operation Manager will be configured in `Chapter 9`, *MicroStrategy System Administration*.

We have finished the installation and configuration of Intelligence Server. Now we need to install the MicroStrategy Client tools on the Windows machine.

We should open a port in the firewall for Tomcat on the Linux machine, in order for the Windows machine to access it:

```
# nano /etc/sysconfig/iptables
```

Add a new line for port `8080`:

```
-A INPUT -m state --state NEW -m tcp -p tcp --dport 8080 -j ACCEPT
```

We should also open a port for Intelligence Server:

```
-A INPUT -m state --state NEW -m tcp -p tcp --dport 34952 -j ACCEPT
```

Then, restart the service:

```
# service iptables restart
```

As a result, we can access MicroStrategy from Windows.

Creating a network

According to our training architecture, we will use at least two machines. One is a Windows machine for client tools and the Oracle database, and a Linux machine for Intelligence Server and the PostgreSQL repository database. Let's look at how we can quickly create a network. This knowledge is very important for BI guys, because usually BI software has complex architecture and communicates with each other through the network. In our small example, the reader can learn basic considerations for building a network between several machines. Let's build a network using VMware:

1. At the top of the VMware Workstation desktop, select **Edit** and then select **Virtual Network Editor**.
2. Change the settings on this screen to match these:

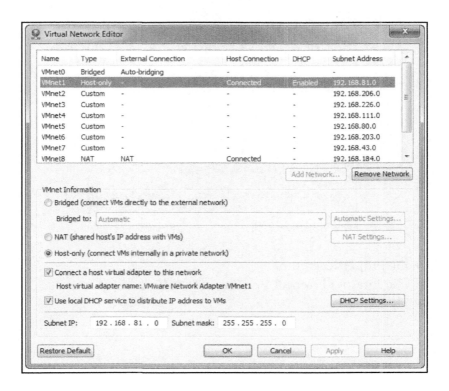

3. Enable **Use local DHCP service to distribute IP address to VMs**.
4. Click the **OK** button. Now the preset IP address included in the images should work for VMware Workstation and VMware Player.
5. Open Control Panel and locate the Network and Sharing Center option. Double-click on it.
6. The private network is the bridged adapter and the public network is host-only. If your image is not making connections, look at the properties of the public network. Select the **Local Area Connection 2** link:

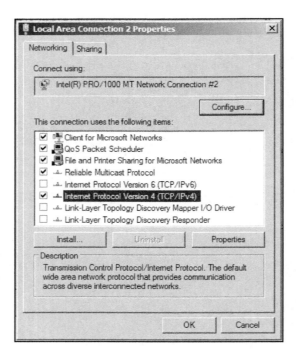

7. Click the **Properties** button.
8. Select the **Internet Protocol Version 4 (TCP/IPv4)** entry and then click the **Properties** button.

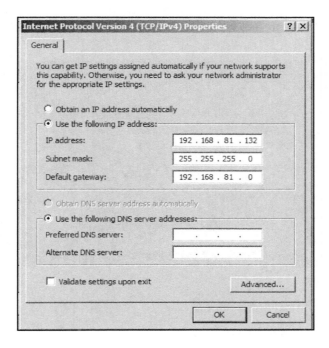

Now we should change the network for Red Hat also. Let's do it:

1. Go to the terminal and run the `system-config-network` utility to change the IP address:

```
# system-config-network
```

2. With the red highlight on the Device Configuration option, press the *Enter* key.
3. If you need to update the IP address, use the cursor keys to move up and down through the fields and then you can make the update. Use the cursor keys or the *Tab* key to move to the **Ok** button and press the *Enter* key or the *spacebar* to select **Ok**.

After you work your way back to the first screen, you'll have to use the *Tab* key to navigate to the **Save** & **Quit** button:

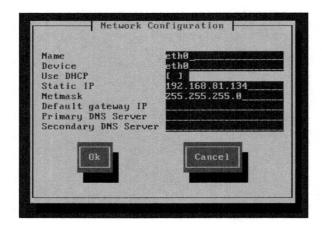

4. Restart the network service:

    ```
    # service network restart
    ```

5. Check the result:

    ```
    # ifconfig
    ```

As a result, the Linux and Windows machines now live on one network and can easy communicate with each other. Using this approach, we can connect other machines that run other software. For example, we could run Oracle on a separate machine. In addition, we can create a cluster of several machines running MicroStrategy.

MicroStrategy prefers up to four nodes in a cluster, but you can install more than four if you want.

Now we can install the MicroStrategy Client tools and connect Intelligence Server.

Installing MicroStrategy 10 tools

One of the simplest tasks is installing the client tools on the Windows machine. We should install the following software:

- MicroStrategy Analyst
- MicroStrategy Developer
- MicroStrategy Architect
- MicroStrategy Server Administrator
- MicroStrategy Object Manager
- MicroStrategy Command Manager
- MicroStrategy System Manager
- MicroStrategy Integrity Manager

We should connect to our Intelligence Server, which is based on RHEL. Let's run Developer on port `34952` with the server name as the IP address `192.168.81.134`. There are not any projects yet, but soon we will create one good project using our great expertise.

Installing Oracle database

For our book, we decided to use Oracle 11g because it is the most popular RDBMS in the world. We can download Oracle from `http://www.oracle.com/technetwork/databas e/enterprise-edition/downloads/112010-win64soft-094461.html`.

In our case, we will install it on the same machine as MicroStrategy, in order to save resources. In the real world, we should use a separate server. The installation process is pretty simple and straightforward. Just download the software and run `setup.exe`.

Deploying data in Oracle database

The last step before finishing this chapter is to deploy our sample database, which we will use throughout this book in order to build advanced visualizations, dashboards, and many other things.

There are SQL files in the attachment that comes with this book. We are going to deploy these in our Oracle database:

- `Schema.sql`
- `dw.sql`

In order to deploy these files in the Oracle database, we should:

1. Run SQLPlus.
2. Connect to the Oracle database as a system user.

3. Run these commands:

```
@<Full_path>/Schema.sql;
@<Full_path>/dw.sql;
```

In the next chapter, we will create a schema based on this database.

BI tips

We want to share some of our tips that help to improve perception of BI users and make their lives a little bit easier. We also want to share some great books and training that can help to increase skills and expertise, in order to grow within your organization or find a better job.

BI skills

We want to share some important skills from experienced BI developers. These cover several areas:

- **BI software**: There are many BI tools on the market but they have many features in common. That's why it is good to master MicroStrategy, then it is easy to understand how others work.
- **Dimensional modeling**: This approach is the most popular design schema.
- **Data modeling**: Before starting to develop schema, we should understand the corporate data model, that's why we should learn how to read models.
- **Databases**: Nowadays, relational databases are the most popular choice for data warehouses. As BI tools, there are plenty of databases, but all of them run SQL and have different advantages and disadvantages.
- **Network knowledge**: Usually BI tools use three-tier architecture; as a result it is good to know how to set up the network, open the network ports, and so on.
- **Visualization**: It is a well-known fact that graphical representation of data is the most effective way to represent data.
- **Security**: There are many users who work with BI and have different levels of access. It is very important to understand security topics and different ways of authenticating users.

- **Unix operational systems**: Usually big companies prefer to use Unix systems as their main operating system for software, because they are reliable. However, they have a console or a terminal, which is why it is good to have knowledge of working with such operating systems.

> According to the MicroStrategy documentation, it runs faster in a Linux environment.

There is no secret to how to master BI. There is only one way – constantly learn through reading and technical exercises. www.packtpub.com offers us plenty of technical books that can help us to solve any technical issues.

The most critical skill for a BI developer is to quickly find a solution using Google. It is impossible to store all relevant information in our head, but we can easily Google it and find the right solution. Do not hesitate to ask Google if you are struggling.

BI users' development

One hot topic is the happiness of business users. Usually they are not technical guys and often struggle with report development. Another difficulty is that there are many attributes and metrics in the data warehouse, and sometimes we can't use them in one query because it could produce cross joins and even crash the database. There is only one solution – constantly train them and give them the opportunity to learn the technical and business sides of BI solutions. As a result, the BI department should develop two streams of training – business and technical. Technical training relates to BI software. For example, our book is an advanced training for MicroStrategy. At the same time, business users should learn different business cases. For example, how they can build reports in order to compare revenue for 2014 and 2015 across all branches in Canada?

The main challenge of this training is to motivate business users. But there is a lack of time to learn. As a result, they make wrong decisions on inaccurate data. In order to involve them in the training process, we want to share one of our success stories.

One of the authors implemented BI Academy. It was an internal brand; users who successfully finish the training and pass the internal exam get a branded T-shirt:

In order to make the training process fun, the author used special software that offers the opportunity to create cartoons:

These guys were very popular because they helped to solve real business problems. Another piece of advice is to contact heads of department and encourage them to make this online training mandatory for employees. There are some training courses based on this approach on YouTube: `https://www.youtube.com/channel/UCAGzL89m1L3c675hn7DE2Uw`

Or you can see the MicroStrategy example here:

`https://www.youtube.com/channel/UCLDoF-D_CH51CfGVEn8PBvQ`

BI portal

The final thing that is good to have in an organization is a BI portal. When companies run BI solutions, they do it for users. Usually, BI users are not technical. The best practice is to build BI and integrate it into an intranet website. For example, in the attachment to this chapter, there is a file called `sweet home.html`. It is not a BI portal, but it demonstrates the idea very well. It helps business users and developers to quickly get the latest news about BI changes and innovations. Moreover, it links to BI environments and training. For example, the company can use Microsoft SharePoint because it is easy to deploy, and we can easily integrate it with MicroStrategy and Office products.

Summary

In this chapter, we talked about BI and shared our thoughts on some BI-related topics, as well as some tips that can improve the BI ecosystem. We then met MicroStrategy 10 and its new features. Finally, we deployed MicroStrategy 10 on top of Red Hat Linux and Tomcat. In addition, we deployed Oracle and a sample database.

In the next chapter, we are going to create a semantic layer and learn best practices for Oracle integration, as well as the creation of schema and schema objects.

2

Setting Up an Analytics Semantic Layer and Public Objects

Semantics in general means the meaning of a message behind the words, so when we say semantic in terms of BI, it means the meaning of data from the user's perspective. It is the keystone of any data warehouse project, as it allows better understanding of requirements, the design of successive data models, and a link between the physical data model and the reporting tool, in our case MicroStrategy. In the previous chapter, we learned about setting up an environment for MicroStrategy, so in this chapter we can dig deeper and understand about the semantic layer and the objects needed to present data to an end user.

This chapter will cover:

- BI architecture
- The project design process
- Defining schema objects
  - Creating attributes
  - Defining parent-child relationships
  - Building hierarchies
  - Creating facts
- Defining public objects
  - Creating simple and complex metrics
  - Adding filters
  - Creating prompts

BI architecture

BI is all about delivering timely and relevant information to the right level of audience, which helps them to make an appropriate decision. In this section, we will learn about BI architecture and the components involved in it.

Components of BI architecture

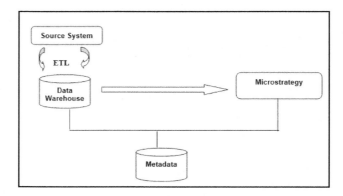

Source system: This is any stored data that will be used for BI projects. It could be a database, mainframe system or flat files, or any other system that stores **Online Transaction Processing (OLTP)** data. This is where data is stored in its raw form.

ETL: This process then pulls the data from the source system and prepares it for the data warehouse. It involves three steps:

- **Extract**: The process of reading data from source systems
- **Transform**: The process of converting data from its previous form to the form it needs to be in, either by combining data from multiple sources or by applying business rules and logic
- **Load**: The process of writing data into the target database, that is, the data warehouse

Data warehouse: This is typically an **Online Analytical Processing (OLAP)** system. It is the way to store data to be used in the analysis. Data can be stored in regular databases such as MS SQL Server, Oracle, and so on.

BI Platform: In our case, this is MicroStrategy. Some of the main components of MicroStrategy are:

- **Metadata**: This is data about data. What that means is that it contains information that facilitates the retrieval of data from the data warehouse using the MicroStrategy application. It stores MicroStrategy object definitions and maps them to the data warehouse's content. The MicroStrategy application uses metadata to translate user requests into SQL queries, and the results from SQL queries into MicroStrategy objects. Therefore, we can say metadata acts as a central repository for all the object definitions, such as facts, attributes, filters, and so on.

- **MicroStrategy applications**: These provide the ability to present the data in a superior form for analysis. Users can create reports, grids, graphs, and dashboards, and access them via MicroStrategy Web, Desktop, and Mobile, and MS Office too. It supports in-memory analytics with intelligent cubes. In addition to this, users can use a **software development kit (SDK)** to customize the application and integrate with other applications.

- **MicroStrategy Architect:** This project design tool allows users to define all the required components to build a project from a centralized interface.

At this point, we know about all the components, but how these components come together is the next thing we will learn in the project design process.

The project design process

Project design is not just about creating a project in MicroStrategy architect; it involves several steps and thorough analysis, such as how data is stored in the data warehouse, what reports the user wants based on the data, and so on. The following are the steps involved in our project design process:

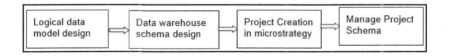

Logical data model design

Once the user have business requirements documented, the user must create a fact qualifier matrix to identify the attributes, facts, and hierarchies, which are the building blocks of any logical data model.

An example of a fact qualifier is as follows:

	A	B	C	D	E	F	G
1	Facts / Dimensions	Country	Product	Company	Department	Employee	Date
2	OrderQuantity	X	X				X
3	SalesAmount	X	X				X
4	SalesAmountQuota	X			X		X
5	Revenue	X		X	X		X
6	Totalcalls					X	X
7	Current year MTD sale	X	X				X
8	Prior year MTD sale	X	X				X
9							

A logical data model is created based on the source systems, and designed before defining a data warehouse. So, it's good for seeing which objects the users want and checking whether the objects are in the source systems. It represents the definition, characteristics, and relationships of the data. This graphical representation of information is easily understandable by business users too. A logical data model graphically represents the following concepts:

- **Attributes**: Provides a detailed description of the data
- **Facts**: Provides numerical information about the data
- **Hierarchies**: Provides relationships between data

Data warehouse schema design

Physical data warehouse design is based on the logical data model and represents the storage and retrieval of data from the data warehouse. Here, we determine the optimal schema design, which ensures reporting performance and maintenance. The key components of a physical data warehouse schema are columns and tables:

- **Columns:** These store attribute and fact data. The following are the three types of columns:
    - **ID column**: Stores the ID for an attribute
    - **Description column**: Stores text description of the attribute
    - **Fact column**: Stores fact data

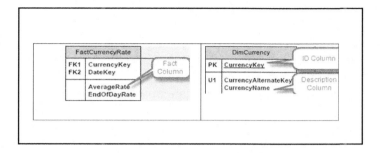

- **Tables:** Physical grouping of related data. The following are the types of tables:
- **Lookup tables**: Store information about attributes, such as IDs and descriptions:

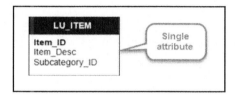

- **Relationship tables**: Store information about the relationship between two or more attributes:

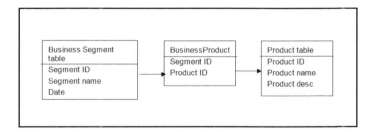

So, here the **BusinessProduct** table is a bridge table between Business Segment and Product table.

- **Fact tables**: Store factual data and the level of aggregation, which is defined based on the attributes of the fact table. They contain base fact columns or derived fact columns:
    - **Base fact**: Stores the data at the lowest possible level of detail:

    - **Aggregate fact**: Stores data at a higher or summarized level of detail:

The following diagram shows a simple data warehouse model for our chapter:

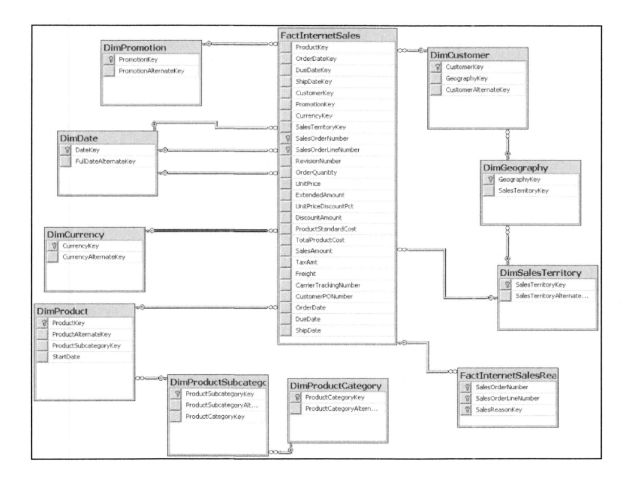

Project creation in MicroStrategy architecture

Once we have a solid foundation, a good logical and physical model design, you can move on to the creation of the actual project in MicroStrategy.

The steps to be followed for project creation are listed here.

Creating a data source

In our chapter, we are going to use Oracle 11g, which we installed in `Chapter 1`, *Getting Started with MicroStrategy*. There are lots of best practices for integrating Oracle and MicroStrategy, such as:

- Enable use of temporary tables for intermediate result sets
- Enable SQL global optimization to reduce the number of SQL passes generated in MicroStrategy
- Instead of ANSI syntax, use Oracle join syntax
- Enable set operator optimization to combine multiple subqueries into a single subquery
- Use bitmapped indexing for performance and storage saving
- Allow Oracle to identify queries coming from MicroStrategy
- Create a single BIGFILE scratch tablespace for MSTR intermediate tables

Users can find more information using this link:

```
https://community.microstrategy.com/mxret26282/attachments/mxret26282/d
atabase/365/1/Integrating%20MicroStrategy%20Analytics%20Platform%20with
%20Oracle.pdf
```

It is very important to use these best practice, because they help to improve performance by reducing execution time.

Here are the creation steps:

1. Navigate to the MicroStrategy bin directory in Linux and type `./mstrconnectwiz.`
2. Click on the **Test** button, enter the username and password, and click **OK**.
3. Enter all the required information and click finish to create a data source:

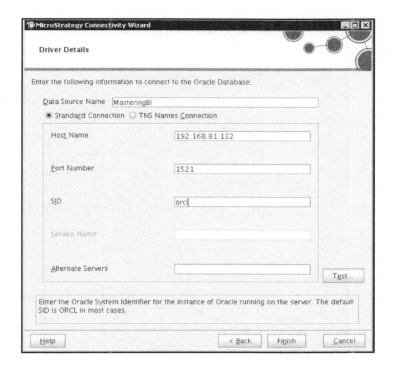

Creating a project

The user can now connect to a data warehouse and everything a user creates will be automatically stored in the metadata repository. There are two ways to create a project in MicroStrategy. These are:

- Using the project creation assistant
- Using MicroStrategy Architect

Using the project creation assistant

1. In MicroStrategy Desktop, click on **Schema** | **Create new project**.
2. Click **Create Project**. On the new project screen, enter the project name and click **OK**:

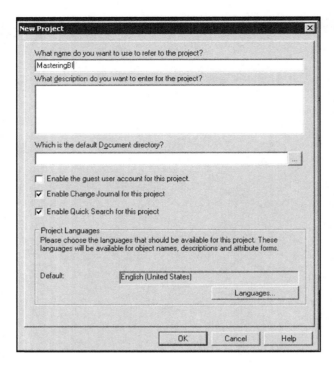

3. This creates the project, enabling the **Select tables from the Warehouse Catalogue** option:

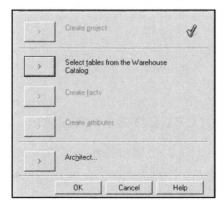

4. Click on **Select tables from the Warehouse Catalogue**. This opens the **Warehouse Database Instance** created by the user in the previous step; select the primary database instance for the project from the dropdown:

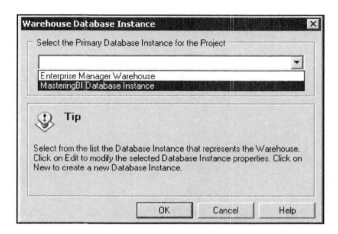

5. Click **OK** after database selection, move the tables from tables available to tables being used, and click **Save** and close in the top-left of the window:

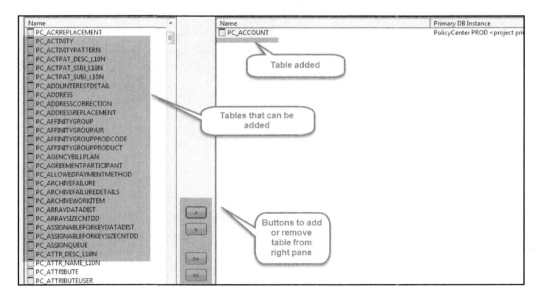

6. This enables the options to create facts and attributes:

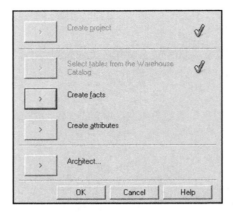

7. Click **Create facts**, which is a column that's going to be used to measure something. So, in our case, we are going to add a numeric column and tell MicroStrategy to use that column while performing numeric operations, such as sum, avg, and so on.
8. In the fact creation wizard, click **Next**.
9. Move the required column names from available to facts and click **Next**:

10. Click **Next | Finish**, which saves facts and lets the user create attributes.
11. Click **Create Attributes** and in the attribute creation wizard, click **Next**.
12. Move the required attributes from available columns to attributes and click **Next**:

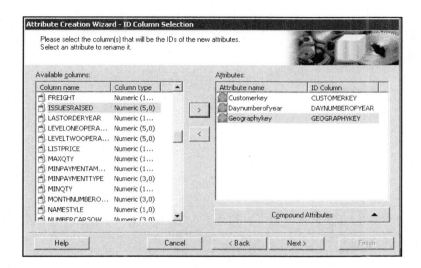

13. Update the description column name, if needed, and click **Next**:

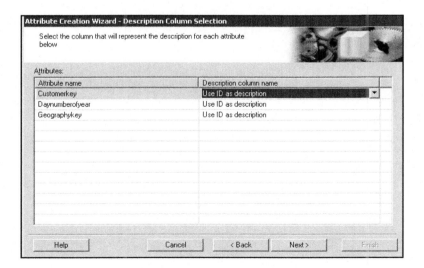

14. Select the lookup tables that contain the description of each attribute and click
Next:

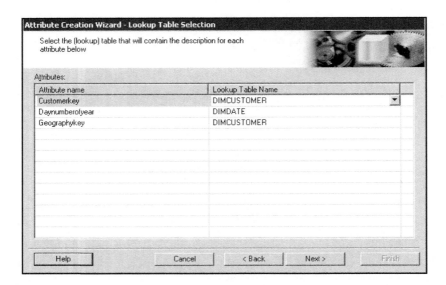

15. Define the attributes relationship based on the relationship created in the logical
data model. The user only creates a relationship between attributes of the same
hierarchy and never with other hierarchies. It is a direct relationship.
16. Click **Next** | **Finish**:

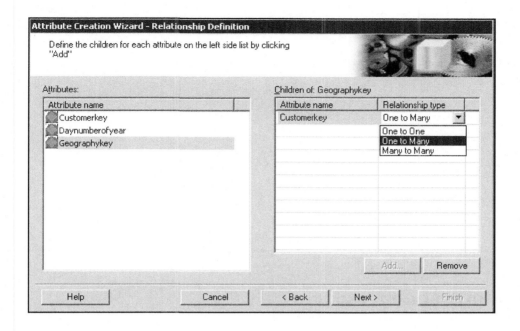

17. Click **OK** on the project creation assistant screen once all the steps are completed to see the project in MicroStrategy Desktop.

Using MicroStrategy Architect

The user can create a project and schema objects that reside within the project. Architect provides a centralized interface where users can define the logical tables, attributes, hierarchies, facts, and metrics that are required during project creation. It usually automatically creates attributes and facts based on the data available in the selected data source, but sometimes the user will have to map it manually. Users can either use the project table view or hierarchy view:

1. In MicroStrategy Desktop, click **Schema | Create new project**. Enter the information in the new project window and click **OK**. Click the arrow for Architect.

2. Select database instance from the drop-down list. Click **OK**. MicroStrategy Architect opens and there the user can add attributes, facts, and hierarchies:

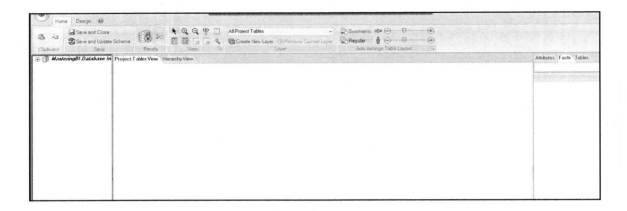

Creating schema objects

This step involves the creation of schema objects such as attribute, facts, and hierarchies, based on the logical model, mapping them to appropriate structures in the data warehouse schema. We will be discussing schema objects in detail in the upcoming sections.

Managing project schema

This is the final and ongoing step in the project design process. Over the life of the project, our physical or logical data models can change, so the user's reporting needs can change, which requires a change of schema objects. So this phase of the project life cycle is responsible for this maintenance and involves tasks such as:

- Creating new objects as needed
- Modifying existing objects
- Removing objects that are no longer needed

In the previous section, we learned that metadata components that represent the physical structure of the data warehouse are called schema objects. In the upcoming sections, we will learn in depth about these schema objects, such as attributes, facts and so on, and based on these schema objects, how we can build more complex objects such as metrics and filters, which are known as **public objects**.

Schema objects

Schema objects represent different components of the logical data model and are directly mapped to a column or columns in the database. Attributes, facts, functions, and operations, hierarchies, partition mappings, tables, and transformations are all schema objects; however, three schema objects comprise the core of project definition and will be covered in this section:

Attributes

Attributes are the descriptive part of the database. They provide information about the data; for example, customer name and city are attributes. The SELECT clause of a SQL statement is based on these attributes.

The following is the report with the Policy Number and Broker Name as an attribute:

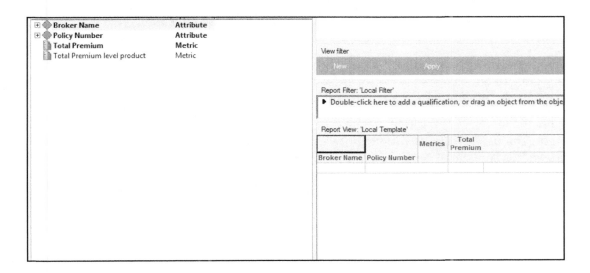

When we see the SQL for this report, the `Policy Number` and `Broker Name` will be shown in the `SELECT` clause as follows:

```
SQL Statements:
create table ZZMD00 nologging as
select     sum(a11.TOTAL_PREMIUM_AMT) WJXBFS1
from       P_DW_DW_ADMIN.POLICY_INFORCE_FACT    a11

create table ZZMD01 nologging as
select     a13.POLICY_NUM  POLICY_NUM,
           a12.BROKER_NAME  BROKER_NAME,
           sum(a11.TOTAL_PREMIUM_AMT) WJXBFS1
from       P_DW_DW_ADMIN.POLICY_INFORCE_FACT    a11
    join       P_DW_DW_ADMIN.BROKER_DIM       a12
    on         (a11.BROKER_KEY = a12.BROKER_KEY)
    join       P_DW_DW_ADMIN.POLICY_DIM       a13
    on         (a11.POLICY_KEY = a13.POLICY_KEY)
group by   a13.POLICY_NUM,
           a12.BROKER_NAME
```

Attribute types

We have three different types of attribute:

- Compound attribute
- Homogenous attribute
- Heterogeneous attribute

Compound attribute: Uses two or more columns as its ID. It is like the compound key of a relational table. You have to look at more than one column to get unique information. For example, let's assume our product attribute is a combination of product_id and product_code_id, which are the primary keys in our table.

Homogenous attribute: Each attribute form points to the same column or set of columns in every table to which it maps. For example, let's assume the ID form for the state attribute maps to two different tables, lu_geography and lu_region; state is still a homogenous attribute because its ID form maps to the same state_id column in each table.

Heterogeneous attribute: This attribute form points to the same column with different names across the database. For example, region_id and reg_id. It's the same column, but with different names.

Attribute form expression types

Attributes have one or more attribute forms that directly map to the data warehouse column. In other words, attributes must have one ID and the other attribute forms are optional. The relationship between all of the attribute forms must be one to one.

Attribute forms can have any number of expressions; primarily we have the following two types of expression form:

- **Simple attribute form expression:** Maps directly to the single attribute column; here is an example:

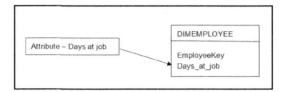

  Here, the ID form of days at job directly maps to the days_at_job column in the LU_EMPLOYEE table, creating a simple attribute expression form.

- **Derived attribute form expression:** Contains multiple attribute columns from the same table, mathematical operators, numbers or other functions such as ApplySimple, and so on. For example:

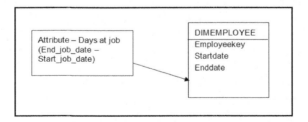

  Here, the ID form for the days at job attribute maps to an expression that combines the Start_job_date and End_job_date columns in the LU_EMPLOYEE table, creating a derived attribute form expression.

General attribute example

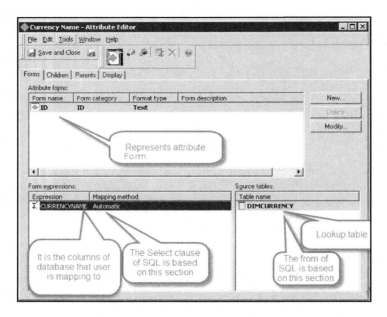

The following are the **Attribute Editor Tabs**:

- **Forms tab:** Defines how an attribute will be displayed. A user can have ID or DESC as a form.
- **Children and parent tabs:** Defines how attributes are directly related to each other. In the case of normalized tables, the table with the primary key is the parent and the table with the foreign key is the child. In the case of denormalized tables, the attribute with high cardinality is the child and the attribute with low cardinality is the parent.

  For example, for the Broker Name attribute we have the Broker Key as a child with a one-to-many relationship, and Broker Number as the parent with a one-to-many relationship:

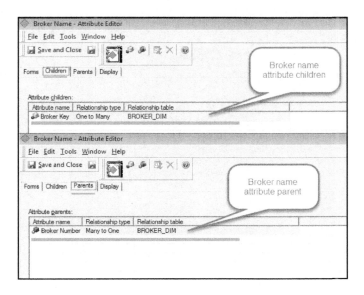

- **Display tab:** Shows how an attribute is represented.

Creating an attribute from Architect

There are two ways of creating an attribute using MicroStrategy Architect:

- **Manual attribution creation**: where the user creates an attribute by themselves, deciding which column to use and designing an attribute and its forms
- **Automatic attribution creation**: where Architect creates the appropriate attribute and attribute forms

The following are the steps for manual attribution creation:

1. Log in to MicroStrategy Desktop.
2. Click on **Schema | Architect**.
3. In the **Project Tables View** tab, find the project table you want to use to create an attribute.

4. Right-click the header of the project table and select **Create Attribute**:

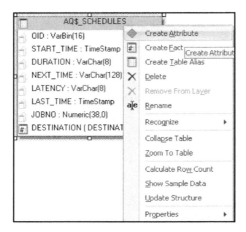

In the MicroStrategy Architect window, in the box, type a name for the attribute and click **OK**.

5. In the **Create New Form Expression** window, define the ID form expression and click **OK**:

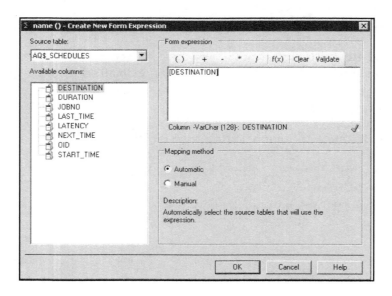

Creating an attribute from the Desktop

1. Click on the **Schema Objects** | **Attributes** folder and right-click on the blank side to select **New** | **Attribute**.
2. This will open three windows: the attributes, forms, and expressions editors.
3. Select the source table under the source table dropdown and drag the column name under the **Form expression** section:

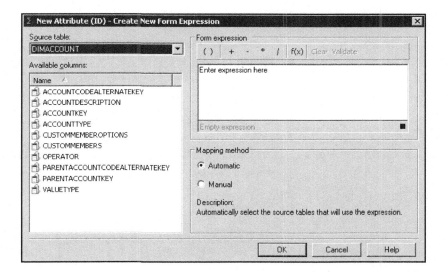

4. After entering the information, click **OK** and it will display the new attribute form window, where the user can add or change the expression form, lookup table, and so on. Click **OK** upon completing the information:

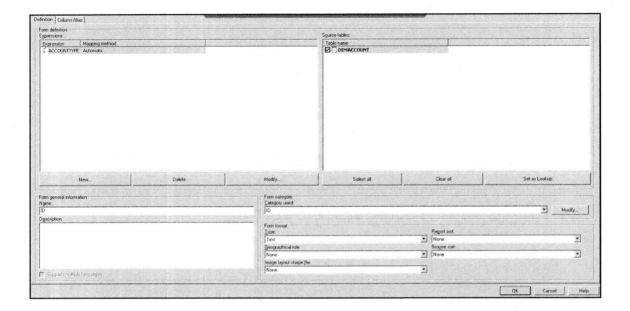

5. Click **Save** and close to save an attribute:

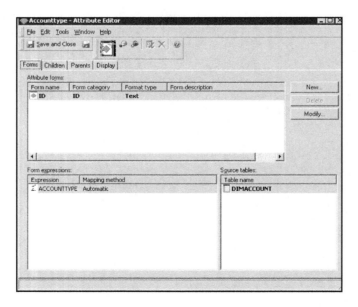

Note: Always update the schema before using newly created schema objects. Without updating, elements will not be available for use.

Facts

Facts are numeric data values, which are generally aggregatable and are used to analyze the business. Facts are the basis of all metrics; facts that create additive metrics exist as a column in fact tables, whereas facts that create non-additive metrics exist as a column in dimension tables. Revenue, sales, and profit are a few examples of facts.

Fact types

There are two primary types of fact:

- Homogeneous
- Heterogeneous

Homogeneous fact: Points to the same column name or set of columns in the table to which it maps.

Here is an example of a homogeneous fact:

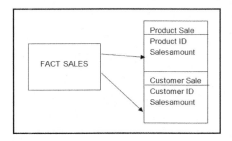

Here we have a sales fact mapping to two different tables, but it is still a homogeneous fact, because it maps to the same `Salesamount` column in each table.

Heterogeneous fact: Points to two or more different columns or sets of columns in the table to which it maps.

Here is an example of a heterogeneous fact:

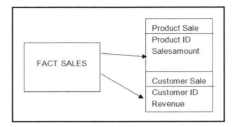

Here we have a sales fact mapping to two different tables, but it is a heterogeneous fact because it maps to two different column names.

Fact expression types

A fact expression is made up of a column or set of columns to which it maps. There are two types of factexpression, and they are:

- **Simple fact**: Maps directly to one column; for example, creating a sales fact using the `Salesamount` column from a table
- **Derived fact**: Contains multiple columns from the same table, mathematical operators, numerical values, or other functions; for example, creating a sales fact using *sales_quantity * unit_price*

SQL representation

In SQL, these are mostly the numeric columns on which a user performs SQL aggregations such as `SUM`, `AVG`, and so forth.

The following is an example of SQL representation.

If a user wants to analyze the sales made by a company during March, sales represents a fact and the company and month represent the attributes:

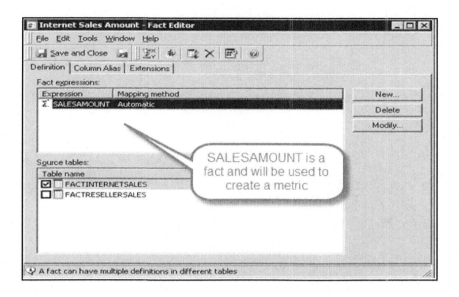

Creating a fact from Architect

There are two ways to create a fact using MicroStrategy Architect. These are:

- **Manual fact creation:** Here a user creates facts themselves, deciding which column to use. This process is time consuming as the user needs to create individual facts one by one.
- **Automatic fact creation:** Let MicroStrategy Architect identify the columns that can be created as a fact, based on a set of heuristics. This method provides a quick way to create facts.

Manual creation of facts:

1. Log in to MicroStrategy Desktop and select the project.
2. Click on **Schema | Architect**.
3. In the Architect graphical interface, click the **Project Tables View** tab.

4. In the **Project Tables View** tab, right-click the header of any table and select **Create Fact**:

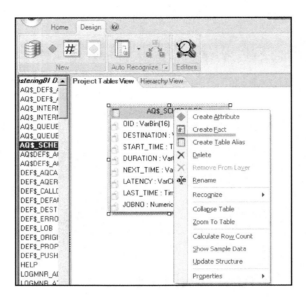

5. In the **MicroStrategy Architect** window, in the box, type the fact name and click **OK**:

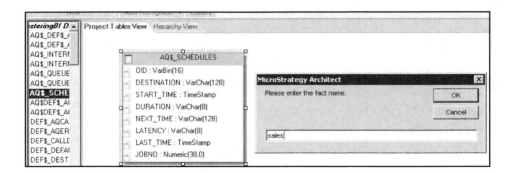

6. In the **Create New Fact Expression** window, define the fact expression and under mapping method, the user can either select the automatic method, which selects for the user all the tables corresponding to the columns that are used in the fact expression, or the manual mapping method, where you manually select each

table corresponding to the columns used. It is preferable to select the automatic mapping method.

7. Click **OK**:

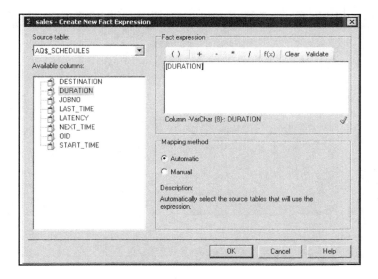

Alternatively, the user can create these facts by right-clicking the appropriate column in the table and selecting **Create Facts**. It will, by default, use the automatic mapping method:

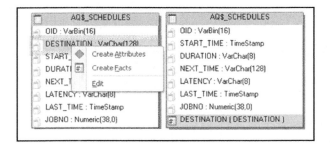

Creating a fact from the Desktop

1. Click on the **Schema Objects** | **Facts folder** and right-click on the blank side to select **New** | **Fact**.

2. Select the source table under the source table dropdown and drag the column name under the form expression section in the expression editor window. Click **OK**:

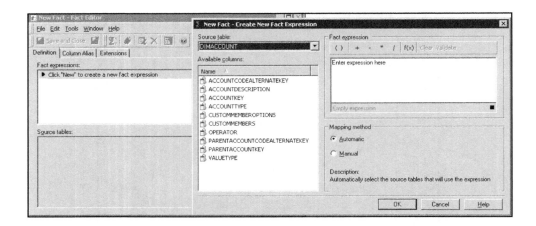

3. On the fact editor screen, click save and close, and provide a name for the fact.

Note: Always update the schema before using newly created attributes or facts in a report or document. Without updating, elements will not be available for use.

Hierarchies

Hierarchies are groupings of attributes that reflect the relationship of one attribute to another. In MicroStrategy, we have following two types of hierarchy:

- System hierarchy
- User hierarchy

System hierarchy: This is based on how data is related in the logical data model. This is the default hierarchy, is automatically created when a user creates a new project, and is not editable. The user cannot directly change a system hierarchy from the hierarchy editor, but can indirectly change it by adding, deleting, or modifying attributes' parent-child relationships. Although the system hierarchy specifies an ordered set of all attributes in the project, it does not define the ordering or grouping among attributes.

User hierarchy: This is based on the user's need to browse the data. The user can always include additional attributes or remove attributes as per the BI need. A user hierarchy provides element browsing and report drilling flexibility.

Example

Consider the logical data model state | country | call_center | agent, which does not have a direct path between country and agent. The user will have to go through the call_center attribute. However, if the user wants to send data directly from country to agent, this could be achieved using a user hierarchy. With a user hierarchy, the user can also define a path between two totally unrelated elements.

Creating a user hierarchy and attribute relationships

A user can create hierarchies and attribute relationships either via Desktop or via Architect; the following section discusses both of these techniques in detail.

Creating a user hierarchy and attribute relationships from Architect

The following are the steps to create an attribute relationship:

1. Log in to MicroStrategy Desktop.
2. Select the project and click **Schema and architect**.
3. In the **Hierarchy View** tab, click the parent attribute and drag the mouse pointer to the child attribute. When the user clicks on the middle of the attribute and drags the pointer, a line is dynamically drawn that links the two attributes:

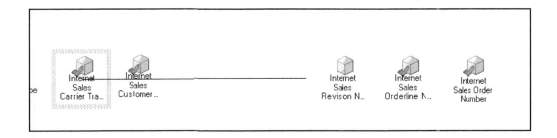

4. If the user needs to change the relationship type, right-click on the line that shows the relationship and select the appropriate relationship type. One to many is the default relationship type:

5. If user need to change the relationship type, right-click the attribute and **Edit Children Relations**:

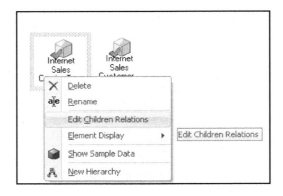

6. To change the relationship table, right-click the line that shows the relationship, point to **Relationship Table**, and select the appropriate table:

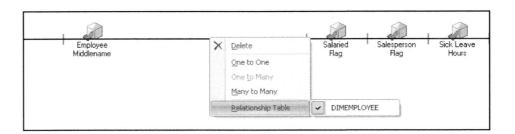

The following screenshot shows the relationship between product and product price:

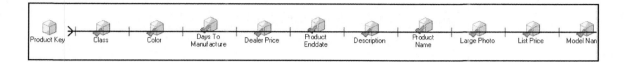

 Note: When a user selects an attribute, the attributes that are child candidates are displayed as regular attributes, whereas others are displayed as ghosted attributes, as shown in the following screenshot:

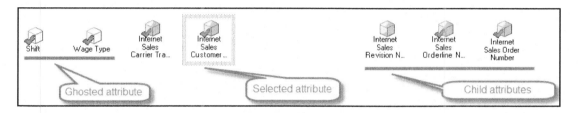

The following are the steps to create a new hierarchy:

1. Log in to MicroStrategy Desktop.
2. Select the project and click **Schema and architect**.
3. In the **Home** tab, select **New Hierarchy**:

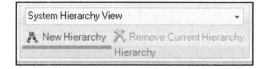

4. Enter the new hierarchy's name:

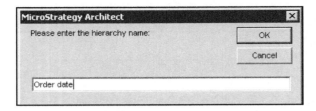

5. When a user creates a hierarchy, it does not contain any attributes. The next step is to add an attribute to the hierarchy.

6. To add an attribute, right-click on the empty space in the hierarchy and select **Add/Remove attributes in Hierarchy**:

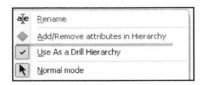

7. Once the attributes are added, the user needs to define the browse attribute for each attribute. Browse attributes are attributes to which you can directly browse from any given attribute. They are indicated by a line that connects the two attributes. The following screenshot shows how to add a browse attribute:

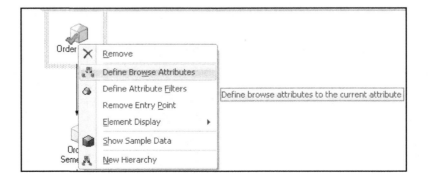

8. The following screenshot shows the order date user hierarchy with a browse path defined:

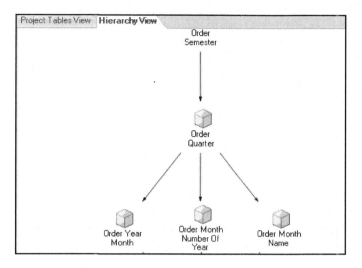

9. Once the user has all the attributes and relationships defined, the user can also set the entry point for the user hierarchy. These are the attributes that are displayed when the user first opens the user hierarchy. Entry point attributes are indicated by a green checkmark beside the attribute icon. The following screenshot shows the option for setting entry points:

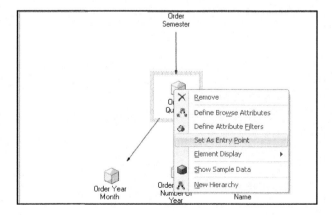

10. A user hierarchy with an entry point set for an attribute is shown in the following screenshot:

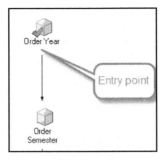

11. User hierarchies are mostly used for browsing attribute data, but the user can configure them for drilling attributes in a report. To configure a user hierarchy for drilling, select the **Use as a Drill Hierarchy** option by right-clicking the empty space in the user hierarchy window:

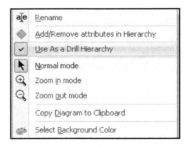

12. The user can even change the element display for an attribute using the element display setting available via right-clicking an attribute. This provides the user with the following options:
    - **Limit:** The user can browse a specified number of elements for an attribute
    - **Unlocked:** The user can browse all the elements of an attribute at one time
    - **Locked:** The user cannot browse the elements of an attribute at all

Creating a user hierarchy and attribute relationships from Desktop

1. Click **File** | **New** | **Hierarchy**, which opens a hierarchy editor with the select Attribute Dialog box.
2. Move the attribute that's needed from available objects to the selected objects list.
3. Click **OK** to view the hierarchy editor, where the user can specify the browse order and make it available for drilling:

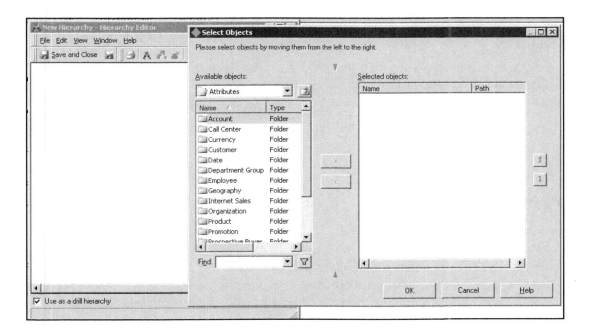

Public objects

Public objects are also known as application objects, and are based on the schema objects. The following diagram shows all the public objects available in MicroStrategy:

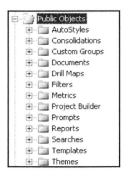

In the following section, we will discuss these public objects in detail.

Metrics

Metrics are public objects that are built from attributes, facts, or other metrics that allow data aggregation. A metric definition contains a formula that determines the calculation to be performed on the data. At a high level, metrics can be categorized as:

- Simple metrics
- Advanced metrics

Types of metric

- Simple metrics include:
    - **Basic metrics**: Simple aggregations of fact, for example SUM (amount), AVG (sale), and so on
    - **Compound metrics**: Combinations of two or more metric objects with one or more constant, mathematical operator, or non-aggregate function, for example, *revenue = quantity * price*, *Runningavg (sales)*, where sales is a metric
- Advanced metrics include:
    - **Level metrics:** Define the level at which the metric aggregates. By

default, all metrics calculate at report level, but the metric-specified attribute levels override the default report level. For example, revenue amount is the sum of revenue calculated at the product category level:

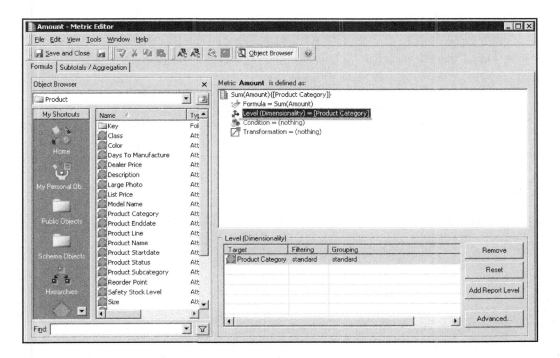

Here is an example of creating a report using simple and level metrics. The following screenshot displays a report where we have total premium amount, calculated at the product level and as a whole:

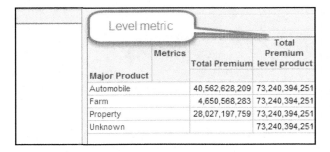

Major Product	Metrics Total Premium	Total Premium level product
Automobile	40,562,628,209	73,240,394,251
Farm	4,650,568,283	73,240,394,251
Property	28,027,197,759	73,240,394,251
Unknown		73,240,394,251

- **Nested metrics:** Use nested functions for aggregation. For example, the average product sales metric formula is defined as: *AVG (SUM (sales){~,product}){~, Region}.*

- **Non-aggregatable metrics:** Metrics that should not be aggregated across a particular attribute or hierarchy. By default, the aggregation function is SUM, which can be set to none, so that the metric does not aggregate to any level. For example, this might include account balance calculations at the end of each day.

- **Pass through metrics:** Metrics created by using pass through functions such as ApplySimple and ApplyComparison. These functions can input a database syntax inside a metric: *ApplyComparison ("#0>#1", [COLUMN_NAME],2).*

- **Conditional metrics:** Metrics with their own filter, which is separate from any other filter specified for the report. For example, let's say the user has a year filter on the report; regardless of that filter, the user wants one of the metrics to calculate 2007 sales. This could be achieved via a conditional metric that ignores the report filter and applies its own filter first:

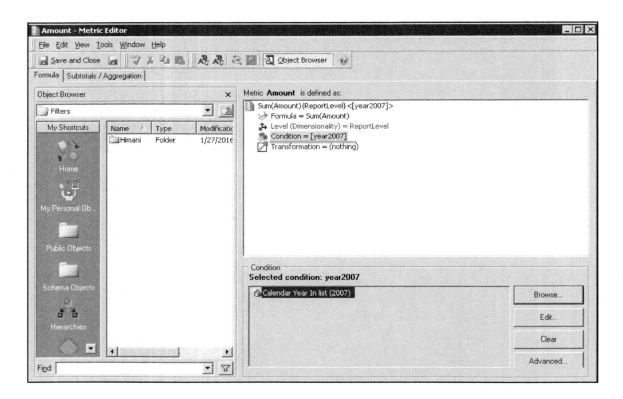

- **Transformation metrics:** Transformation is the schema object that is used in metrics for time-based analysis. Examples of transformation metrics can be month-to-date, year-to-date, year-over-year, and so on:

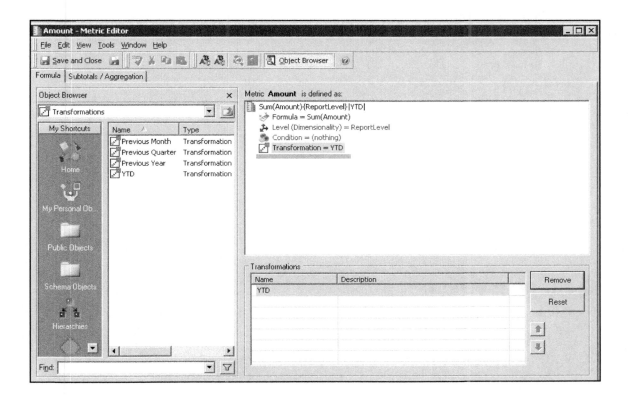

- **Derived metrics:** Metrics created within a report or document using the same report or document objects. These metrics cannot be reused in another report or document. For example, here we have internet sales and reseller sale as metrics, and we want to find the total sales, which can be achieved using derived metrics, by adding internet sales and resellers sale, as shown here:

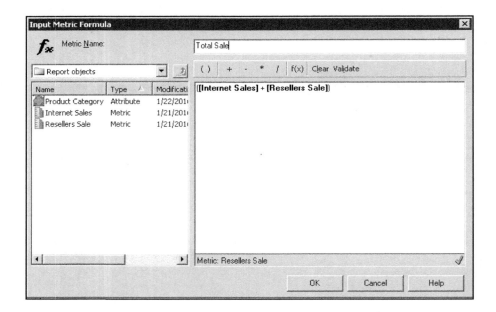

Creating metrics

The following are the steps to create metrics:

1. Log in to MicroStrategy Developer.
2. Navigate to the **Project | Public Objects | Metrics folders**.
3. To create metrics, either Select **File | New | Metrics**, or right-click within the metrics folder and select **New | Metrics**.
4. Select **Empty Metric** and click **OK**.
5. The Metric Editor window opens. In the object browser panel on the left, navigate to **Schema Objects | Facts**.

6. Drag one of the facts to the definition box on the right. By default, the Sum function is applied to the fact:

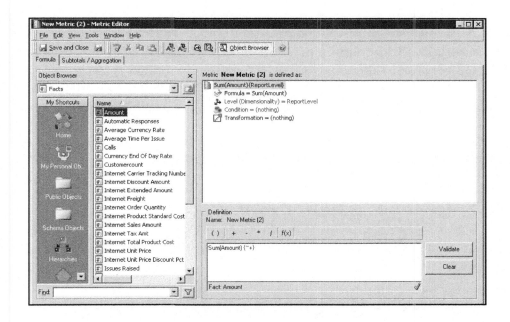

7. Click on **Validate** to check the formula.
8. Click **Save and Close**, and enter the name for the metric.

Prompts

These public objects present users with a set of questions that users may need to answer in order to run the reports. Some prompts are mandatory and some are optional. There are the different types of prompt:

- Filter definition prompt
  - Hierarchy qualification prompt
  - Attribute qualification prompt
  - Attribute element list
  - Metric qualification prompt
- Object prompt
- Value prompt

- **Hierarchy qualificationprompt** allows the user to qualify attributes and elements from a specific hierarchy
- **Attribute qualificationprompt** allows the user to qualify an attribute's ID, description, or other form
- **Attribute element list** allows the user to choose from a list of elements
- **Metric qualificationprompt** allows the user to qualify one or more metrics
- **Object prompt** allows the user to select from one or more objects, such as attributes, metrics, or filters, and also allows them to add more data to the report
- **Value prompt** allows the user to enter a text, date, number, or other value

Example of creating an Object prompt

1. Start MicroStrategy Desktop and log in to the project.
2. Navigate to **Public Objects | Prompts**.
3. Under the `prompts` folder, click **File | New | Prompt**.
4. From the **Prompt Generation Wizard**, select **Filter definition prompt | Qualify on an attribute**:

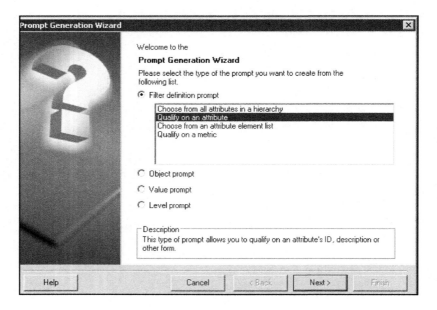

5. Click **Next** and choose the attribute that the user wants as a prompt:

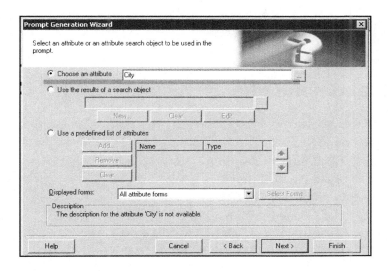

6. Click **Next** and on this screen select prompt answer required (this selection will make this prompt mandatory):

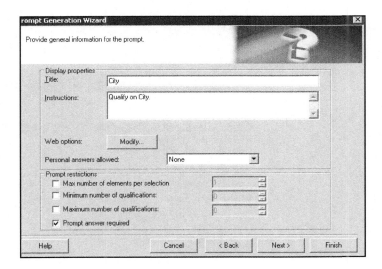

7. Click **Next** and **Finish**.

Filters

Filters define the conditions that are applied to the report or metric, based on which the data is displayed or returned to the report from the data warehouse. It basically limits the report's dataset.

Create a standalone filter

1. Log in to MicroStrategy Developer.
2. Navigate to the **Project** | **Public Objects** | **Filter** folder.
3. To create a filter, either select **File** | **New** | **Filter**, or right-click within the `filter` folder and select **New** | **Filter**.
4. Select **Empty filter** and Click **OK**.
5. Select the appropriate filtering option:
   - **Attribute qualification**: Creates a filter based on an attribute, such as customer name, customer ID, and so on
   - **Set qualification**: Creates a filter based on the metrics or the relationship between the attributes
   - **Shortcut qualification**: Creates a filter based on the results of existing reports or an existing filter

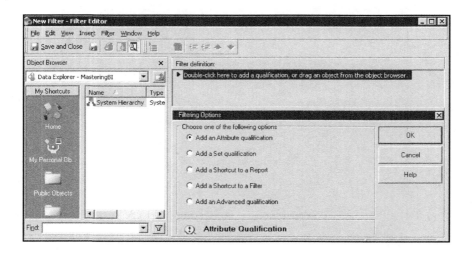

6. Enter all the required information and click **Save and Close**.

7. Enter the filter name.

Filter operators

Filter operators describe how the user wants to filter data. In the following example, Base Year Month can use any of the following operators:

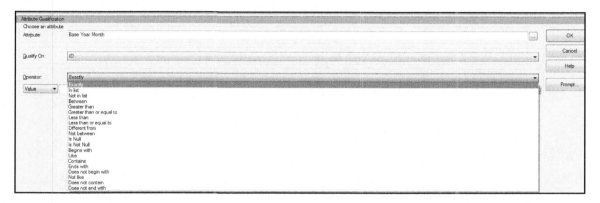

So if we say Base Year Month is exactly 201601, then it will give us data only for that time period.

Example of how these filters are used

Let's say the user wants to display the revenue of an organization for the year 2007; this could be achieved using a filter on the report like this:

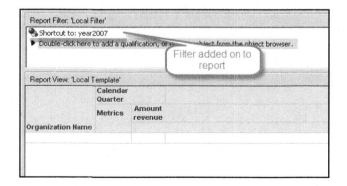

SQL based on report filter

The SQL engine deals with report filters and adds the condition to the report as a where clause. So in our case, the SQL view shows this:

```
select    a14.ORGANIZATIONNAME  ORGANIZATIONNAME,
          a13.CALENDARQUARTER  CALENDARQUARTER,
          sum(a11.AMOUNT)  WJXBFS1
from      EDW.FACTFINANCE          a11
          join      EDW.DIMACCOUNT          a12
          on        (a11.ACCOUNTKEY = a12.ACCOUNTKEY)
          join      EDW.DIMDATE      a13
          on        (a11.DATEKEY = a13.DATEKEY)
          join      EDW.DIMORGANIZATION    a14
          on        (a11.ORGANIZATIONKEY = a14.ORGANIZATIONKEY)
where     (a12.ACCOUNTTYPE in (N'Revenue')
and a13.CALENDARYEAR = 2007)
group by  a14.ORGANIZATIONNAME,
          a13.CALENDARQUARTER
```

Summary

In this chapter, we learned about BI architecture, which is a framework for organizing data and technology components that builds BI systems for data analytics. The project design process is not just the creation of a project; it involves lots of analysis, planning, deployment, development, and maintenance. Schema objects are the building blocks of any MicroStrategy project, and include attributes, facts, and so on. Public objects are based on schema objects and provide the user with the flexibility to generate analytical data; examples of these include metrics, reports, documents, and so on.

In the next chapter, we will be going into more detail about other public objects, such as reports, drill maps, custom groups, consolidations, and so on.

3
Building Advanced Reports and Documents

In the previous chapter, we learned about the creation of schema designs and different schema and public objects; so, in this chapter, we can dig deeper and understand some advanced techniques for presenting data to end users.

This chapter will cover:

- Creating consolidations
- Building different types of custom group
- Creating transformations
- Working on your first advance report
- Creating and adding data to the document
- Dashboard creation and usage

Advanced reporting components

A **report** is an object that provides a multi-perspective view of our data. Reports are the starting point for further business investigations and decisions. Advanced reporting allows us to create complex and sophisticated reports using several advanced objects such as advanced metrics, transformations, consolidations, custom groups, freeform SQL, and intelligent cubes.

Before you begin with this chapter, you should be familiar with basic reports and components.

- Real-life scenarios using advanced reporting features include:
- Top N products with highest sales
- Sales of current year versus previous year
- Yearly revenue splits by territory
- Sales based on seasons

Custom groups

A **custom group** is used to group attribute elements and aggregate results in a report. This report is made up of custom group elements that consist of a header and filter condition. Each custom group element can have its own banding or filtering condition. A custom group allows us to group elements with the same or different attributes and metrics.

In the following example, if a data warehouse contain different countries but you want to group those countries by region, you can use custom groups; the American region custom group element displays countries such as Canada, the USA, and so on as other custom group elements:

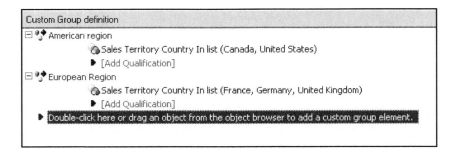

A custom group definition is made up of:

- A **name**, which we define while creating a custom group element. Under this name, we group different attribute elements. This is displayed as a row in the report.
- **Qualification**, which is a condition that should be met to display data on the report. There are different qualification types and we can combine them in the same custom group. Qualification types include:

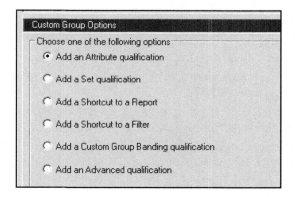

Custom group options are:

- **Attribute qualification**: Displays data based on a value of an attribute
- **Set qualification**: Displays data based on the value, rank, or percentage of a metric
- **Shortcut to a Report**: Displays data based on existing reports
- **Shortcut to a Filter**: Displays data by using existing filters
- **Custom Group Banding qualification**: Displays data into multiple ranges; bands are based on the metric selected
- **Advanced qualification**: Allows the user to use pass-through functions

Note: By default, an advanced qualification is not displayed as an option.

To enable advanced qualification:

1. Select **Tools** | **My preferences**.
2. Select the **Editor** tab and then **Custom Group Options**.
3. Check the **Show advanced filter qualification** checkbox.

Creating a custom group

1. Browse the folder in which you want to create a new custom group; best practice is to create a custom group under public objects and a custom group folder.
2. Select **File** | **New** | **Custom Group** | **Empty custom group**, and **OK**. The custom group editor is displayed.
3. Under custom group definition, create the custom group element either by double-clicking or by dragging the object onto the editor.
4. Give a name to the group element and then define conditions to filter data by selecting an attribute, metric, report, or filter, based on the options provided.
5. Repeat steps 3 and 4 to define additional custom group elements.
6. Click **Save and Close** and type the name of a custom group.

Custom group examples

Attribute qualification: Show the revenue generated between 2005 and 2009, so the qualification is based on the attribute **Calendar Year**:

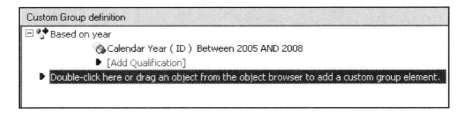

Based on the selection, the data on the report will be displayed as follows:

Custom group		Metrics	Amount revenue
Based on year			134,117,770
	2005		23,486,861
	2006		46,189,611
	2007		43,453,065
	2008		20,988,233

Set qualification: Show the top three organizations with the highest revenue, so the qualification is based on the metric **Total Sales**:

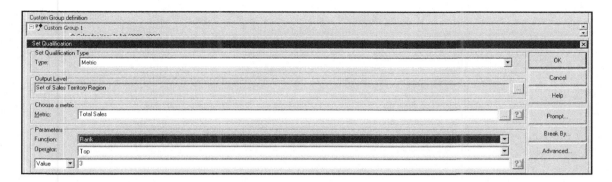

Based on the selection, the data on the report will be displayed as follows:

Top 3 organizations	79,353,874
Canadian Division	34,471,460
Central Division	17,215,212
Southwest Division	27,667,203

Custom group banding qualification: Rank and group the organizations, according to the revenue generated:

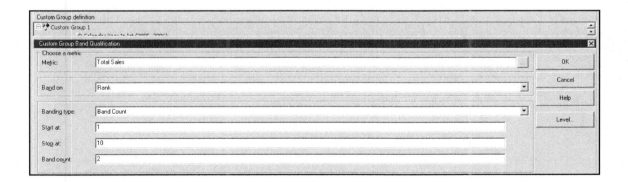

Based on the selection, the data on the report will be displayed as follows:

Revenue range			134,117,770
	Band (1)		108,482,415
		Canadian Division	34,471,460
		Central Division	17,215,212
		Northeast Division	13,877,401
		Northwest Division	15,251,140
		Southwest Division	27,667,203
	Band (2)		25,635,355
		Australia	3,641,063
		France	6,309,020
		Germany	2,763,040
		Southeast Division	12,922,231

We can have different attributes in the same custom group; the following is an example.

- **Custom group**: See the following screenshot:

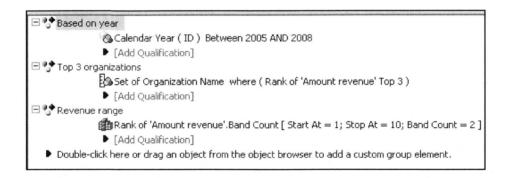

- **Report**: See the following screenshot:

		Metrics	Amount revenue
Custom group			
Based on year			134,117,770
	2005		23,486,861
	2006		46,189,611
	2007		43,453,065
	2008		20,988,233
Top 3 organizations			79,353,874
	Canadian Division		34,471,460
	Central Division		17,215,212
	Southwest Division		27,667,203
Revenue range			134,117,770
	Band (1)		108,482,415
		Canadian Division	34,471,460
		Central Division	17,215,212
		Northeast Division	13,877,401
		Northwest Division	15,251,140
		Southwest Division	27,667,203
	Band (2)		25,635,355
		Australia	3,641,063
		France	6,309,020
		Germany	2,763,040
		Southeast Division	12,922,231

Custom group SQL

Custom groups generate at least one query per element. Many temporary tables may be created to hold intermediate data. They are SQL-intensive and generate many passes. So, if we see the SQL for the previously mentioned custom group, we will see multiple passes and three different queries for each element.

The user can change the way MicroStrategy treats SQL using the intermediate table type. For that, in SQL view, go to **Data** | **VLDB properties** | **Tables** | **Intermediate table types**.

Select **Temporary View** to make SQL more presentable and understandable.

Custom group display options

We can modify the display of custom group at different levels, as follows:

Individual element of the custom group:

In the custom group editor, right-click on the custom group element and select a display option:

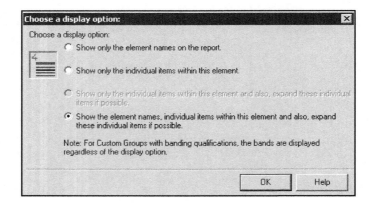

All elements of the custom group:

In the custom group editor, select **Custom Group | Options**:

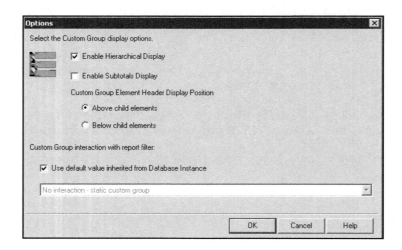

All custom groups on the report:

In the report editor, select **Data** | **Report Data Options** | **Object display**:

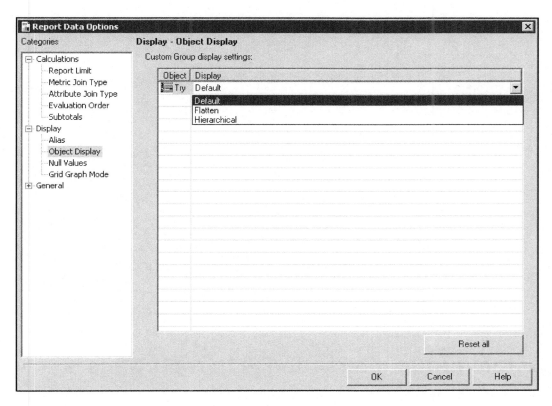

All custom groups in the project for a specific user:

Within the developer, select **Tools** | **My Preferences** | **Editors** | **Custom Group**:

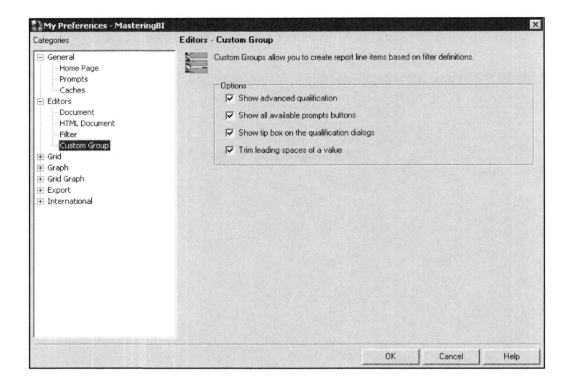

Custom group interaction with report filters

When we create a custom group using attribute qualification, a report filter will be applied to the custom group element. Whereas, in the case of a custom group with metric qualification, a report filter will not be applied to the custom group element causing inaccurate data on the report. For example, if the custom group is created to display a product with sales greater than 50,000 and the report filter is created to display the sales for the year 2005. Here, even if the sales of the product are 25,000 in 2005, the product will still be displayed on the report, which means the report filter is evaluated after the custom group. We can avoid the previously mentioned scenario and define the interaction between the report filter and custom group by using the **custom group interaction with report filter** property, which is available under database instance level VLDB properties and is accessed by taking the following steps:

1. Right-click the project.
2. Select **Project Configuration** ❘ **Database Instances** ❘ **VLDB Properties**:

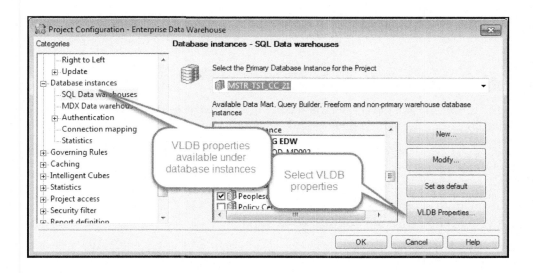

Consolidation

Consolidation allows you to group attributes to define a *virtual attribute*, which does not exist in the project schema. This virtual element could be placed on a report just like an attribute and is calculated on the Intelligence Server side, causing no load on the database. The consolidation element does not have to be based on a single attribute. Also, we cannot group metrics using consolidations. The two main uses of consolidation are:

- To create a virtual attribute
- To perform row-level math

Consolidation elements

Attribute elements define the consolidation. They can be any of the following:

- Elements from the same attribute, such as month-January and February
- Elements from different attributes in the same hierarchy, such as month and quarter from the time hierarchy
- Elements from different attributes in different hierarchies, such as month from the time hierarchy, and region from the territory hierarchy

- Elements from the same consolidation
- Elements from different consolidations within the project

Creating consolidations

Browse the folder in which to create new consolidation; the best practice is to create the consolidation under the public objects and consolidation folder:

1. Select **File** | **New** | **Consolidation**. The consolidation editor is displayed.
2. Under consolidation definition, create the consolidation element by double-clicking an attribute and then dragging its element onto the editor section from the data explorer section.
3. Give a name to the group element and then define the logic in the editor:

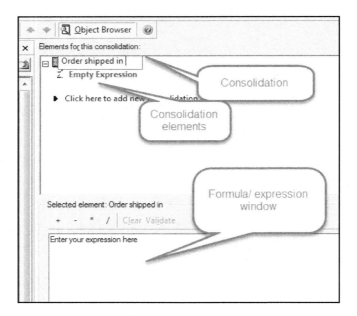

4. Click **Save and Close**, and type the name of a consolidation.

Consolidation examples

Using Arithmetic operator and element from the same attribute

Let's say your database contains data based on months or quarter, but you want a report to display data on a semester basis. You can create a consolidation with elements representing each semester. Basically, you will create a semester as a virtual attribute without changing your data model. In the following image, we have explained the usage of an arithmetic operator and an element from the same attribute by creating a consolidation and a report:

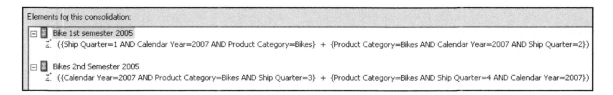

Using logical operator and element from a different attribute

Let's say you want a report showing bikes ordered and shipped in semester one and semester two, 2005. You can use a consolidation such as the following:

Elements for this consolidation:
⊟ 🔲 Bike 1st semester 2005   ž⁻ ({Ship Quarter=1 AND Calendar Year=2007 AND Product Category=Bikes} + {Product Category=Bikes AND Calendar Year=2007 AND Ship Quarter=2})
⊟ 🔲 Bikes 2nd Semester 2005   ž⁻ ({Calendar Year=2007 AND Product Category=Bikes AND Ship Quarter=3} + {Product Category=Bikes AND Ship Quarter=4 AND Calendar Year=2007})

Here, you have used a Logical operator (AND) to consolidate data from different attributes, namely, Product and Date. The report generated based on this consolidation:

Consolidation-logical	Ship Year	Metrics	Total Order Quantity
Bike 1st semester 2005	2007		14,225
Bikes 2nd Semester 2005	2007		22,560

Row-level math

Consolidation allows us to perform a row-level mathematical operation, which makes it a powerful tool for reporting. We can perform addition, subtraction, and so on, between the elements or element groups. Continuing with the bike example, the difference between the first semester and second semester shipping order quantity is calculated using row-level math in a consolidation, as shown here:

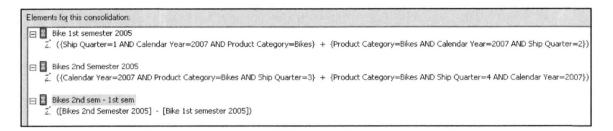

Report

	Metrics	Total Sales
Consolidation-logical		
Bike 1st semester 2005		13,358,304
Bikes 2nd Semester 2005		21,552,573
Bikes 2nd sem - 1st sem		8,194,269

Similarly, we can have a ratio between the two semesters' sales amount and can format elements differently within the same consolidation, as shown here:

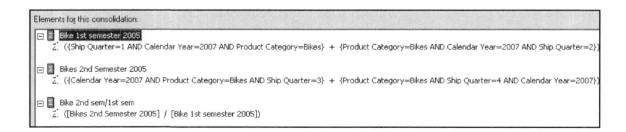

Consolidation

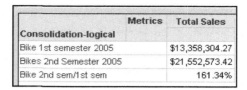

	Metrics	Total Sales
Consolidation-logical		
Bike 1st semester 2005		$13,358,304.27
Bikes 2nd Semester 2005		$21,552,573.42
Bike 2nd sem/1st sem		161.34%

Report

To format each element individually, we right-click on an element within a consolidation, as shown, and then select **Formatting properties**:

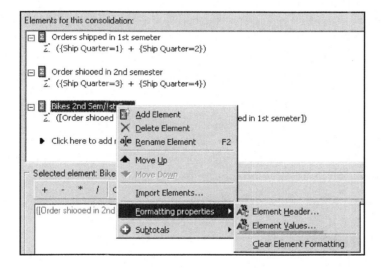

SQL based on consolidation

MicroStrategy generates a query; the SQL engine generates the SELECT and then the consolidation and the calculation are performed on the Intelligence Server/analytical engine using three-tier mode if available. If not, the developer will perform those calculations.

Following is the SQL view of the report with a consolidation that shows the calculation performed by analytical engine:

```
[Analytical engine calculation steps:
    1. Calculate consolidation: <Consolidation-logical>
    2. Perform cross-tabbing
]
```

Consolidation and custom group comparison

See the following for a comparison:

- Consolidation use attributes are a grouping of attribute elements, whereas a custom group is based on filters
- Consolidation allows a user to perform row-level math, which is not possible in a custom group
- Consolidation is faster than custom groups as it may need just one pass for all the elements of the consolidation
- Consolidation can be used to create other consolidations, whereas that's not possible with custom groups
- Consolidation calculates data at the analytical engine level, whereas a custom group calculates at the warehouse-level
- Hierarchical display in consolidation is fixed at the element level only, whereas in a custom group it is flexible and expandable

Transformations

A transformation is a schema object that is created using other project attributes and can only be assigned to metrics. This is used for time series analysis; say, you want to calculate the growth percentage, namely how much your company revenue has grown this year compared to how much it grew last year. The transformation, once created, can be used for n number of reports that require time-based analysis.

Building a transformation

For **table based transformation** (YTD), we create a reference table with two columns, where the first column is the current date and the second column holds the date, required to calculate the running total based on the current date.

The reference table in our case looks like the following:

	DateKey	YTD_key
1	20050101	20050101
2	20050102	20050101
3	20050103	20050101
4	20050104	20050101
5	20050105	20050101
6	20050106	20050101
7	20050107	20050101
8	20050108	20050101
9	20050109	20050101
10	20050110	20050101
11	20050111	20050101
12	20050112	20050101
13	20050113	20050101

As we migrated from SQL server to Oracle, all the tables we created were based on SQL server. Use the following query:

```
with report as
(
select cast('2005-01-01' as datetime) DV1
union all
select DV1 + 1
from report
where DV1 + 1 < '2010-10-31'
)
,md as
(
select cast('2005-01-01' as datetime) DV2
union all
select DV2 + 1
from md
where DV2 + 1 < '2010-10-31'
)
select cast(convert(varchar, DV1, 112) as integer) DateKey,
cast(convert(varchar, DV2, 112) as integer) YTD_Key
into DimYTD
from report, md where DV1 >= DV2 and DV2 >= DateAdd(yy,
DateDiff(yy,0,DV1),0)
order by DV1, DV2
OPTION (MAXRECURSION 0)
```

Once the table is created, we need to import that table to the project using a warehouse catalog and then we can start creating the transformation based on the following steps:

1. Select **File | New | Transformation**. In the transformation editor, select the attribute from, say, YTD_key, which in our table maps this year to the previous year.
2. Click **Save and Close** on the toolbar. Name the transformation Last Year.

The transformation creation screen is as follows:

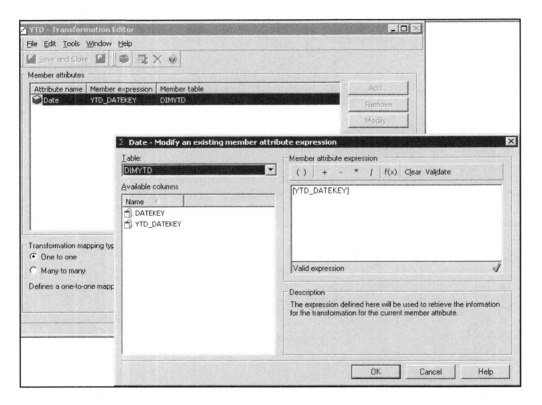

One can use transformation within the report as follows:

1. Go to the report folder and create a report.
2. Add the required objects; in our example, add the date, organization name, and revenue.
3. Also, we must have attribute onto the report being used on the transformation.

4. Now, right click on the revenue metric and select **Insert** | **Transformations** | **YTD** | **Normal**:

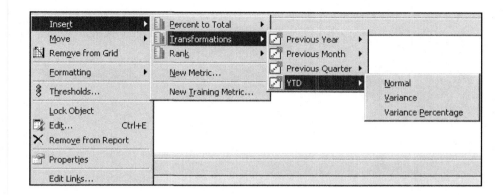

5. After adding the transformation, run the report and the result should be like the following:

Date	Organization Name	Metrics Amount	YTD (Amount)
20070801	Southeast Division	13,007,531	62,477,384
20070901	Canadian Division	12,726,619	79,667,776
20071201	Canadian Division	12,214,191	110,629,436
20070901	Southeast Division	11,230,446	73,707,830
20060801	Canadian Division	11,144,848	59,048,149
20060901	Canadian Division	11,102,116	70,150,265
20060801	Southeast Division	11,064,163	59,180,426
20060701	Canadian Division	11,062,948	47,903,301
20071101	Southeast Division	10,964,078	91,969,595
20051101	Southeast Division	10,670,564	29,545,473
20070801	Canadian Division	10,578,138	66,941,157

For **expression based transformation**, the steps to create a last-year transformation based on an expression are:

1. Select **File** | **New** | **Transformation**. In the **Transformation Editor**, click **Add** and select the attribute, in our case, year.
2. Define the attribute expression; say, for a previous year, type –1 after the year attribute (*year-1*). This will subtract *1* from the selected year and calculates the previous year.

3. Click **Validate** to confirm the accuracy of an expression. Once a green check mark displays, click **OK**.

4. Click **Save and Close** on the toolbar. Name the transformation **Last Year**:

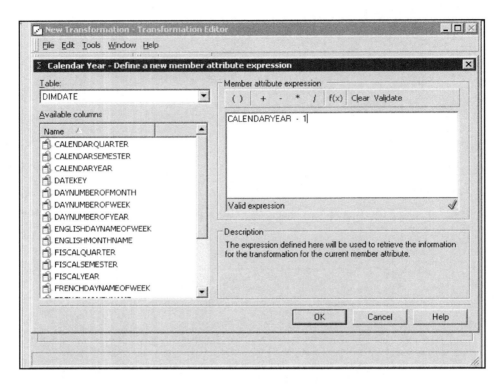

In the following sample report, we have created a transformation which selects the year as 2008 and subtracts 1, giving us the revenue for 2007. To validate our transformation, we have created a metric with a filter of 2007; so, based on that, we can see that the result from the transformation is the same as the result from the metric with a filter. We can use either, but transformation provides us with reusability:

Organization Name	Metrics	Revenue 2008	Transformation -year-1 (Revenue 2008)	Revenue 2007
Australia		1,655,326	1,985,737	1,985,737
Canadian Division		4,507,458	10,954,950	10,954,950
Central Division		2,087,646	5,108,907	5,108,907
France		1,858,094	3,288,195	3,288,195
Germany		1,150,205	1,574,373	1,574,373
Northeast Division		1,710,389	4,622,633	4,622,633
Northwest Division		2,718,923	4,695,559	4,695,559
Southeast Division		1,418,765	2,855,418	2,855,418
Southwest Division		3,881,428	8,367,292	8,367,292

Transformation components

Member attributes: Transformation is applied to this component. For example, in year to date transformations, the member attributes are the year and day.

Member tables: This component stores the data for the member attribute. For example, for a table-based transformation, it could be a logical table, such as LU_Year.

Member expression: This is the expression that is associated with the member attribute. For example, for expression-based transformations it could be logical, arithmetic operator, or a function such as applysimple.

Mapping type: This component determines the creation of the transformation based on the nature of the data. Mapping can be:

- One-to-one
- Many-to-many

Drill maps

Drill maps provide users with the capability of viewing data that is not available on the report. It allows analyzing the data within the same or a different context of data on the report. Let's say report 1 is created to view the annual sales of a company, but then the user wants to view the quarterly sales of the company; this can be achieved by drilling.

The user can drill on any object by right-clicking or double-clicking via the developer, or by a single click via the Web, and selecting the direction of the drill. If the user right-clicks on an element, it will drill for that particular element only, whereas if the user selects the header, it will drill for all the elements on that column. If user hierarchies are not defined, then system hierarchies create a default drill map. The drill path includes the destination of the drill, which could be an attribute, a hierarchy, or a template.

Creating drill maps and paths

You can open the drill map editor in various ways, as follows:

- From **Project**: Select **File** | **New** | **Drill map**
- From **Report**: Select **Data menu** | **Edit drill map**
- From **Attributes**: Select **Tools** | **Edit drill map**
- From **Consolidation**: Select **Tools** | **Edit drill map**
- From **Custom group**: Select **Custom group** | **Edit drill map**

Selecting any of the preceding options opens a drill map editor, as follows:

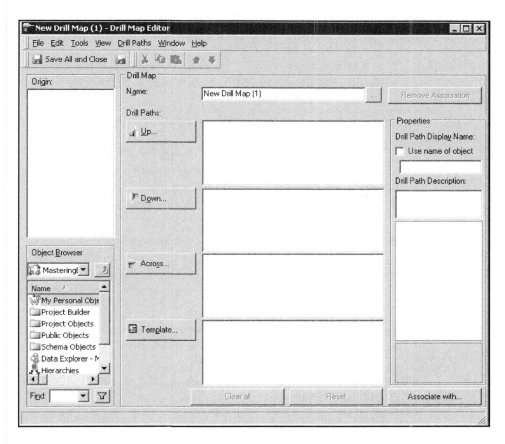

Enter the values of the different components of a drill map editor. The components are:

- **Origin**: This displays the object for which we want to create a drill map or the objects that are present in a report. Origin can either be empty or have values, depending on the method of our drill map creation.
- **Object browser**: Displays the objects of the project in hierarchical order. We can drag and drop the objects from here to any of the drill paths or to the origin section.

- **Drill map section**: This section has following components:
  - **Name**: This is the name of the drill map; upon selecting any object, the drill map name changes to `ProjectDrillMap`
  - **Browse**: Allows the user to edit the existing drill map
  - **Remove association**: Allows the user to disassociate the object from the current drill map
- **Drill Paths**: Here the user defines the destination to be drilled. This section contains the following drill paths:
  - **Up**: Allows a user to select an object, which could be an attribute, custom group, or consolidation. The object selected will be shown under the drill up menu on the report.
  - **Down**: The object selected will be shown under the drill down menu on the report.
  - **Across**: The object selected will be shown under the drill other directions menu on the report.
  - **Template**: This is where objects are displayed in a report. It allows the user to replace the report template with the destination template.
- **Properties**: This section contains the following components:
  - **Drill path display name**: Name displayed on the right; click while drilling on the report.
  - **Drill path description**: Description of drill path, with a limit of 250 characters.

Let's look at a drilling example:

We create a report showing Internet sales by region. We can drill down from the country level to see the sales in the states that make up the country and drill up from products. The relationship between attributes defines how we can drill between them. The drill map editor and report based on our example are as follows.

The **Drill map editor** is as follows:

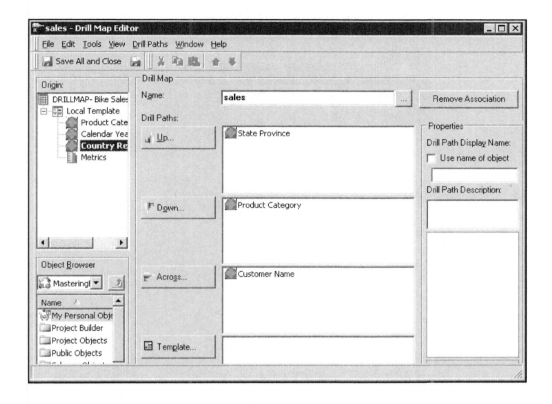

A report based on the drill map is as follows:

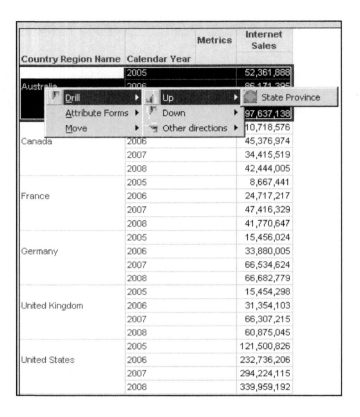

Freeform SQL

Freeform SQL gives you full control over accessing data; you can run your query directly against a data warehouse, bypassing the MicroStrategy SQL engine. Using Freeform SQL, you can access data from several ODBC sources such as Excel flat files. After writing the query in the Freeform SQL editor, we create a managed object or map it to an existing attribute. It is good to use Freeform SQL while creating static reports, fetching data from other sources, or using OLTP tables that are not set up for OLAP analysis.

You can have element prompts or security filters on Freeform reports, but you cannot include custom groups, consolidations, transformations, and existing filters on the report.

Creating a Freeform SQL report

The steps to create a Freeform SQL report are:

1. Select **File** | **New** | **Report**. A new grid dialog box opens.
2. Select the **Free Sources** tab; on this tab, select or create the database instance using the new ODBC source.
3. Select create **Freeform SQL** report and click **OK**.
4. This opens a Freeform SQL editor where we can type our SQL query, create or reuse existing attributes and metrics, and insert a prompt or security filters as needed.
5. Once SQL creation completes, click **OK** and this will close the Freeform SQL editor and open the report editor.
6. Select **File** and **Save** report.

An example:

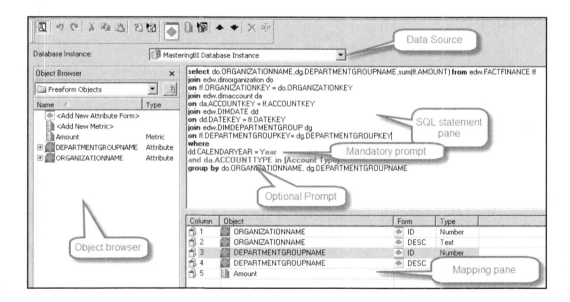

Freeform SQL features

Let us describe a few Freeform SQL features.

Prompt

Prompt controls the data display. Data will only be displayed based on the user input at runtime. In freeform, we can only have the value prompt and element prompt.

There are two options to add a prompt on to the freeform SQL editor:

- **Add New Prompt**: This allows you to create a new prompt.
- **Insert Prompt**: This allows you to select an existing prompt.

The different prompts are:

- **Value Prompt**: For a text value prompt, we need to manually add a single quote to the prompt name, whereas the date and number prompt can be used without a quote
- **Element Prompt**: For element prompts, if we are using the keyword IN, then we need parentheses around the prompt, but in the case of any other operator, such as >=, =, and so on, we need not have parentheses

Defining an optional prompt:

- In the SQL pane, highlight the line containing the prompt
- Right-click the highlighted part and select **Prompt-dependant SQL**; this will turn the whole line pink
- At runtime, even if we leave this prompt empty, the report will be executed properly

Security filters

Security filter provide us with control at the MicroStrategy level and restricts the result set that the user or group can view while executing the report. If the user belongs to a specific group, by default the security role assigned to that user is not applied to the report filter. To apply the security filter, we have to insert it within the SQL statement of the report. Security filters are created based on the project attributes.

The components of security filters are:

- **Attribute mapping pane**: Contains the column that replaces the attribute form contained in the security filter
- **Replacement string**: This will be inserted into the SQL pane and replaced by a security filter upon report execution

- **Select level**: Defines the level of detail the user or group can view upon executing the report
- **Ignored attributes**: Contains the attribute form that needs to be ignored while creating a security filter:

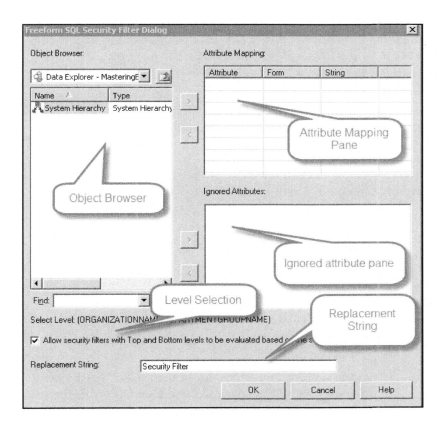

Intelligent cube

Intelligent cubes are multi-dimensional, in-memory copies of data that can be queried and accessed by many different documents and reports. Basically, the cube is allocated on the Intelligence Server machine and uses either memory or disk to store the definition and perform fast data retrieval.

We can treat it as a database where data is pre-cached and quickly accessed. To improve the report execution performance and response time, it's good to run the report with significant wait time and high usage against intelligent cubes. We cannot include custom groups, consolidations, derived metrics, prompts, or view filters in an intelligent cube.

The steps to create an intelligent cube are as follows:

1. Navigate to the folder where you want to create an intelligent cube; the best practice is to create it under **Public Objects** | **Reports**.
2. Select the report from which you want to build an intelligent cube. Edit and enter the report editor.
3. Select **Data** | **Intelligent Cube Options** | **Convert to Intelligent Cube**.
4. Click **Save and Close**, and enter an intelligent cube name.

This gives us a cube, but it has not been processed so it cannot be used for reporting. To make it usable, right-click on a cube and click **Run**. Once execution completes, it shows an **Execution complete** screen, giving us the provision to create reports out of a cube.

We can publish intelligent cubes as follows:

- Publish manually:
    1. Browse to the intelligent cube that needs to be published.
    2. Right-click the intelligent cube and click **Run.**
- Publish with schedule:
    1. Select **Administration** | **Configuration Managers** | **Subscriptions**.
    2. Right-click and select Subscription creation wizard.
    3. On the welcome page, click **Next**.
    4. On the specify characteristics screen, select the project that contains the intelligent cube and select **Cube refresh** as the delivery type. Click **Next**.

5. On the **Choose Report/Document** screen, browse to the intelligent cube to be published and click the right arrow to move it to the selected objects pane. Click **Next**.
6. On the choose recipient screen, select **Schedule** or **Run Subscription Manually**. Click **Next**.
7. On the **Specify Subscription Properties** screen, select **Expire Subscription** if subscription should expire on and the recipient email id who receives mail after the intelligent cube runs. Click **Next**.
8. The summary page is displayed; review the information and click **Finish** creating a subscription.

- Alternate way to publish an intelligent cube:
    1. Right-click the intelligent cube and select **Schedule Delivery To | Refresh Cube**.
    2. In **Refresh Cube Subscription Editor** enter the **Name, Schedule, Delivery Notification** and click **OK**.

Based on the schedule selected, the intelligent cube will be refreshed.

Republishing an intelligent cube using the preceding options will reload data from the data warehouse causing existing data to be overwritten. To avoid this, we can use the **incremental refresh intelligent cube** option.

Incremental refresh type options are:

- **Update**: Add new data if not in a cube, or else just update where applicable
- **Insert**: Add new data if available
- **Delete**: Based on the filter or report definition, data is deleted from the cube
- **Update only**: No new data is added, it is just updated where applicable

Types of object used for incremental fetching:

- **Filter**: This is used for incremental refresh; data returned by a filter is compared to an existing cube data
- **Report**: This is a template for an intelligent cube, and the cube is populated based on the report's data

To create an incremental refresh:

1. Right-click on an intelligent cube and select **Define Incremental Refresh Report**.
2. Select the options from the following screen for incremental refresh:

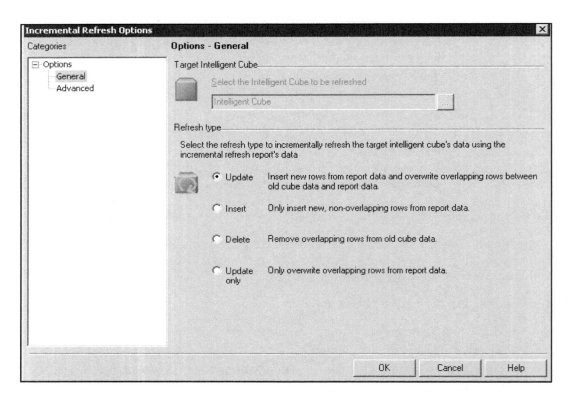

An example:

Let's say we have an intelligent cube which stores weekly sales data, so we would like an intelligent cube to update weekly sales data by the end of the week. We can use incremental refresh so that the data for one week is added without affecting the existing data.

Enabling and disabling intelligent cube usage

By default, reports can use an intelligent cube within the project, but we can enable or disable this as follows:

1. Right-click the project | **Project Configuration** | **Intelligent Cube** | **Dynamic Sourcing**:

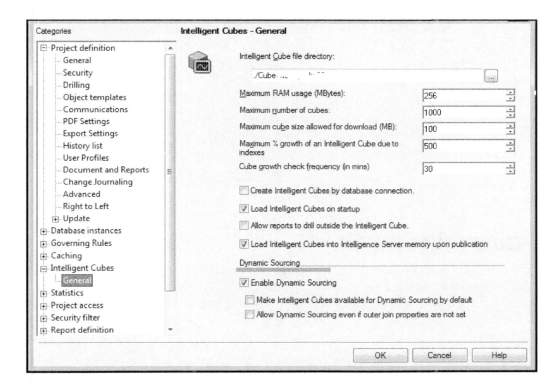

2. Select data | **VLDB properties** | **Dynamic Sourcing**:

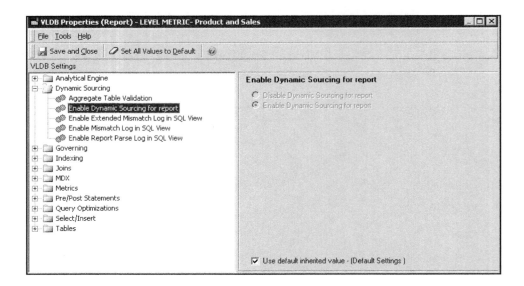

Advanced reports

A report represents the formatted data from the data warehouse, allowing a user to gather business insights and make decisions. All the previously mentioned components we discussed form an advanced report. The following screenshot displays a report in design view:

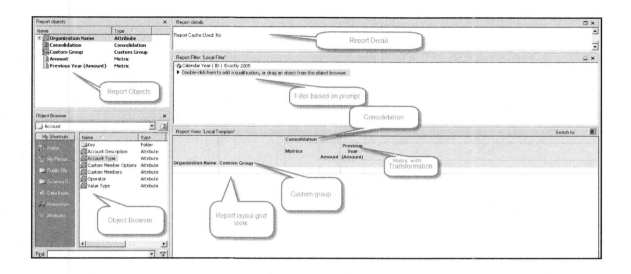

Creating and adding data to the document

A document is an object that displays data from one or more reports, intelligent cubes, or any other external data source. Documents have different visualization modes in different environments.

The visualization modes in Web are as follows:

- **Presentation mode**: With MicroStrategy 10, express mode is renamed as presentation mode. It allows you to view the result of the document. In this mode, we cannot make any changes to the document. Before MicroStrategy 10, express mode was used to display the results of the document.
- **Editable mode**: Allows you to quickly see the changes made to the document, that is, we can see all the results as we work.
- **Design mode**: Allows you create a document, display structure, or placeholder for the document, but not the actual results.

The visualization modes in Desktop are as follows:

- **Design mode**: Displays the structure or placeholder for the document object, but not the actual results.
- **PDF mode**: Allows you to view the final or result view of the document.

- **HTML mode**: Allows you to see the document as it will be displayed in Web, but sometimes with a few formatting differences.

To create a document from a report:

1. Right-click the report via MicroStrategy Web or developer.
2. Select create a document, or execute a report and then under the **Tools** menu in web, select create a document. This opens a report in express mode. If we want to edit it, we can select the design mode on the toolbar.

All the document sections are displayed in the layout area. The following screenshot displays the document sections:

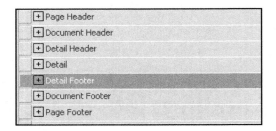

- **Page Header**: Any data field placed in the page header is displayed at the top of every page in the document.
- **Document Header**: Any data placed in this section is displayed once at the beginning of the document.
- **Detail Header**: This section comes before the detail section and is mostly used to display the column heading for the column used in the detail section.
- **Detail**: This section displays the main section, where we mostly place all our attributes and metrics.
- **Detail Footer**: This section is used to display information such as totals, that is, it sums up the information of the detail section.
- **Document Footer**: Any data placed in this section is displayed once at the end of the document. So, it is a good place to summarize the document.
- **Page Footer**: Any data placed in this section is displayed at the end of each page; an example is the page number.

Document controls

The following screenshot displays document objects:

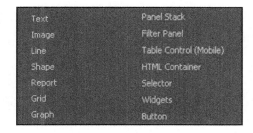

- **Text field:** displays data such as static labels, report names, page numbers, attributes, metrics, and so on.
- **Image:** This could be a logo on a document. To insert an image into the document, it should be present in an image folder inside the intelligence, web, and mobile servers. We can also insert an image from an external URL.
- **Line:** This is used to create a line, for example, underlining the report name.
- **Grid/graph:** Displays data for interpretation in a tabular or graphical manner.
- **HTML container:** This is used to display another report or document, real-time information from the Web, for example, displaying a real-time stock market report,
- **Panel stack:** Multiple panels are bundled together using panel stack. The user can move between the panels within panel stack, viewing one panel at a time. For example, let's say we need a document company's sales information and employees' information. We can create two different panels within panel stack to hold all the information about a company. Following is a sample image:

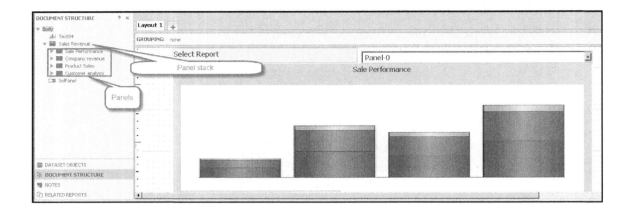

- **Selector:** This object gives you the option to flip between the panels or display results based on different attributes and metrics. There are different types of selectors, such as drop-down, slider, radio button, and so on. The following screenshot shows of the drop-down selector for flipping between different panels:

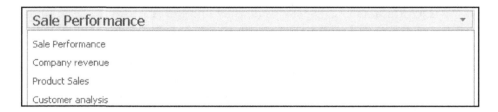

Following are the steps to add a selector:

1. On the document, click **Insert | Selector**, and then select the type of selector you want to insert into the document.
2. Once a selector is added to the document, select **Properties and Formatting** by right-clicking on the selector.
3. Navigate to the selector tab and select any of the action types from the drop-down, as required. Action type allows us to choose between attribute, metric, panels, and attribute element.
4. Click **Apply** and **OK** to return to the document.

Note: The user cannot add a selector to the details section of a document.

- **Widgets:** This object allows a user to visualize data in different ways in MicroStrategy Web.

Look at the following sample document:

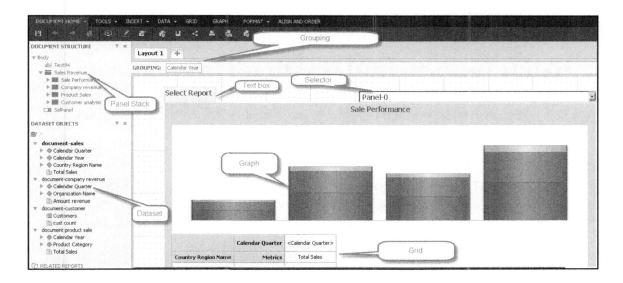

Moving towards a dashboard

A dashboard is a one-page long, interactive, special type of document. It gives a more flexible way of presenting data, as each user is capable of changing their dashboard view based on their permissions. It uses the same components as documents, and in the next chapter, we will learn about layering data, selectors, and widgets in detail.

This chapter is intended to provide you with the basic steps for dashboard creation.

To create a dashboard do the following:

- Click **Create | New Dashboard**
- Select a document dataset, which could either be a report, intelligent cube, or any other external source data:
- From the **Data** menu, select **Add data set**
- Browse and select the data source and click **OK**
- Add controls or objects to the dashboard as needed
- After we have entered all the required information, click the **Save** icon and give the dashboard a name.

Linking reports and documents

The link allows executing a report/document from within the report even if the destination report is not related to the original report. We can execute a link from a report, grid/graph within the document, attributes, metrics, and prompts.

The components of links are as follows:

- **Name**: This is the descriptive name of the link, which helps in identifying the target. By default, it is Link1 for the first link.
- **Target**: This is the report or document that we want to execute from within the report.
- **Prompt based on target**: Gives the user a way to answer the prompt in a target, if any.

To create a link:

1. Open the report on which you want to create a link.
2. To create a link, right-click the object (attributes, metrics, and hierarchies) and select **Edit Links.**
3. If this is the first link, browse for a report or a document under run this report and document heading, and select target report/document.
4. Select the target prompt from the drop-down.
5. Select **Prompt Answer Method** from the drop-down. The options displayed are:
   - **Answer with the same prompt from the source**: Source reports and prompt answers are used for the target. It is only applicable if both source and target use the same prompt.
   - **Prompt user**: While executing a target report, the user manually

answers the prompts.

- **Use default answer**: Default answers are considered while executing the target.
- **Answer with an empty answer**: No prompt answer is needed or provided while executing the target.

6. Repeat the steps to answer all the prompts; once completed, click **OK**.
7. Now we can navigate from `Report 1` to `Report 2`.

An example of linked reports:

Let's say we have one report, which displays the sales by region, and another report further divides it into sales by region-product and sales based on the year prompt. We have followed the preceding steps and created a link from a sales-region report to a sales-product report at the attribute level. Now, right-clicking on the attribute points to the link and shows the report sales-product as follows:

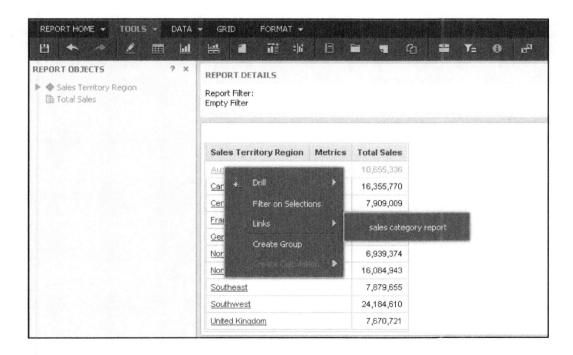

Selecting sales category executes that report and displays the result as follows:

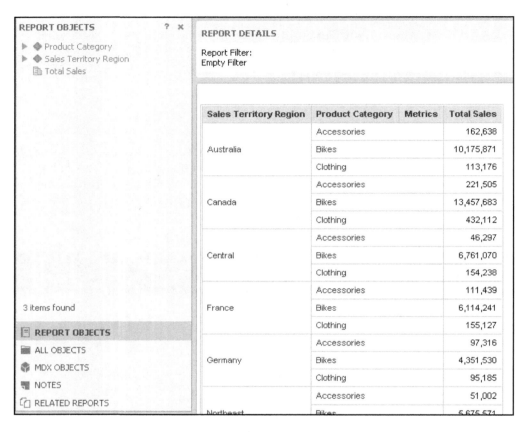

Similarly, we can create a link to a document from metrics or hierarchies.

Summary

In this chapter, we learned about consolidations, which are made up of an ordered collection of consolidation elements; this is the grouping of attribute elements. It allows inter-row arithmetic operations. A custom group is made up of an ordered collection of custom group elements, which contains its own set of filtering qualifications, a special type of document that displays data and summarizes all the key metrics for business use. We learned about drill maps to view additional information after the report has been executed.

We also discussed Freeform SQL, which allows the creation of customized SQL for data retrieval from a database, and in-memory copying of data, which is used for fast reporting and data fetching, known as intelligent cubes. In the next chapter we will cover graphical techniques for presenting data for analysis using maps, graphs, and advanced charts. We will also discuss integrating third-party ESRI map tools with MicroStrategy for creating geo-based reports.

4
Advanced Visualization Techniques

Visualization makes understanding data easier than a grid display of data. An appealing, understandable image can engage the user and transmit concepts more rapidly than a grid with some numbers. Trends and patterns that are not revealed in text-based data are easily identified by placing data in a visual context.

In the previous chapter, we learned about the basics of document creation and its components, such as panels and selectors. This chapter will cover:

- The dashboard style document and its components
- Basic and advanced visualization techniques
- MicroStrategy and ESRI integration

Dashboard style document

The dashboard style document is an interactive document, which is usually one-page long and is used to summarize and present key business indicators. The user can control the view of the data using several features, such as widgets, selectors, filters, and so on. There are different types of dashboard that provide different business values, and are listed as follows:

- **Performance Summary dashboard**: They present data in graphical and tabular form. This type of dashboard is ideal for communicating summary information as a high-level view of the business.
- **Metrics dashboard**: They present status and trends with graphical indicators, basically displaying metrics to compare the actual performance to goals.

- **Dynamic content dashboard**: They present many reports in a single dashboard, using multiple layers or panels.
- **Dynamic visualization dashboard**: They present more data within less space, using interactive widgets and sophisticated formatting.

The following dashboard components help the user to view subsets of data.

Panels

A panel is a holder that groups several elements such as a selector, line, image, grid/graph object, and so on. A group of panels is known as a panel stack. Individual panels are stacked on top of each other and the user can flip between these panels using selectors.

Insert panelstack and panels by the following steps :

1. Open the document in design mode via MicroStrategy Web.
2. Select **INSERT** | **Panel stack** and click on the desired location where you want to add the panel stack.
3. This adds the panel stack with a single panel.
4. Now, to add another panel to the stack, **Select** the panel stack and place your cursor under the title bar. The toolbar is displayed.
5. Click **Add panel**.
6. This adds a new panel and sets it as the current panel:

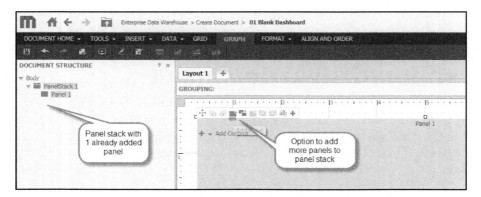

Note: We can also click **Duplicate Panel** if we want to copy panels.

Filter panel

This panel only contains selectors which gives provision to select the data as needed. This component can only be added using Web.

Insert a filter panel as follows:

1. Open the dashboard in design mode.
2. Expand the document section and select the panel where you want to insert a filter stack:

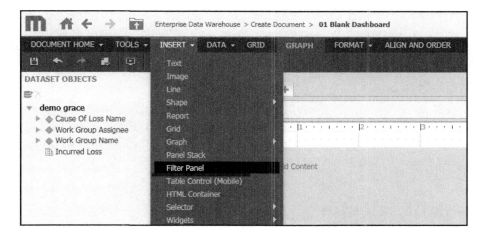

3. A filter stack can be inserted either by clicking the plus sign (+) next to **Add Content** on the panel, or clicking **INSERT** | **Filter Panel** and then dragging the cursor over the panel. This adds the **Filter Panel**.

By default, a filter panel is added with a title bar that lets the user clear, expand, or collapse all filters. For example, let's say we need a dashboard to display data for a region where the total sales of bikes was more than 114,000 in 2007; this could be achieved by a filter panel as shown here:

Here, in one filter panel, we have three different selectors to filter the data as the user needs. So now we will define the dashboard's other components in the next section.

Selectors

A selector provides interactivity for the user and lets the user flip between the panels of the panel stack, target a panel stack to filter the components within it, and display different contents for another selector, metrics, attributes, consolidation, and so on within a grid/graph.

Types of selector

The selector type defines how and what the selector controls. The choice of a selector depends on the target and source selection and the user's interface preference:

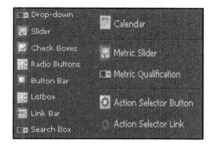

Selector types

Add and format a selector as follows:

1. Open a document in design mode.
2. Select the section in which the **Selector** needs to be inserted:

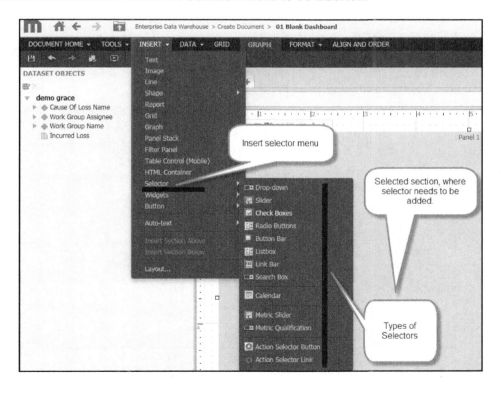

3. To add a selector, either click **INSERT** | **Selector** or, at the top of the panel, click the **+** sign and select a **Selector**.

4. Drag the cursor to the location where the selector needs to be added.

5. Once a selector is added, we can right-click **Selector** and select **Properties and Formatting** to format the selector.

6. On the **Selector** tab in the **Properties and Formatting** window, we can select the action type of the selector, source, and target (most important when defining a selector):

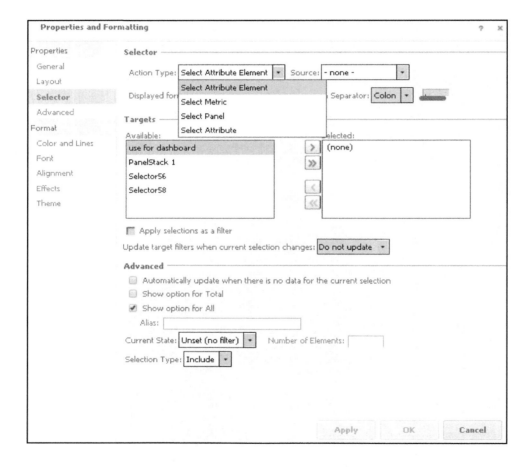

Creating a selector based on the target can be done by clicking the section where the user wants to add an element selector:

Selector source	How to create
Attribute of dataset as source	Under the dataset objects, right-click on an attribute and then select `Add Element Selector`.
Attribute within grid as source	Within the grid, right-click on any of the attributes and select `Create Selector Control`.
Metric within grid as source	Within the grid, right click on any of the metrics and select `Create Selector Control`.
Panel as source	Under the document structure, right-click on the panel structure and select `Create Panel Selector`.
Filter metric value	Click **Insert** menu, point to **Selector**, then select either **Metric Slider** or **Metric Qualification**.

Let's take the example of a selector that targets other selectors. We want to display a dashboard with a product subcategory and name. One selector displays the product subcategory and the other selector displays the product name, based on the product subcategory. This can be achieved when the subcategory targets the product name selector. Say the user selects **Mountain Bikes** in the subcategory; the other selector should only display product names associated with **Mountain Bikes**. This is shown in the following screenshot:

Basic visualization (graphs)

Graphs allow the user to analyze data quickly by providing a visual view of data. In MicroStrategy, there are a number of graph styles, such as vertical, polar, bubble and so on, depending on the user's needs. The following screenshot shows the types of graph in MicroStrategy:

These graphs can have further subtypes; a **Vertical bar** graph can be further divided into absolute, clustered, stacked, and so on:

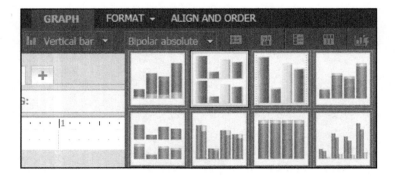

Steps to add a graph are as follows:

1. Open the document in design mode.
2. Click **INSERT | GRAPH** and select the appropriate graph type.

Graph type selection depends on the number of objects in the report, as we cannot display the graphs until a certain number of attributes or metrics appear in the report. The following table displays the minimum number of objects needed for different types of graph:

Minimum objects needed	Graph style
One attribute, one metric	Area (Vertical, Horizontal)
	Bar (Vertical, Horizontal)
	Line (Vertical, Horizontal)
	Pie
	Radar
	Histogram
	3D: Riser
	3D: Floating
	3D: Connect Series
	3D: Surface
	Gauge
	Funnel
	Pareto
One attribute, two metrics	Scatter: XY
	Polar
	Stock: Hi-Lo
	Pareto: Percent
	Budgeting
	Gantt
One attribute, three metrics	Scatter: XYZ
	Bubble
	Stock: Hi-Lo-Open
	3D: Connect group
	3d: Scatter
One attribute, four metrics	Stock: Hi-Lo-Open-Close
One attribute, five metrics	BoxPlot

One attribute, one metric – Vertical Line – Absolute graph

The following graphs displays the amount of revenue generated by various bike subcategories in 2005, on a monthly basis. The following screenshot shows design mode:

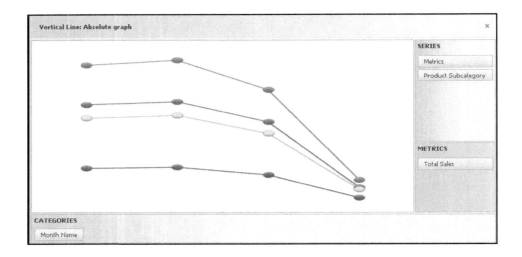

Vertical Line graph in design mode

The following screenshot shows presentation mode.Once the graph is created in design mode, we can run it in presentation mode for the final output:

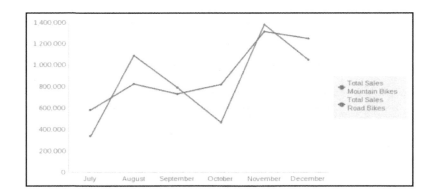

Vertical Line graph in presentation mode

One attribute, two metrics – Budgeting

These graphs are used to compare two sets of closely related data, such as when comparing actual revenue against forecasted revenue or prior revenue. In this example, we are comparing actual sales with expected sales.

The following screenshot shows this graph in design mode:

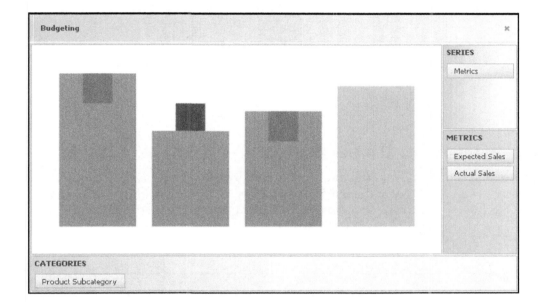

Budgeting graph in design mode

Once the graph has been created in design mode, we can run it in presentation mode for the final output:

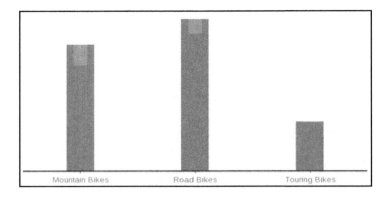

Budgeting graph in presentation mode

One attribute, three metrics – Bubble chart

The following graph displays the total order quantity, sales, and profit earned by products in different years. The size of the markers gives the actual picture of the metric. The position of the object determines how the object will be displayed in the resulting graph.

The following screenshot shows this graph in design mode:

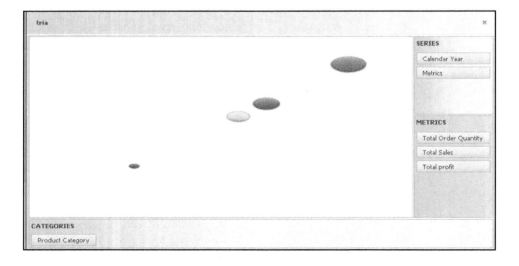

Bubble graph in design mode

The following screenshot shows this graph in presentation mode:

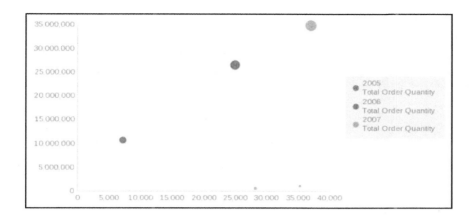

Bubble graph in presentation mode

One attribute, four metrics – Stock: Hi-Lo-Open-Close

This type of graph allows the user to view high, low, opening, and closing values, all in one graph. While creating this graph, the user should arrange the columns of the graph in the proper order. In this graph:

- The first metric is for the high value
- The second metric is for the low value
- The third metric is for the open value
- The fourth metric is for the close value

The following graph displays a company's monthly stock prices. We can create a graph to analyze company stocks and inventories on a daily, monthly, and so on basis.

The following screenshot shows this graph in design mode:

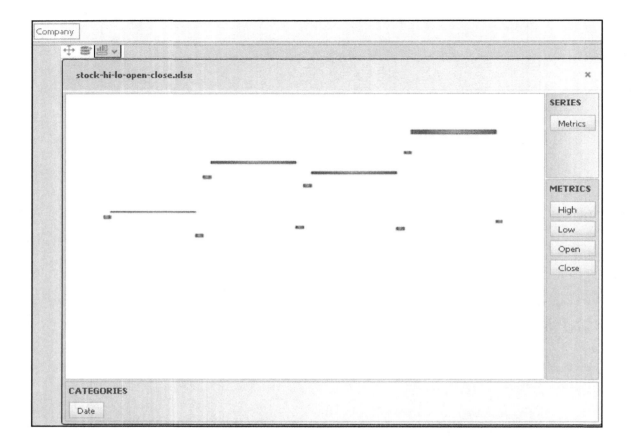

Stock: Hi-Lo-Open-Close graph in design mode

The following screenshot shows this graph in presentation mode:

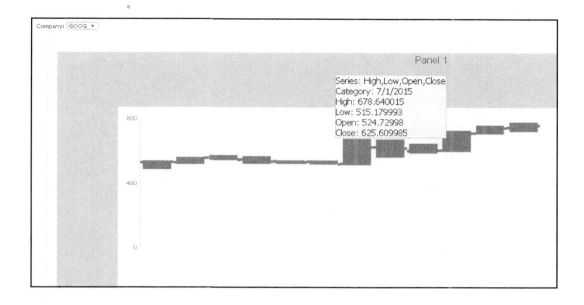

Stock: Hi-Lo-Open-Close graph in presentation mode

One attribute, five metrics – Boxplot

A **boxplot** lets the user depict a grouping of numerical data based on its quartiles. It is also known as a box and whisker plot; the "whiskers" are the lines extending vertically from the box. It helps us compare similar distributions at a glance; the goal is to make the center, spread, and overall range of values immediately apparent.

The box and whisker plot includes:

- Lower quartile: Middle point of lower half of data
- Upper quartile: Middle point of upper half of data
- Minimum value: Largest value
- Maximum value: Smallest value
- Median: Middle point of ascendingly arranged data

These are five different metrics and one attribute.

The easiest way to explain this graph is to say a company wants to identify the age group of prospective buyers; this could be done using a boxplot graph.

The following screenshot shows this graph in design mode:

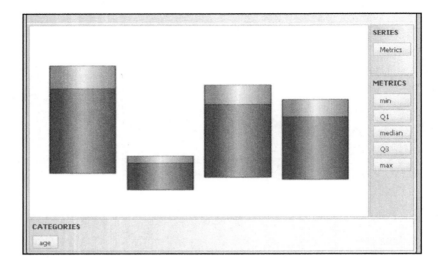

Boxplot in design mode

The following screenshot shows this graph in presentation mode:

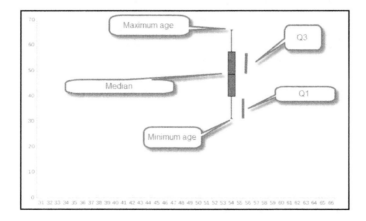

Boxplot in presentation mode

Similarly, we can use a boxplot to analyze the company's sales in different quarters, as follows:

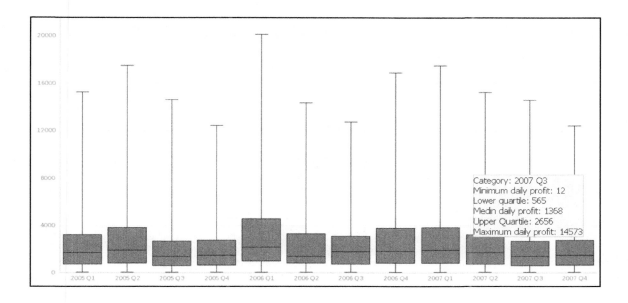

Boxplot in presentation mode

Clicking on individual boxes provides related information within a tooltip.

Complex graph – Gantt

This type of chart is useful for presenting project schedules, human resources-related activities, and so on. It basically displays the start, end, and duration of an activity. In the following example, we have created a chart to identify the length of time an employee has been at the company.

The following screenshot shows this graph in design mode:

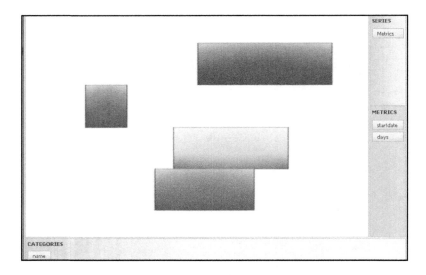

Gantt graph in design mode

The following screenshot shows this graph in presentation mode:

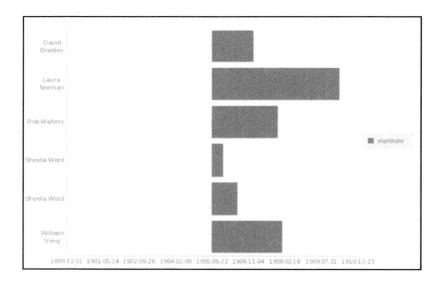

Gantt graph in presentation mode

Widgets

Widgets provide the user with a visual and interactive look for their data. In this section, with MicroStrategy 10 we will discuss DHTML widgets. We will also talk about replacing Flash widgets with other components, such as graph or selectors.

The following screenshot shows the types of DHTML widget available with MicroStrategy 10:

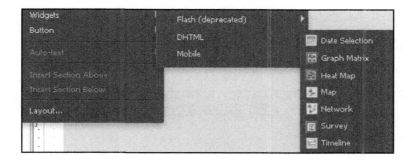

Perform following steps to create widgets:

1. In MicroStrategy Web, open the document in `Design Mode`.
2. Click **Insert | Widgets | DHTML** and select the appropriate widget.
3. Click on the location in your document where you want to place the widget. The grid/graph containing the widget is displayed. A small icon at the bottom-right corner of the grid/graph identifies the type of widget you have added to the document.
4. Add objects to the grid/graph from the **Dataset Objects** panel on the left, select objects, and drag them on top of the widget, based on the requirements of a selected widget type.

Date selection widget

This is a calendar selector that lets the user view data based on the date selected. The date selection widget displays a calendar where the user can select the date for which data is needed.

The minimum requirement for the date selection wizard is at least one date attribute.

To create a date selection widget:

1. Open the document in MicroStrategy Web, in design mode.
2. Create the grid/graph or panel stack to be used as the target.
3. Once a target is created, follow the steps to create the selector widget.
4. Click the **Insert** menu | **Widgets** | **DHTML** | **Date Selection**.
5. Click on the location in the document where you want to place the widget. The grid/graph containing the widget is displayed.
6. From the **Dataset Objects** panel on the left, select one date attribute and drag it on top of the grid/graph's rows.

Now to connect the selector to the target, right-click the attribute to be used as the selector, and choose **Use As Selector**.

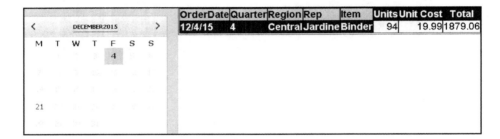

Sample document with date selection wizard

Graph matrix widgets

A graph matrix widget allows the user to analyze trends in various metric dimensions. Basically, a graph matrix is composed of several area graphs. The graphs should have either three attributes in a row and one metric in a column, or two attributes in a row and one attribute and one metric in a column.

For example, in the following widget, the rows of the report display two attributes, sales territory region and product category, and the column displays one attribute, calendar year, and one metric, total sales:

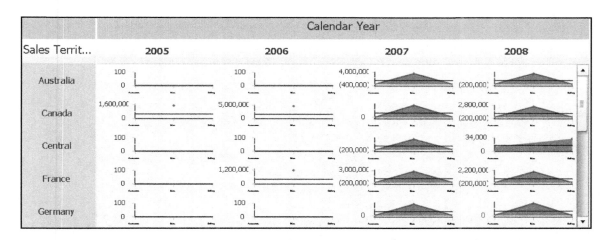

DHTML view graph

In Flash (deprecated) view the graph location is displayed as follows:

A separate graph is displayed for each combination of objects. To view a document in Flash view:

1. Select the graph.
2. Click **Tools | Report custom visualization.**

3. Move the graph matrix (deprecated) from available to selected.
4. Click **OK.**

Heat map widget

A heat mapwidget represents different attribute elements using combinations of colored rectangles. In a heat map:

- Rectangle size represents the relative weight
- Rectangle color represents the relative change in the value of the rectangle (a percentage term)
- Hovering over a rectangle displays complete information about the associated metrics and attribute values

The minimum requirement for a heat map is at least one attribute in a row and two metrics in a column. Based on the attributes selected, the rectangles are created and grouped.

In the following example, we show the total profit and sales made by a product in different regions on a yearly basis. To do this, we have selected three attributes, product, year, and region, and two different metrics, total product and total sales.

The following is the DHTML view of the heat map:

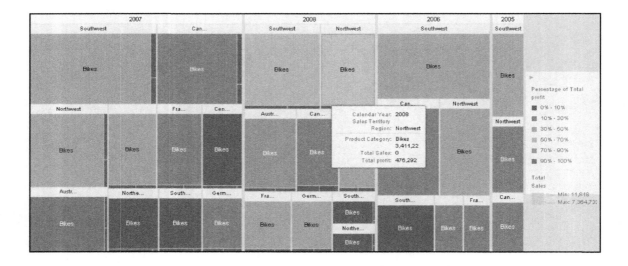

Map widget

A map widget provides data for location-based analysis. We will discuss this widget in detail in the section covering the integration of ESRI maps with MicroStrategy.

Network widgets

Network widgets allow the user to identify an individual item and the relationship between these items. With this widget, the user can choose from one of the following three layout options:

- Force-directed layout
- Circular layout
- Linear layout

The minimum requirements for a network widget are two attributes, which act as starting and ending nodes for the edges, and three metrics, used to size the edges and nodes, and color the edges.

Let's say the user wants to identify the relationship between the products sold in different regions based on profit, cost, and revenue; the following network graph displays this:

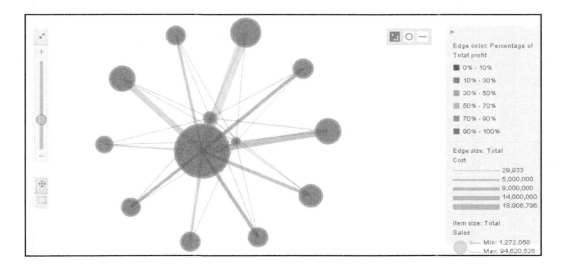

Forced-directed layout

A different representation is used to display the relationship between attributes and metrics:

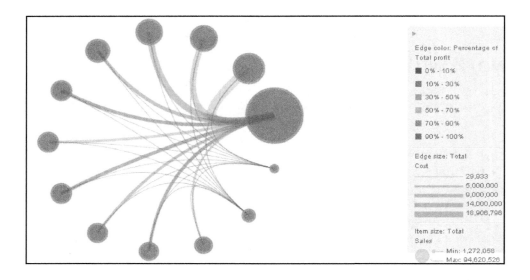

Circular layout

And now the linear representation of attribute and metric connectivity:

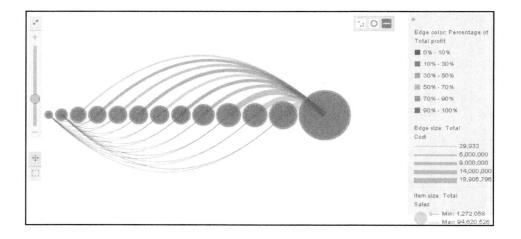

Linear layout

Survey widget

A survey widget lets the user create a survey in the database. The user can answer survey questions, which are then stored in the data source. This widget allows the user to dynamically generate and maintain surveys.

Prerequisites for creating a survey widget are as follows:

- Create table access in database
- MicroStrategy 9.4 or above
- Transaction service license

To create a survey widget:

1. Create or import a table with the information needed to create or display a survey, for example `questionID`, `questiontitle`, `answertitle` and so on:

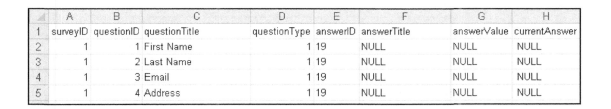

	A	B	C	D	E	F	G	H
1	surveyID	questionID	questionTitle	questionType	answerID	answerTitle	answerValue	currentAnswer
2	1	1	First Name	1	19	NULL	NULL	NULL
3	1	2	Last Name	1	19	NULL	NULL	NULL
4	1	3	Email	1	19	NULL	NULL	NULL
5	1	4	Address	1	19	NULL	NULL	NULL

2. Add the created or imported table to the warehouse catalog and import the table prefix.
3. Create the attributes based on each of the columns in the added table.
4. Create a report with the newly created attributes.
5. Create another table to store the survey response.
6. Create a transaction report using freeform SQL.

7. Create transaction reports.

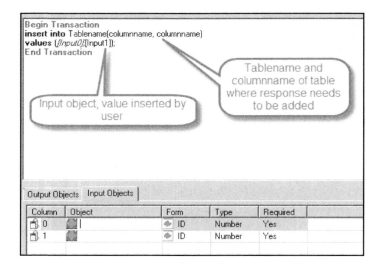

Freeform SQL editor

8. Go to MicroStrategy Web and create a document based on adding the report created in step *4*.
9. Right-click on the added report and click **Properties and Formatting**.
10. Under **Properties and Formatting,** go to the grid and uncheck **Enable incremental fetch on grid**, then navigate to widgets and set it as DHTML survey.
11. Click **Widget Properties**, match the survey elements to the appropriate template units, and click **OK.**
12. Again, right-click on the report and select **Configure Transaction.**
13. In the configure transaction dialog box, browse for the report created in step *6* and update the input properties accordingly.
14. Create an **Action Selector** button to submit the survey.
15. Save and run the document.
16. In presentation mode, fill in the survey answers and press **Submit**.

17. The table created in step 5 should be updated based on the user's response:

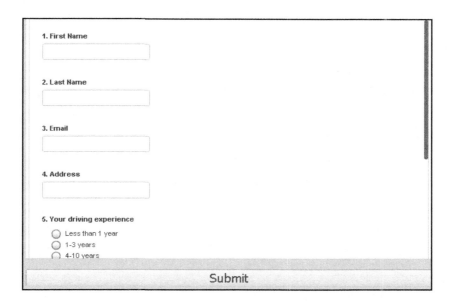

Sample of a survey widget on a document

Timeline widget

A timeline widget provides the ability to look at data from different time frames on a single page, allowing the user to quickly spot repeating trends.

The minimum requirements for a timeline widget are as follows:

- The report must have the first two attributes on the row axis, and the first attribute must have its first form.
- The first attribute has the following forms:
    - **Event name**: This mandatory form is displayed on the horizontal bar () representing the event on the timeline
    - **Event description**: This optional form displays the description in the tooltip
    - **Event image**: This optional form displays the image in the tooltip that opens when an event is clicked on in the timeline
    - **Event color**: This optional form is the color of the horizontal bar

- **Event icon**: This optional form is the source for the image displayed on the horizontal bar
- **Event text position**: This optional form determines whether to start the text of the event name to the right of or on top of the horizontal bar

- The second attribute represents the start date of the event
- The third attribute is optional and represents the end date of the event

Let's say an HR department wants to understand the trends for employee retention by seeing the start date and end date for an employee, and how long the employee stayed with the company; this is achieved using a timeline:

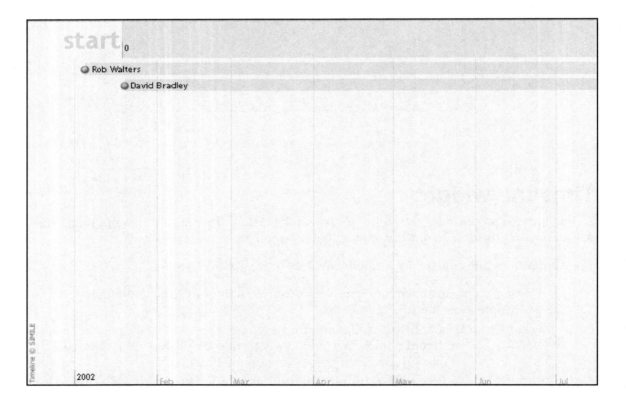

Sample document with a timeline widget

In MicroStrategy 10, use the following rules to replace Flash widgets with a graph:

Flash widget	Graph
Funnel	Funnel
Interactive bubble graph	Bubble
Interactive stacked graph	Vertical Area (change the graph sub-type to Stacked in the Graph toolbar)
Time series slider	Vertical Area

Flash widget	Selector
Date selection	Calendar
Fish eye	Listbox

Visual insight

Visual insight provides the user with the ability to create quick, interactive dashboards. It allows the user to import data from several different sources, manipulate the data, and apply visualization techniques as per business needs. Basically, a quick dashboard is like a document, but the process of creating this dashboard is easier and faster. A quick dashboard can display multiple visualizations with data from different datasets; however, each visualization can display data from only one dataset at a time. Visual insight lets the user share a quick dashboard through e-mail, embedding it in web or linking it to a quick dashboard. To share a dashboard, it must be saved. We can share the dashboard by clicking on the following icon:

To create a quick dashboard, the user can select data from the following datasets:

- Import data from external data sources, as shown in the following screenshot:

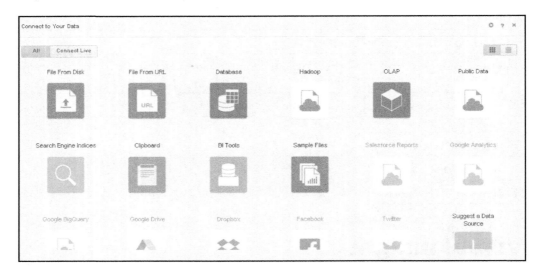

- Import data based on existing reports, cubes, or objects

To add a new quick dashboard, you must have the following:

- The MicroStrategy report service product
- Document designer privileges
- Web edit, create, and run dashboard privileges

Create a quick dashboard as follows:

1. Select the dashboard dataset, which can be added as in the following ways:
   - Add external data
   - Create new report
   - Add existing dataset

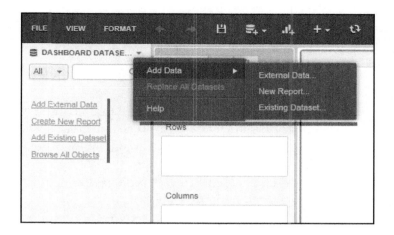

2. On the home screen, click **Create | New Dashboard:**

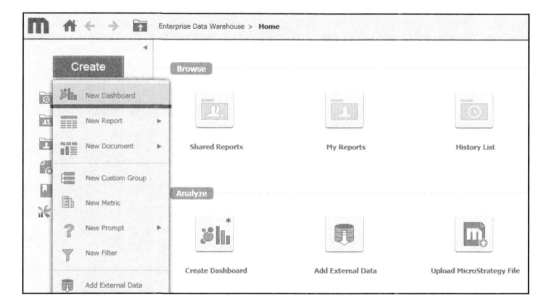

3. Browse all objects.
4. Select the visualization technique.
5. Based on the visualization technique, update the selected fields within the editor panel.
6. Once completed, click **Save** and run the newly created dashboard.

Types of dashboard visualizations

In the previous sections, we have discussed these visualization techniques in detail. Visual insight is just a faster and easier way to insert these visualizations:

- **Grid:** Data is displayed in grid format and this allows the user to sort, pivot, drill, and filter data
- **Graph:** Data is displayed in graphical format and the user can choose between different graphs, such as area graphs, line graphs, and so on
- **Heat map:** Data is displayed as a combination of colored rectangles, each rectangle representing an attribute
- **Map:** Data is displayed as a geographical location on a map and markers are displayed based on metric values
- **Network:** Data is displayed as a network of nodes, where each node represents an attribute

In the following dashboard, we have used different visualization techniques:

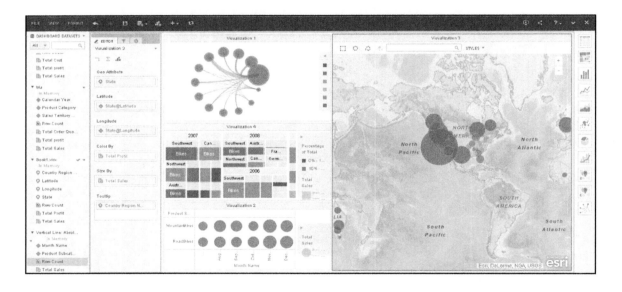

Sample quick dashboard

Adding additional visualizations

In MicroStrategy 10, the user can add new visualizations using JavaScript graph tools such as D3, Highchart, and so on. The user can use already-created visualizations from `https:/ /community.microstrategy.com/t5/Custom-Visualization-Gallery/bg-p/vizga llery`.

To use this new feature, we just have to insert the folder that contains your graph into the plugins folder of MicroStrategy Web.

In our case, we have inserted a **D3 Bubble Chart** for visualization, and this is available under DHTML as follows:

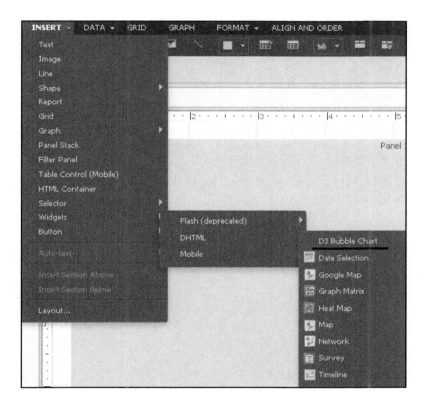

MicroStrategy and ESRI map integration

Location-based analytics or geospatial analytics allow companies to gain better and additional insights into their market and growth opportunities. This lets users make faster and more informed decisions. This can be achieved by integrating MicroStrategy with either ESRI Maps or Google Maps. ESRI Maps for MicroStrategy allows the user to deploy dynamic maps and perform rich geoanalysis. In this section, we will discuss MicroStrategy's integration with MicroStrategy.

Integration types are:

- ESRI cloud-based map integration
- ESRI on-premises map integration

ESRI on-premises integration requires the user to purchase an on-premises ArcGIS server, or use a publicly available ESRI server. In the following section, we will discuss ESRI cloud-based map integration.

To set up or configure cloud-based ESRI maps obtain an ESRI map key:

1. Navigate to the MicroStrategy download site: `https://software.microstrat egy.com/Download/index.aspx`.
2. Locate the ESRI map keys link in the left-hand navigation.
3. On the next screen, select **release and DSI**, and click **Retrieve License key(s)**. This will provide you with the key.

Once you have the ESRI key, follow these steps to configure the ESRI map:

1. Navigate to the `esriConfig.xml` file located in the MicroStrategy Web directory`\WEB-INF\xml\config`.

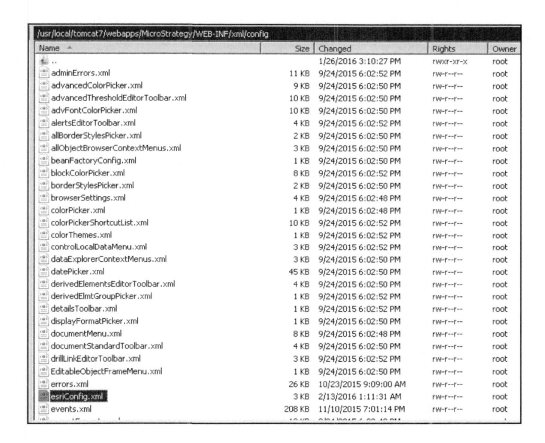

/usr/local/tomcat7/webapps/MicroStrategy/WEB-INF/xml/config

Name	Size	Changed	Rights	Owner
..		1/26/2016 3:10:27 PM	rwxr-xr-x	root
adminErrors.xml	11 KB	9/24/2015 6:02:52 PM	rw-r--r--	root
advancedColorPicker.xml	9 KB	9/24/2015 6:02:50 PM	rw-r--r--	root
advancedThresholdEditorToolbar.xml	10 KB	9/24/2015 6:02:50 PM	rw-r--r--	root
advFontColorPicker.xml	10 KB	9/24/2015 6:02:50 PM	rw-r--r--	root
alertsEditorToolbar.xml	4 KB	9/24/2015 6:02:52 PM	rw-r--r--	root
allBorderStylesPicker.xml	2 KB	9/24/2015 6:02:50 PM	rw-r--r--	root
allObjectBrowserContextMenus.xml	3 KB	9/24/2015 6:02:50 PM	rw-r--r--	root
beanFactoryConfig.xml	1 KB	9/24/2015 6:02:50 PM	rw-r--r--	root
blockColorPicker.xml	8 KB	9/24/2015 6:02:52 PM	rw-r--r--	root
borderStylesPicker.xml	2 KB	9/24/2015 6:02:50 PM	rw-r--r--	root
browserSettings.xml	4 KB	9/24/2015 6:02:48 PM	rw-r--r--	root
colorPicker.xml	1 KB	9/24/2015 6:02:48 PM	rw-r--r--	root
colorPickerShortcutList.xml	10 KB	9/24/2015 6:02:52 PM	rw-r--r--	root
colorThemes.xml	1 KB	9/24/2015 6:02:52 PM	rw-r--r--	root
controlLocalDataMenu.xml	3 KB	9/24/2015 6:02:52 PM	rw-r--r--	root
dataExplorerContextMenus.xml	3 KB	9/24/2015 6:02:50 PM	rw-r--r--	root
datePicker.xml	45 KB	9/24/2015 6:02:50 PM	rw-r--r--	root
derivedElementsEditorToolbar.xml	4 KB	9/24/2015 6:02:50 PM	rw-r--r--	root
derivedElmtGroupPicker.xml	1 KB	9/24/2015 6:02:52 PM	rw-r--r--	root
detailsToolbar.xml	1 KB	9/24/2015 6:02:52 PM	rw-r--r--	root
displayFormatPicker.xml	1 KB	9/24/2015 6:02:50 PM	rw-r--r--	root
documentMenu.xml	8 KB	9/24/2015 6:02:48 PM	rw-r--r--	root
documentStandardToolbar.xml	4 KB	9/24/2015 6:02:50 PM	rw-r--r--	root
drillLinkEditorToolbar.xml	3 KB	9/24/2015 6:02:52 PM	rw-r--r--	root
EditableObjectFrameMenu.xml	1 KB	9/24/2015 6:02:50 PM	rw-r--r--	root
errors.xml	26 KB	10/23/2015 9:09:00 AM	rw-r--r--	root
esriConfig.xml	3 KB	2/13/2016 1:11:31 AM	rw-r--r--	root
events.xml	208 KB	11/10/2015 7:01:14 PM	rw-r--r--	root

2. Edit the `esriConfig.xml` file in any text editor and enter the ESRI map key obtained from ESRI between the `<apps>` `</apps>` tags, as shown in the following screenshot:

```
<ec>
   <!-- The following nodes are used for on-premises map integration -->
   <bms>
     <bm key="default"> </bm>
   </bms>
   <pjs>
   </pjs>
   <!-- End of nodes used for on-premises map integration -->

   <!-- The following nodes are used for cloud-based map integration -->

   <!-- Please insert keys obtained from MicroStrategy Map key from Technical Support in apps node -->
   <apps>
ADD KEY HERE|
</apps>

   <layers>
     <layer id="1"
         title="US-States"
         ml="http://services.arcgis.com/P3ePLMYs2RVChkJx/arcgis/rest/services/USA_States_Generalized/FeatureServer/0"/>
     <layer id="2"
         title="US-ZipCodes"
         ml="http://services.arcgis.com/P3ePLMYs2RVChkJx/arcgis/rest/services/USA_ZIP_Codes/FeatureServer/0"/>
     <layer id="3"
         title="US-Counties"
         ml="http://services.arcgis.com/P3ePLMYs2RVChkJx/arcgis/rest/services/USA_Counties_Generalized/FeatureServer/0"/>
     <layer id="4"
         title="World-Countries Detailed"
         ml="http://services.arcgis.com/P3ePLMYs2RVChkJx/arcgis/rest/services/World_Countries/FeatureServer/0" />
     <layer id="5"
         title="World-Countries Generalized"
         ml="http://services.arcgis.com/P3ePLMYs2RVChkJx/arcgis/rest/services/World_Countries_(Generalized)/FeatureServer/0" />
     <layer id="6"
         title="World-Admin-Divisions"
         ml="http://services.arcgis.com/P3ePLMYs2RVChkJx/arcgis/rest/services/World_Administrative_Divisions/FeatureServer/0"/>
```

3. Save the `esriConfig.xml` file.
4. Restart the web server for the changes to take effect.

For this book, we used Tomcat on Linux. Navigate to the Tomcat bin directory in Linux and issue the following commands to stop and then start the server:

```
./shutdown.sh
./startup.sh
```

Creating reports in MicroStrategy for Geo-based analysis

ESRI map has following map types:

- The Marker map type is useful when the user wants an individual marker for each location
- An Area map colors areas based on their metric value
- A Density map is useful when the user wants to understand trends for many geographic locations based on the concentration of geographic data

Prerequisites before designing a document using ESRI map are as follows:

- To display markers or density maps, the user must have latitude and longitude values. This is achieved with either one attribute or two separate attributes.
- To display areas on the map, the user must create an attribute with the name of the location.
- At least one metric must be used if the user wants to use color formatting.

To create an ESRI map visualization:

1. In MicroStrategy Web, click **Create | New dashboard**.
2. Select the map icon from the **Visualization** gallery. If the **Visualization** gallery is not available, select it from the **View** menu.
3. Select the dataset needed for document creation. It can be an existing dataset, or data from an external source.
4. Click the **PROPERTIES** panel (shown in the following screenshot) and select the appropriate options for **Map style**, **Map type**, **Map Options**, and so on. If the **PROPERTIES** panel is not available, select it from the **View** menu:

5. Based on the map type selected, we can update the fields of the editor panel.

The following screenshots show different map types:

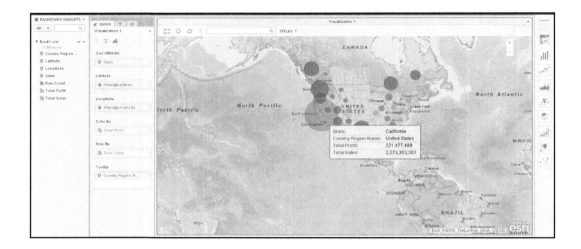

Marker map

The following screenshot shows an Area map:

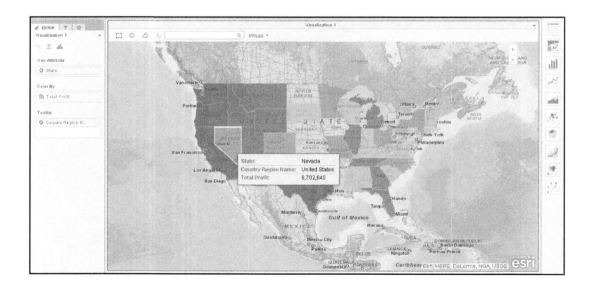

Area map

Note: We have used a tool called `MapMarker` to obtain the latitudes and longitudes corresponding to the states.

MicroStrategy and Google Maps integration

To use Google Maps with MicroStrategy, the user needs to have a Google Maps API key. The following are the steps to obtain this key:

Firstly we need to get a license key using the following steps:

1. Access `https://developers.google.com/maps/`.
2. Select the platform for which you need the Google key. In our case, we will select **Web**.
3. On the next screen, select the **Google Maps JavaScript API**.
4. Click **GET A KEY**.
5. On the **Activate the Google Maps JavaScript API** screen, click **CONTINUE**.
6. Create a new project.
7. On the next screen, under the **Credentials** tab, provide the URL. In our case, as we are using J2EE, the URL will be `http://SERVERNAME:PORTNUMBER/MicroStrategy/servlet/mstrWeb*`.
8. If you are using `ASP.NET`, the URL will be `http://SERVERNAME/MicroStrategy/asp/Main.aspx*`.
9. Click **Create.**
10. This will generate a key for MicroStrategy integration.

To deploy and configure a map visualization are as follows:

The GIS connector for Google Maps allows us to integrate MicroStrategy with Google Maps. The following are the steps to do this:

1. Navigate to `GISConnectors` in the MicroStrategy installation folder.
2. Click on the `GoogleMap` folder under the `GISConnector` folder.
3. Now, based on the operating environment, select the next folder:
     - For a J2EE environment: Open the `ConnectorForGoogleMap` folder,
     - For a .NET environmentL: Open the `ConnectorForGoogleMap_ASP` folder
       In our case, it will be the `ConnectorForGoogleMapfolder`.

4. From the folder we just opened, copy the second `ConnectorForGoogleMap` folder.

5. Now, navigate to the plugins folder inside the MicroStrategy Web installation folder and paste the `ConnectorForGoogleMap` folder.

6. Within this folder, navigate to `WEB-INF/xml/config/google` and edit the `googleConfig.xml` file to add the key obtained from Google in the getting license section.

7. Add your API key between the `<mk>` and `</mk>` tags, and, as we are using the standard Google Maps API, we set the `isPremier` attribute to `False`. The following is the file structure:

```
<gc>
    <mk isPremier="false">Add key obtained from Google</mk>
</gc>
```

8. Restart your web server.

After restarting, the Google Maps visualization should be available in DHTML, mobile, and visual insight modes in MicroStrategy Web, as shown here:

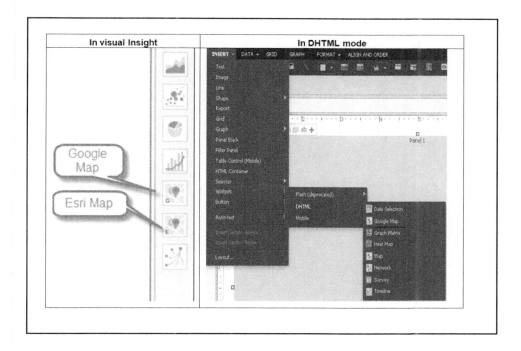

Summary

In this chapter, we learned about dashboards, which are a special type of document that displays data and summarizes all the key metrics for business use; panels, holders that group several elements such as selectors, lines, images, grid/graph objects, and so on; panel stacks, which are groups of panels; selectors, which provide interactivity to the user and let them flip between the panels of the panel stack; graphs and charts, which are diagrammatical representations of sets of data; widgets, which are another way of visualizing data, combined with rich interactivity for users; and visualization techniques, which provide the user with the ability to create quick, interactive dashboards.

In the next chapter, we will cover the MicroStrategy **Software Developer Kit (SDK)**, which allows users to extend and customize MicroStrategy's functionality, and integrate it with third-party applications.

5
Customization of MicroStrategy

Business requirements are constantly growing, and often exceed what can be offered by MicroStrategy built-in functionalities. Fortunately, MicroStrategy provides **software development kit (SDK)**. SDK is a set of tools which can extend MicroStrategy capabilities, such as programming tools, libraries of classes, and functions.

MicroStrategy SDK gives us access to the whole platform and has all the important elements required to build a great business intelligence solution that meets all the requirements of business people. Moreover, MicroStrategy allows customizing native mobile applications on Android or iOS with SDK.

There are many use cases of MicroStrategy customization, such as making dashboards more engaging, improving customer experience, and making data more accessible. The following topics are covered in this chapter:

- Overview of Web SDK
- Web Beans
- Customizing style with CSS
- Advanced visualization with SDK
- Overview of advanced web customization with API
- Overview of Mobile SDK: rebranding

Before we start

In this chapter, we discuss SDK customization capabilities, required development environment, SDK definition, and where to get documents.

What types of customizations can we do? Following are some options:

- Rebranding
- Consuming data externally
- Modifying MicroStrategy objects
- Creating new visualizations

Development environment requirements are as follows:

- Development machine with Windows/Linux/Mac OS with Java JDK installed
- Tomcat web server with MicroStrategy web server deployed
- Connectivity to MicroStrategy Intelligence Server can be deployed locally

What is SDK

SDK is a set of tools that helps you to integrate functionalities into any application, including Web SDK, Mobile SDK, Visualization SDK, Web Services SDK, Office SDK, and Intelligence Server SDK.

Where to get documentations and resources

There are several websites you can get more information from, including **MicroStrategy Community** (https://community.microstrategy.com/), **MicroStrategy Developer Zone** (https://community.microstrategy.com/t5/custom/page/page-id/developer-zone), API reference, MicroStrategy discussion forums, and MicroStrategy knowledge base:

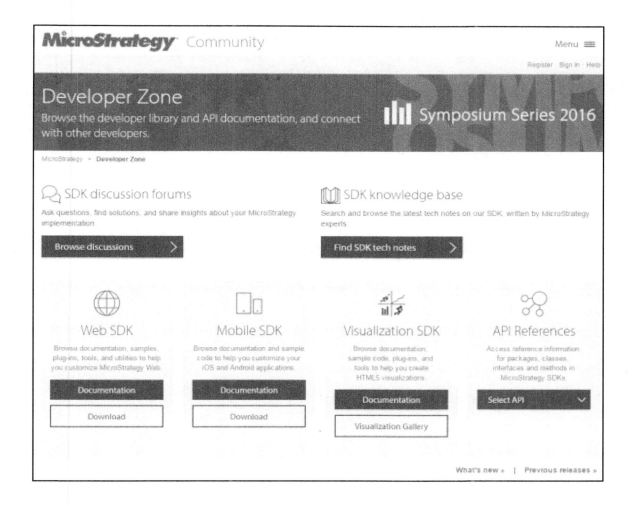

Overview of Web SDK

In this section, we introduce MicroStrategy web architecture, plugin architecture, deploying SDK, and configuring **Web Customization Editor** (**WCE**) both in Linux and in Windows, and discuss some best practices for customizations and upgrades.

MicroStrategy Web architecture

The layers that make up the MicroStrategy Web application are as follows:

- XML API layer
- Web Objects layer
- Web Beans layer
- Web Transforms layer
- Application Objects layer
- Presentation layer

Application programming interface (API) is an interface that enables the user to access information from other applications, and allows the user to integrate services to their own applications. A **Web Bean** is a Java class that contains business logic and accepts no parameters, which includes JavaBean and Enterprise JavaBean:

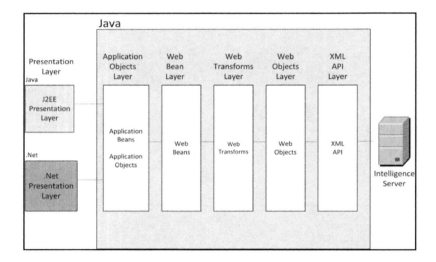

MicroStrategy plugin architecture

MicroStrategy separates its main codes from plugins. Extra functionalities and customizations are implemented by using plugins, without modifying its main codes. Plugins are organized as subfolders in the `plugins` folder:

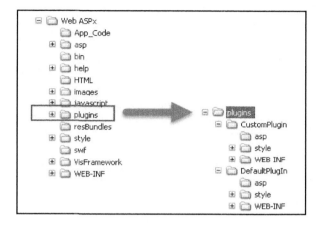

Deploying SDK and configuring WCE in Linux

Let us deploy the WCE plugin in order to change the appearance of MicroStrategy Web:

1. We can download MicroStrategy SDK from
   `http://community.microstrategy.com/t5/custom/page/page-id/devel`
   `oper-zone`.

There are rich documentations here: `https://lw.microstrategy.com/`
`msdz/MSDL/_CurrentGARelease/docs/projects/WebSDK/default.`
`htm#topics/other/Introduction_to_the_Web_SDK.htm%3FTocPat`
`h%3DWeb%2520SDK%7C_0`

2. Moreover, we need Eclipse in order to work with MicroStrategy SDK. Let's
   download Eclipse SDK using this URL: `http://archive.eclipse.org/eclip`
   `se/downloads/drops4/R-4.4.2-201502041700/`.

   Choose Red Hat Linux for Windows: `eclipse-SDK-4.4.2-linux-gtk-`
   `x86_64.tar.gz`

3. Create a folder for MicroStrategy SDK:

   #cd /root/
   #mkdir WebSDK

4. Extract `eclipse-SDK-4.4.2-linux-gtk-x86_64.tar.gz` to `/root/WebSDK`.
   As a result, we get Eclipse.

5. Extract `MSTRSDK.zip` to `/root/WebSDK` and then find JAR files:

    # **cd /root/WebSDK/SDK/tools/WebCustomizationEditor**

6. Extract `com.microstrategy.web.sdk.webcustomization.zip` into this folder:

    # **cd /root/WebSDK/SDK/tools/WebCustomizationEditor/plugins**

    Then copy the JAR file to `/root/WebSDK/eclipse/plugins`.

7. In addition, we should deploy Apache Ant.

Apache Ant is a Java library and command-line tool that helps build software.

Go to `https://ant.apache.org/bindownload.cgi` and download zip archive: `apache-ant-1.9.6-bin.zip`. Extract to `/root/WebSDK`.

8. Finally, we need to deploy Apache Axis 2.

Apache Axis2TM is a Web Services/SOAP/WSDL engine, the successor to the widely used Apache Axis SOAP stack. There are two implementations of the Apache Axis2 Web services engine-Apache Axis2/Java and Apache Axis2/C

Go to `http://axis.apache.org/axis2/java/core/download.html`.

9. Choose Binary distribution – `axis2-1.7.1-bin.zip` and extract to `/root/WebSDK`.

10. Now we can run Eclipse in `/root/WebSDK/eclipse`:

    # **./eclipse**

11. Set preference for MicroStrategy Plugin. Go to **Window** | **Preferences** in order to add settings to the MicroStrategy plugin accordingly:

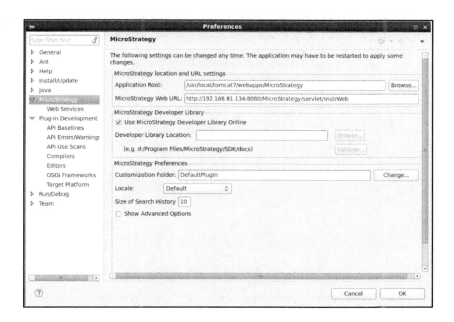

12. Go to **Web Services** and fill in the information, like in the following screenshot:

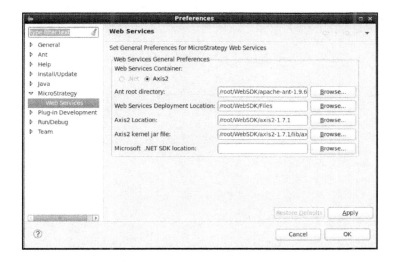

13. Now you can go to **Window** | **Show View** | **Other** and choose `MicroStrategy`:

As a result, we deployed MicroStrategy customization plugin into Eclipse and now we are able to modify MicroStrategy Web.

Installing SDK and configuring WCE in Windows

If you are in a Windows environment, you need to download Web SDK (`MSTRSDK.zip`) from MicroStrategy Community (`https://community.microstrategy.com/`), unzip it, then cut and paste the SDK folder into the MicroStrategy installation folder:

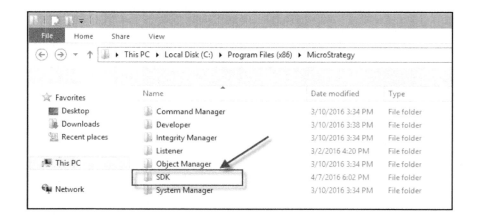

The WCE is a tool provided by MicroStrategy to make developing easier, by automatically creating plugins inside the plugins folder, according to your customization requirements. It is possible to create plugins without WCE, but it will be hard and prone to mistakes. WCE is essentially a plugin of Eclipse **Integrated Development Environment (IDE)**. It can automatically create folders and template files, so that the user can concentrate on the critical parts of the code.

The plugin is included in the SDK folder as a ZIP file. You need to locate it in `/SDK/tools/com.microstrategy.web.sdk.webcustomization.zip`:

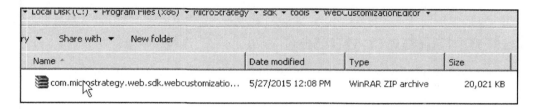

Unzip it, and put it into the Eclipse `plugins` folder:

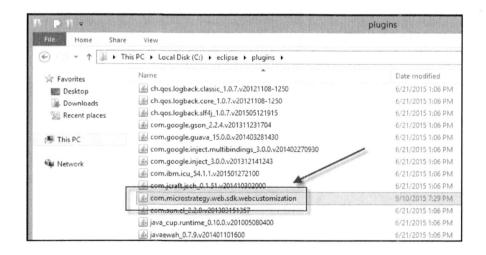

Best practices for customizations and upgrades

There are some tips to follow that will save you time and increase your work's durability:

- Always encapsulate all the changes in plugin inside plugins
- Do not change any code outside the `plugins` folder
- Before an upgrade, always back up the content of the `plugins` folder, and redeploy the `plugins` folder after the upgrade
- After upgrading, remember to check if there is a new version of WCE

Customization pages

The page configuration file defines the framework for the entire MicroStrategy web application. It is located in `WEB-INF\xml\pageConfig.xml`.

Web Beans

In MicroStrategy, Web Beans are simply Java beans. Beans are simply blocks of MicroStrategy data which enable you to bring MicroStrategy data onto the page.

Beans can have the following characteristics: name, type, source (including request parameters, name of enumeration constant, constant, preference, browser setting, and feature), and value.

Applications of Web Beans

Consider that your company wants to restrict the end report users from accessing the full functionality of the `Report Execution` page. Instead, end-users should be restricted to viewing the report results only. The steps to do this are as follows:

1. Create a new plug-in called `EmbedSingleReport`
2. Duplicate the report (`Report Execution`) page to create the `beansExercise` page

3. Modify the first link in the `exerciseLinks.jsp` file so that it uses the following anchor tag:

```
<a href="mstrWeb?pg=beansExercise&reportID=271209CD11D3EA25C000B3B2D8
6C964F">Embed a Single Report on a Page</a>
```

4. Verify your new link by logging in to your MicroStrategy project in MicroStrategy Web, accessing the `exerciseLinks` page, and clicking the **Embed a Single Report on a Page** link

5. After customization, clicking the first link on the `exerciseLinks` page displays the report

Consider that your company wants you to create a report showing the contents of two reports. That is, you need to combine the outputs of two reports into one. The steps to do this are as follows:

1. Create a new plugin called `EmbedMultipleReports`

2. Duplicate the report (`ReportExecution`) page to create the `multipleBeansExercise` page

3. Modify the second link in the `exerciseLinks.jsp` file to use the following anchor tag:

```
<a href="mstrWeb?pg=multipleBeansExercise&reportID=271209CD11D3EA25C0
00B3B2D86C964F&reportID2=D1AE56B011D5C4D04C200E8820504F4F">Embed
Multiple Reports on a Page</a>
```

4. Verify your new link by logging in to your MicroStrategy project in MicroStrategy Web, accessing the `exerciseLinks` page, and clicking the **Embed Multiple Reports on a Page** link

5. After customization, clicking the second link on the `exerciseLinks` page should display both the SDK Sample Report and the `Call Center Timeliness` report on your page:

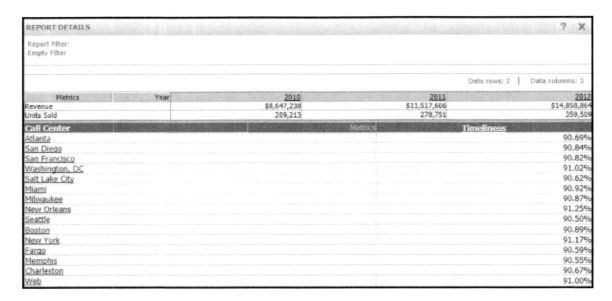

Consider that you need to refine the report created in the previous example, by making the contents of the two reports expandable and collapsible web panels, like the following:

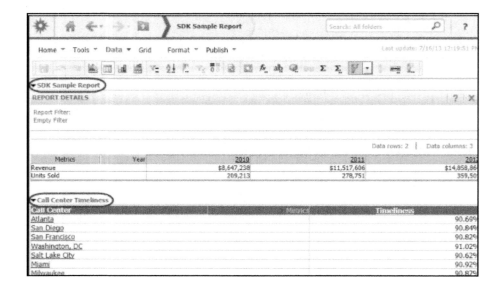

The steps to do this are as follows:

1. Under MicroStrategy Web configuration, expand Pages.
2. Double-click **multipleBeansExercise (multipleBeansExercise)** to open its editor.
3. Click the **Template Properties** tab.
4. In the **Template Properties Editor**, under **Page Templates**, on the **Default** tab, right-click the content page section and select **Edit current file**.
5. Near the middle of the file, after the `</web:ifFeature>` tag, add the following custom code:

```
<%--Adding panel around the report bean for the first report --%>
<web:panel name="report1Panel" language="1" useImage="true">
<web:panelTitle><B>SDK Sample Report</B></web:panelTitle>
<web:panelCloseInfo width="13" height="13" img="1arrow_down.gif">
Hide Report </web:panelCloseInfo> <web:panelOpenInfo width="13"
height="13" img="1arrow_right.gif">Show Report </web:panelOpenInfo>
<web:panelContent>
```

6. After the next `<fweb:ifBeanValue>` closing tag, add the following custom code:

```
</web:panelContent> </web:panel>
```

7. Toward the bottom of the file, find the following custom HTML:

```
<%--Adding new report bean for the second report --%>
<web:displayBean beanName="rb2"/>
```

8. Replace the preceding code with the following custom HTML:

```
<%--Adding panel around the new report bean for the second report --
%>
<br><br> <web:panel name="report2Panel" language="1" useImage="true">
<web:panelTitle><B>Call Center Timeliness</B></web:panelTitle>
<web:panelCloseInfo img="1arrow_down.gif">Hide
Report</web:panelCloseInfo><web:panelOpenInfo img="1arrow_right.gif">
ShowReport</web:panelOpenInfo><web:panelContent><web:displayBean
beanName="rb2" /></web:panelContent></web:panel>
```

   Click **Save**.

9. Close the `Report_Content.jsp` file.
10. In Eclipse, click **Restart Tomcat**.
11. In your web browser, navigate to `http://localhost/MicroStrategy/servlet/mstrWeb`, or your MicroStrategy web starting page.

12. Log in to your MicroStrategy project as administrator.
13. Click the MicroStrategy icon and select the `exerciseLinks` shortcut to navigate to the `exerciseLinks` page.
14. Click the **Embed Multiple Reports on a Page** link.

Customizing MicroStrategy styles with CSS

Cascading Style Sheets (CSS) is a tool to apply formatting to HTML elements, such as fonts, font sizes, and alignments. It enables the web developer to separate contents from formats. MicroStrategy Web uses the CSS files to provide centralized formatting to its web pages.

There are three kinds of CSS files in MicroStrategy:

- Application-wide CSS files in the `/style/mstr` subfolder: `mstrTheme.css`, `mstr.css`
- Page-specific CSS files in the `\style\mstr` subfolder: `pageProjects.css`, `pageLogin.css`, `pageDesktop.css`, `pageFolder.css`, `pageCreateReport.css`, `pageCreateDocument.css`, `pageWait.css`, `pagePrompts.css`, `promptIndex.css`, `pageReport.css`, `pageRW.css`, and so on
- Browser-specific CSS files are used to handle cross-browser discrepancies

Applications of CSS customization

The customizing project icon on the welcome page enables you to access projects such as `MicroStrategy Tutorial`, `My First Projects`, and so on:

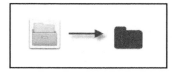

The steps to do this are as follows:

1. Create a new plugin called **WelcomePageIcon**
2. For the welcome page, change the value of the background-position property associated with the `#mstrIconProject` rule in `pageProjects.css` to PX –7 PX
3. For the welcome page, change the value of the background-image property associated with the `#mstrIconProject` rule in `pageProjects.css` to URL (`images/project.gif`)
4. Verify your customization by logging in to your MicroStrategy project in MicroStrategy Web and accessing the welcome page

Let us consider another application. Suppose we want to change the color of the font that displays the text links for `Shared Reports`, `My Reports`, and so on, from gray to blue:

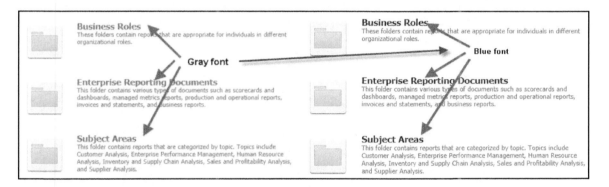

The steps to do this are as follows:

1. Create a new plugin called **FolderBrowsingFont**
2. Change the value of the color property associated with the folder browsing page to `#000099` by modifying the CSS
3. Verify that you have applied the new font color by logging in to your MicroStrategy project in MicroStrategy Web and accessing the shared report page to check the display of text links with the new font

Adding advanced visualization with SDK

MicroStrategy Visualization Builder is a new feature of MicroStrategy 10 which allows you to import and create custom HTML5 visualizations using the Visualization SDK kit:

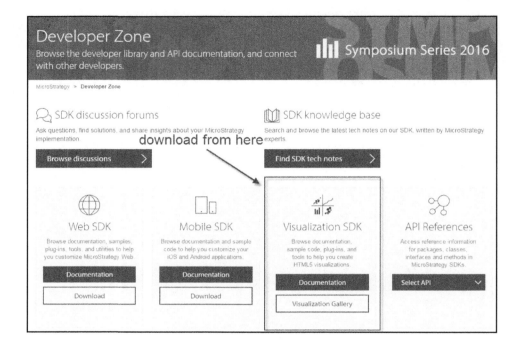

Installing Visualization SDK

- Choose **Download a local copy of the Visualization SDK**
- Extract the downloaded zip file, and then put the `_VisBuilder` folder into the `MicroStrategy/plugins` folder
- Restart your Tomcat server:

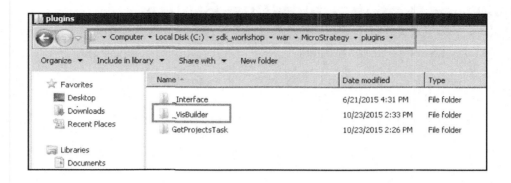

Introduction to Visualization Builder

Visualization Builder is based on the dashboards page. All the settings are conveniently displayed on the user interface. MicroStrategy data structure knowledge is not required. It enables live JavaScript code and live CSS code changes, and no web server restarts are required to enable changes. In addition, it has features like auto completion of JavaScript code, live validation of JavaScript and CSS, supporting third-party libraries such as D3, Google Charts, HighCharts, and so on:

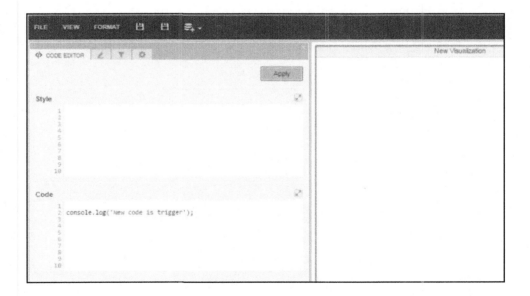

Application of Visualization Builder

Consider that we need to implement a new type of visualization based on the Google Charts library. The steps are as follows:

1. Install Visualization Builder by pasting the unzipped folder into the `plugins` folder of MicroStrategy Web.
2. A new shortcut will show on the side menu of the home page:

3. Left-click on the **Visualization Builder**.
4. Load a dataset, and select it by using the **Selecting Existing Dataset** function on the top bar:

5. Use the `SDK Sample Report`.

6. Add `Year` to `Attributes` and `Units Sold` and `Revenue to Metrics`. You will see a blank screen as there is no code to display yet. You can still see the data by clicking the top-right corner and choosing **Show Data to See Popup with Data Grid** or **Change Visualization to Grid**.

7. Go to the **Properties** tab, set the **Visualization name** to `Google Chart Line Graph`, set **Minimum number of metrics** to 2, check **Available for dashboards**, add `http://www.google.com/jsapi` to the list of libraries, and click **Apply**:

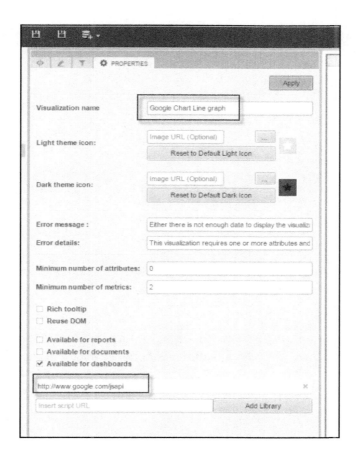

8. Click **Save** and set the **Folder name** as `GoogleVis`. After the new plugin has been created, you can go to the `plugins` folder of your MicroStrategy Web folder to check it.

9. Now we use the **Code Editor** tab, to create code to support our visualization.

10. Make the dataset usable by Google Charts:

```
var data = {};
var gridata = this.dataInterface;
data.cols = [];
data.cols[0] = {"id": "ATT_NAME_JS", "label": "Attribute", "type":
"string"};
var i;
for (i = 0; i < gridata.getColumnHeaderCount(); i++) {
var metricName = gridata.getColHeaders(0).getHeader(i).getName();
data.cols[1 + i] = {"id": metricName, "label": metricName, "type":
"number"};
}
data.rows = [];
for (i = 0; i < gridata.getTotalRows(); i++) {
data.rows[i] = {};
var c = [], attributesValue = "", a, z;
for (a = 0; a < gridata.getRowHeaders(i).size(); a++) {
attributesValue += gridata.getRowHeaders(i).getHeader(a).getName()
+ " ";
}
c[0] = {"v": attributesValue};
for (z = 0; z < gridata.getColumnHeaderCount(); z++) {
c[1 + z] = {"v": gridata.getMetricValue(i, z).getRawValue()};
}
data.rows[i].c = c;
}
```

11. Before working with the data, make it variable to hold some parameters:

- `var domNode = this.domNode` is a DOM node where the visualization will be rendered.

- `var width = this.width, height = this.height`. Read width and height dynamically from the Visualization container so it will occupy all available space.

12. Load the Google visualization code to render the graph:

```
google.load("visualization", "1", {"callback": function () {
var gdata = new google.visualization.DataTable(data);
var options = {'title': 'Google chart', 'width': width, 'height':
height};
var chart = new google.visualization.LineChart(domNode);
chart.draw(gdata, options);
}, "packages": ["corechart"]});
```

13. Save the visualization. Now you have it in the Visualization gallery.

Overview of advanced web customization with MicroStrategy API

MicroStrategy Web API is fundamental for any advanced MicroStrategy Web customization. For example, we can create a Java application to connect to MicroStrategy and export results as a JSON object in order to feed into other systems.

Overview of Mobile SDK

The Mobile SDK provides tools to customize mobile applications. It can enable you to:

- Rebrand your application and preconfigure it
- Customize to use custom help files or perform actions such as disabling software encryption
- Perform specific checks before launching
- Use MicroStrategy's security and authentication functionality
- Integrate with Google Maps and Newsstand
- Use MicroStrategy's widgets, as well as create custom ones
- For iOS devices, you can use MicroStrategy Command Center to create a mission control center, with multiple iPads controlling a wall of HDTV screens

Mobile SDK for iOS

Mobile SDK for iOS allows you to compile the MicroStrategy Mobile application for iOS mobile devices. It includes the Mobile application, along with documentation in the MSDL. It works with Xcode and the iOS SDK.

Mobile SDK for Android

Mobile SDK for Android enables you to compile the MicroStrategy Mobile application for Android mobile devices. It includes a Mobile application, along with documentation in the MSDL. It works with the Eclipse IDE and the Android SDK.

Application of Mobile SDK – Rebranding

We can rebrand the MicroStrategy Mobile application for iOS by changing the name, the application icon, and the splash screen. Typically, system administrator provides the mobile configuration URL to users. Firstly, we need to set up the MicroStrategy Mobile project; secondly, we rebrand the application.

Set up the MicroStrategy Mobile project

For setting up the MicroStrategy Mobile project:

1. Open the MicroStrategy Mobile project in Xcode.
2. Choose whether to deploy the project to an iPhone or iPad.
3. Update the bundle identifier with your application ID.
4. Update the URL scheme.
5. Build the project to confirm that it compiles and deploys successfully.

Rebranding the application

1. Change the name of the application:
    1. Double-click the appropriate property list file (`Info_IPhone.plist` or `Info_IPad.plist` for iPhone and iPad, respectively), to open it in the editor.
    2. Configure the Bundle display name property. This property is the name used for the application. Update the value of this property with the name of your application.
    3. Save changes.
2. Change the URL scheme for the application.
3. Change the icon of the application:

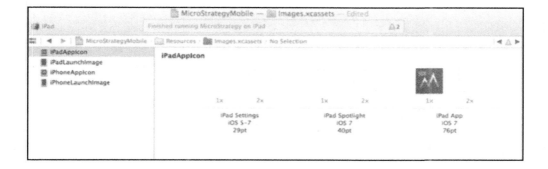

4. Change the splash screen of the application:
    1. Splash screen is simply a PNG graph file which will be displayed during lunch. It can be replaced under `images.xcaseets`.
    2. Right-click the iPhone/iPad folder and select **Add Files** to **MicroStrategyMobile**. This displays an editor for setting properties.
    3. Navigate to the new PNG file(s) you created for the splash screen, and select the check box for **Copy items into destination group's folder** (if needed) in the dialog.
    4. Select the appropriate target (**MicroStrategyMobileIPhone** and/or **MicroStrategyMobileIPad** for iPhone and iPad respectively) in the **Add To Targets** panel, and click **Add**. The editor closes.
    5. Save changes.
5. Add custom help.

Finally, build the project to confirm that the application compiles and deploys successfully.

Summary

In this chapter, we discussed using SDK to customize MicroStrategy. We also demonstrated several use cases, such as how to rebrand mobile application, and how to customize web reports.

In the next chapter we will discuss predictive analysis. We will go beyond the simple statistical functionalities provided by internal functions. MicroStrategy predictive analysis gives our business an edge by enabling us to combine the predictive mechanism with automation, which is the true strength of MicroStrategy 10.

6
Predictive Analysis with MicroStrategy

Predictive analysis can give our business an edge. In this chapter, we will go beyond the simple descriptive statistical functionalities of MicroStrategy. We will discuss how to make predictions based on existing data in hand. We will also discuss how to automate the predictive mechanism using MicroStrategy 10.

The predictive power of a model depends on data quality, and identified patterns and trends remaining unchanged. MicroStrategy is not the ideal tool for discovering these patterns and trends; SAS, R, Stata, or EViews might be better suited to the model developing stage. The strength of MicroStrategy lies in its ability to implement and automate pre-built prediction models into our database, thus saving us time and greatly increasing productivity. MicroStrategy can integrate with third-party solutions, especially with R.

This chapter will cover the following topics:

- Integrating R with MicroStrategy
- Data mining overview
- Steps for doing data mining in MicroStrategy
- Several business applications of predictive analysis
- Automating the predictive mechanism

Predictive analysis in MicroStrategy 10

Predictive analysis is part of **Data Mining Service**, and we need to meet certain licensing requirements. With the license, we have access to native analytical functions, as well as many features provided through R integrations.

Licensing requirements

Data Mining Service is part of **Intelligence Server**, and we need a **Developer Designer** license to access it.

Native analytical functions in MicroStrategy 10

According to the MicroStrategy 10 documentation, there are 270 native functions built into MicroStrategy, covering basic, OLAP, mathematical comparison, financial, predictive, and statistical areas. With them we can conduct linear regression, logistic regression tree regression, decision trees, association rules models, and time series models.

Integrating R with MicroStrategy

R is an open source programming language and software environment for statistical analysis and graphics. MicroStrategy can use R to do the predictive model estimations. By using R Integration Pack, MicroStrategy can get the inputs, pass them to R, get the computation results back from R, and then pass those to predictive metrics.

In MicroStrategy version 10, we need the following steps to integrate R:

1. Install MicroStrategy.
2. Install R from `https://www.r-project.org/`.
3. Install R Script functions from `https://rintegrationpack.codeplex.com/`.

Installing R

Use the following commands to install R on Red Hat Enterprise Linux 6.6:

```
wget
http://download.fedoraproject.org/pub/epel/6/x86_64/epel-release-6-8.noarch
.rpm
```

```
yum localinstall epel-release-6-8.noarch.rpm
yum install R
```

If there are dependency issues, you will find an error message similar to this:

```
--> Finished Dependency Resolution
Error: Package: R-core-devel-3.1.1-3.el6.x86_64 (epel)
         Requires: lapack-devel
Error: Package: R-core-devel-3.1.1-3.el6.x86_64 (epel)
         Requires: blas-devel >= 3.0
```

R installation failed because neither the EPEL nor the RHN repositories have all of the prerequisite packages available. To fix this, we need to enable the repository by changing the appropriate enabled = 0 line to enabled = 1:

```
vim /etc/yum.repos.d/redhat.repo
[rhel-6-server-optional-rpms]
...
enabled = 1
```

Executing yum installs R again; the R installation now should work (source: Engineering Walden, https://bluehatrecord.wordpress.com). Check your R after installation. MicroStrategy may require the R 64-bit version as shown in the following screenshot:

```
[root@localhost tmp]# R

R version 3.2.3 (2015-12-10) -- "Wooden Christmas-Tree"
Copyright (C) 2015 The R Foundation for Statistical Computing
Platform: x86 64-redhat-linux-gnu (64-bit)
```

Installing R Integration Pack

First, we need to download **R IntegrationPack** from https://rintegrationpack.codeplex.com/.

Then unpack the archive, and run `setup.sh` in the terminal. Follow the instructions to finish the installation:

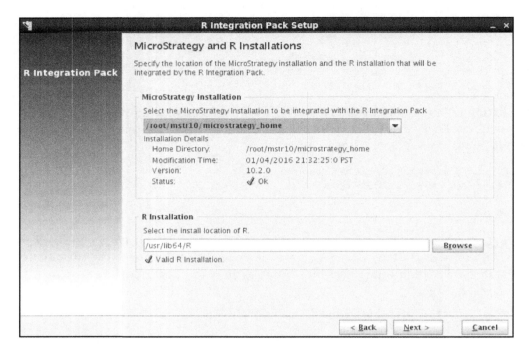

Now you need to upgrade existing projects; run **Configuration Wizard** in the terminal, and the following command:

```
/mstrcfgwiz
```

If you have problems, a good source to refer to is *R Integration Pack User Guide*, which is a PDF file you can download from `https://rintegrationpack.codeplex.com/`:

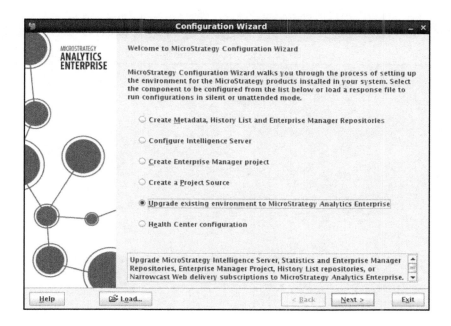

Creating a neural network model in R and exporting it as a PMML file

Let's build a simpleneural network model, and export the model as a PMML file:

```
library(nnet)
Iris <-
read.csv("https://raw.githubusercontent.com/uiuc-cse/data-fa14/gh-pages/dat
a/iris.csv")
IrisNet <- nnet(species~., data=Iris, size=4)
str(IrisNet)
library(pmml)
pmml(IrisNet)
```

`library(nnet)` will load the neural network package, and `str(IrisNet)` will show the structure of the neural network:

```
> library(nnet)
> Iris <- read.csv("https://raw.githubusercontent.com/uiuc-cse/data-fa14/gh-pages/data/iris.csv")
> IrisNet <- nnet(species~., data=Iris, size=4)
# weights:  35
initial  value 165.456625
iter  10 value 51.617848
iter  20 value 7.132479
iter  30 value 5.109677
iter  40 value 4.924437
iter  50 value 4.922125
iter  60 value 4.922013
iter  70 value 4.921957
iter  70 value 4.921957
iter  70 value 4.921957
final  value 4.921957
converged
> str(IrisNet)
List of 19
 $ n            : num [1:3] 4 4 3
 $ nunits       : int 12
 $ nconn        : num [1:13] 0 0 0 0 0 0 5 10 15 20 ...
 $ conn         : num [1:35] 0 1 2 3 4 0 1 2 3 4 ...
 $ nsunits      : num 9
 $ decay        : num 0
 $ entropy      : logi FALSE
 $ softmax      : logi TRUE
 $ censored     : logi FALSE
 $ value        : num 4.92
 $ wts          : num [1:35] -2.32 -31.29 7.65 -65.78 -25.51 ...
 $ convergence  : int 0
 $ fitted.values: num [1:150, 1:3] 1 1 1 1 1 1 1 1 1 1 ...
  ..- attr(*, "dimnames")=List of 2
  .. ..$ : chr [1:150] "1" "2" "3" "4" ...
  .. ..$ : chr [1:3] "setosa" "versicolor" "virginica"
 $ residuals    : num [1:150, 1:3] 0 0 0 0 0 0 0 0 0 0 ...
  ..- attr(*, "dimnames")=List of 2
  .. ..$ : chr [1:150] "1" "2" "3" "4" ...
  .. ..$ : chr [1:3] "setosa" "versicolor" "virginica"
 $ lev          : chr [1:3] "setosa" "versicolor" "virginica"
 $ call         : language nnet.formula(formula = species ~ ., data = Iris, size = 4)
 $ terms        :Classes 'terms', 'formula' length 3 species ~ sepal_length + sepal_width + petal_length + petal_width
  .. ..- attr(*, "variables")= language list(species, sepal_length, sepal_width, petal_length, petal_width)
  .. ..- attr(*, "factors")= int [1:5, 1:4] 0 1 0 0 0 0 1 0 0 ...
  .. .. ..- attr(*, "dimnames")=List of 2
  .. .. .. ..$ : chr [1:5] "species" "sepal_length" "sepal_width" "petal_length" ...
  .. .. .. ..$ : chr [1:4] "sepal_length" "sepal_width" "petal_length" "petal_width"
  .. ..- attr(*, "term.labels")= chr [1:4] "sepal_length" "sepal_width" "petal_length" "petal_width"
  .. ..- attr(*, "order")= int [1:4] 1 1 1 1
  .. ..- attr(*, "intercept")= int 1
  .. ..- attr(*, "response")= int 1
  .. ..- attr(*, ".Environment")=<environment: R_GlobalEnv>
  .. ..- attr(*, "predvars")= language list(species, sepal_length, sepal_width, petal_length, petal_width)
  .. ..- attr(*, "dataClasses")= Named chr [1:5] "factor" "numeric" "numeric" "numeric" ...
  .. .. ..- attr(*, "names")= chr [1:5] "species" "sepal_length" "sepal_width" "petal_length" ...
 $ coefnames    : chr [1:4] "sepal_length" "sepal_width" "petal_length" "petal_width"
 $ xlevels      : Named list()
 - attr(*, "class")= chr [1:2] "nnet.formula" "nnet"
```

`library(pmml)` will load the PMML package, and `pmml(IrisNet)` will show the PMML code of the estimated neural network model. We can copy and save the PMML code as an XML file. MicroStrategy can import this neural network model from the XML file, or directly:

```
R RGui (32-bit) - [R Console]
R File Edit View Misc Packages Windows Help

> library(pmml)
Loading required package: XML
> pmml(IrisNet)
<PMML version="4.2" xmlns="http://www.dmg.org/PMML-4_2" xmlns:xsi="http://www.w3.org/2001/XMLSchema-instance" xsi:schemaLocatio
  <Header copyright="Copyright (c) 2016 John" description="Neural Network PMML Model">
   <Extension name="user" value="John" extender="Rattle/PMML"/>
   <Application name="Rattle/PMML" version="1.4"/>
   <Timestamp>2016-02-18 23:59:41</Timestamp>
  </Header>
  <DataDictionary numberOfFields="5">
   <DataField name="species" optype="categorical" dataType="string">
    <Value value="setosa"/>
    <Value value="versicolor"/>
    <Value value="virginica"/>
   </DataField>
   <DataField name="sepal_length" optype="continuous" dataType="double"/>
   <DataField name="sepal_width" optype="continuous" dataType="double"/>
   <DataField name="petal_length" optype="continuous" dataType="double"/>
   <DataField name="petal_width" optype="continuous" dataType="double"/>
  </DataDictionary>
  <NeuralNetwork modelName="NeuralNet_model" functionName="classification" numberOfLayers="2" activationFunction="logistic">
   <MiningSchema>
    <MiningField name="species" usageType="predicted"/>
    <MiningField name="sepal_length" usageType="active"/>
    <MiningField name="sepal_width" usageType="active"/>
    <MiningField name="petal_length" usageType="active"/>
    <MiningField name="petal_width" usageType="active"/>
   </MiningSchema>
   <Output>
    <OutputField name="Predicted_species" feature="predictedValue"/>
    <OutputField name="Probability_setosa" optype="continuous" dataType="double" feature="probability" value="setosa"/>
    <OutputField name="Probability_versicolor" optype="continuous" dataType="double" feature="probability" value="versicolor"/>
    <OutputField name="Probability_virginica" optype="continuous" dataType="double" feature="probability" value="virginica"/>
   </Output>
```

Data mining overview

In MicroStrategy, predictive analysis is a subset of Data Mining Services; we cannot do predictive analysis well without knowing the basics of data mining. In this section, we will learn some basics.

Purpose of data mining

The purpose of data mining is to discover useful information from the data, to help us make better business decisions. Data mining is also about automation, reusable methods, and time saving. We want to implement a pre-built model into our database and automate the use of mathematical and statistical processes to predict future outcomes, in short, to build an automated predictive mechanism. Examples include instant credit scoring, fraud detection, marketing campaign management, interactive marketing, market basket analysis, failure rate prediction, and so on.

Limitations of data mining

First, data mining reveals patterns, but we are responsible for deciding how valuable these patterns are. Second, data quality affects model quality; poor data will produce poor predictive models. Third, accuracy of prediction depends on discovered patterns and trends remaining unchanged. If there is a structure change (you may be familiar with the concept from Chow's test in econometrics), big discrepancies between actual values and model predictions are expected. Fourth, we need to understand data mining tools before using them. Finally, yet importantly, data mining may cause legal issues and ethical challenges.

Terminologies

Let us review some frequently used data mining terminologies in MicroStrategy.

Target variable, explanatory variable

Consider a simple linear model:

$$\text{Probility of Response} = 0.02 + 0.04\ \text{Age} + 0.02\ \text{Gender} + 0.06\ \text{Income}$$

On the left hand side, probability of *Response* is called a dependent variable, or Target variable. On the right-hand side, *Age*, *Gender*, and *Income* are called independent variables, predictors, explanatory variables, predictive variables, or input variables.

Continuous variable, categorical variable

Continuous variable is about numerical values we can perform arithmetic operations on, for example, price, income, and salary. Categorical variable is about non-numerical values, such as true or false, or numeric values that are just labels, for example, 1 for January and 2 for February; social security numbers; and US zip codes.

Training, validation, modeling

In order to increase our confidence in our models, we often go through training, validation, and modeling stages. Training uses part of the data, say 80%, with target values known to build our model. Validating uses part of, say 20%, the available data with known target values to apply the model we built and to verify the computed results with the actual results. Modeling applies our model to the data with target variable values unknown.

The effectiveness of going through these steps, in my humble opinion, is doubtful, because how accurately our models predict depends on two things and two things only: one, the data quality; two, the discovered patterns and trends remaining unchanged. Even if our model gives fabulous prediction results in the validation stage, its prediction could fail miserably when applied to out of sample data, because the patterns and trends in the data we built the model upon are different from those in the data we applied our model to.

The solution is to ensure the data we built the model upon is *representative* enough. That is, it has the same patterns and trends as the data we intend to apply our model to. This is a challenging task.

Supervised learning, unsupervised learning

According to *Pattern Recognition and Machine Learning, Bishop, Springer-Verlag New York*, supervised learning refers to input data with a known target variable, while unsupervised learning has no known target variable. The goal in unsupervised learning problems may be to discover groups of similar data points, which is called clustering.

Classification, prediction

When a target variable is categorical, we often refer to related data mining techniques as classification, for example, predicting whether a customer will churn or not. Classification data mining techniques include decision tree and logistic regression.

When a target variable is continuous, we often refer to related data mining techniques as prediction. For example, predicting the monthly revenues for the next year. Prediction data mining techniques include linear regression, time series analysis, and so on.

Data mining techniques

Some commonly used techniques include decision tree, regression model, cluster model, and neural network. The following graph shows the level of prediction accuracy, and how hard it is to understand different techniques. In general, decision tree is easy to understand but the least accurate, neural network is the most accurate but also the most difficult to understand, while regression model and cluster model are somewhere in between:

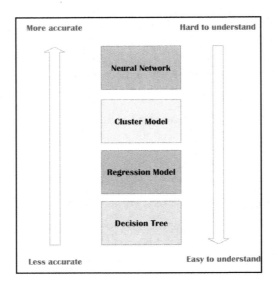

Four steps to achieve data mining in MicroStrategy

Typically, we follow four steps to perform data mining: creating a dataset, selecting variables, developing the model, and deploying the model:

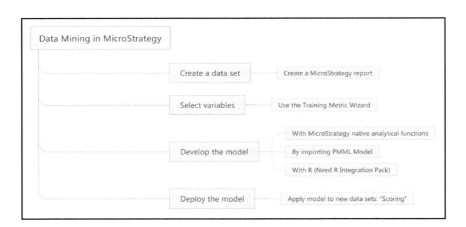

Let us try doing some data mining and predictive analysis following these steps. Let's say we need to prepare a back-to-school marketing campaign by sending out promotional mail. Our resources are limited, so we want to reduce costs by sending only to those that are most likely to respond. We have customers' demographic information and their previous response records from the last campaign.

Creating a dataset

Suppose we have the following demographic information: **Age**, **Education Level**, **Gender**, and **Household Count**. In addition, we have the response records of the last campaign. In our data, the previous campaign shows 1,002 positive responses out of 5,612 customer orders:

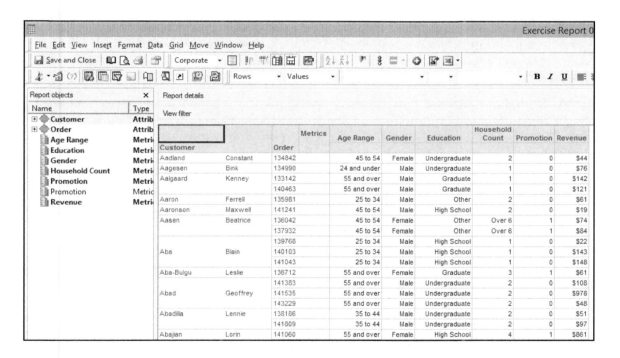

Selecting variables

Selecting variables needs both domain expertise (experience) and statistics knowledge. We use our experience to pick the most influential factors, and use statistics to take care of those variables that would cause model-estimating problems, for example, those variables that cause multicollinearity. In this process, we may need to do principal component analysis, or variable transformations. For our example, we choose all the variables.

Developing the model

In this step, we need to decide what kind of model to use: decision tree, regression model (linear, non-linear, which functional form), or neural network, and so on, then do model estimation.

Developing a model needs expertise. As a quantitative researcher who worked for many years in econometric modeling with business and financial data, I know this task can be very tricky and complicated. In many cases, business analysts find it more productive to outsource this task to responsible and well-trained statisticians or economists.

In this example, we assume that this model developing work is outsourced. An economist used a third-party application (R, SAS, Stata, or EViews, and so on), connected to the dataset and built a Neural Network model. He exported the model as a PMML file, and sent it back to us. We simply need to import this PMML file:

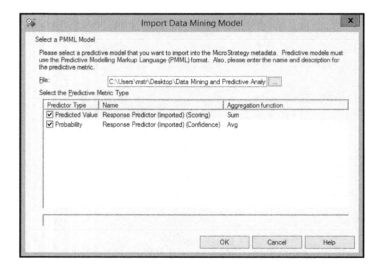

We may want to have a closer look at the imported model. MicroStrategy can give us details of this neural network model. Here is how to do it: right-click the **Response Predictor (Imported) (Scoring)** metric and select **Edit**. In the **Metric Editor**, on the **Tools** menu, select **View Predictive Model**. A graphical representation of the model appears:

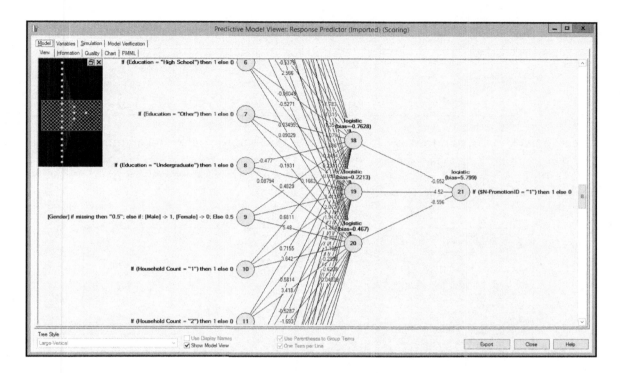

Creating a validation report

After importing the model, we may want to verify how well this model predicts before deploying it. This task can be done by applying this model on a dataset with known target variable values. We run the model, and compare actual target variable values with the estimated values. This process is model validation. In our example, we can create this dataset with known target variable values by simply using a filter, to include the data between 8/1/2013 and 9/30/2013, in which period responses to previous promotion are known:

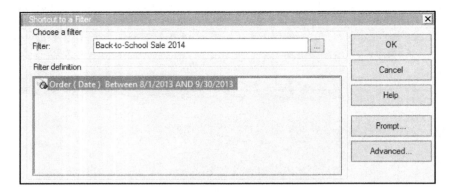

Create a new report, add the `Customer` attribute, and add the following metrics: `Back-to-School Responder`, `Response Predictor (Imported) (Scoring)`, `Response Predictor (Imported) (Confidence)`. Run the report. Now we can compare the actual response with the predicted response side by side:

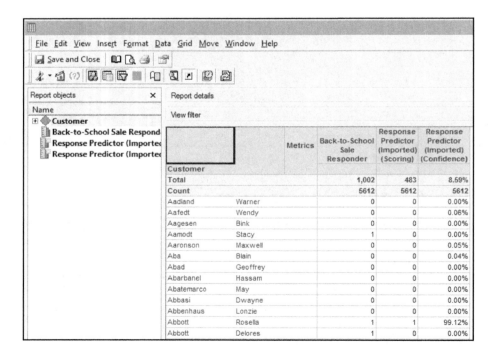

Deploying the model

After model verification, if we are satisfied with the predicting accuracy of the imported model, we can deploy it. That is, we can apply the model to the modeling dataset (the dataset with the target variable unknown). In our example, we can create such a modeling dataset by changing First Order Date (ID) to after 9/30/2014:

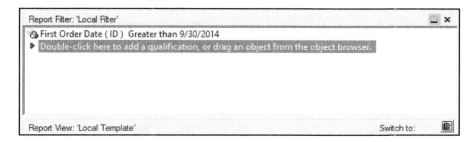

Run the report. Now we get a list of 23 customers we should send promotional mail to:

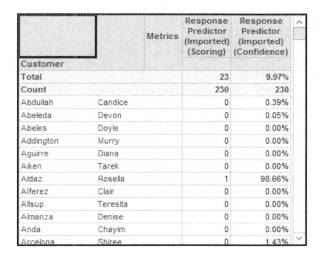

Business applications of predictive analysis

Forecasting is using data trends and cycles to predict future values. For example, claims, sales, and expenses data have seasonality and trends. When we count their cycles and trends, we can predict their future values reasonably well. There are two commonly used forecasting techniques: regression analysis and time series analysis. In terms of regression analysis, MicroStrategy supports linear regression, exponential regression, tree regression, and logistic regression. Logistic regression generally applies to predicting categorical target variables, while other regressions models generally apply to predicting numerical target variables.

In this section, we will demonstrate MicroStrategy's predictive analysis capabilities with several business applications. You will see that MicroStrategy has simplified the work to the extent that using different types of data mining model is simply a single mouse click away.

Forecasting quarterly revenues using linear regression and exponential regression with seasonality

Suppose we have a company's quarterly revenue data from 2012 Q1 to 2014 Q4. Based on these data, we want to forecast its quarterly revenues in 2015. Values for Revenue variable are given. Quarter Index, and Quarter of the Year metrics can be created:

The Quarter Index metric is defined as:

$$((Max(Quarter@ID) \{\sim\} - (10 * Max(Year@ID)) \{\sim\}) + ((Max(Year@ID) \{\sim\} - 2012) * 4))$$

The Quarter of the Year metric is defined as:

$$(Max(Quarter@ID) \{\sim\} - (10 * Max(Year@ID) \{\sim\}))$$

Quarter	Metrics Revenue	Quarter Index	Quarter of the Year
2012 Q1	$1,682,656	1	1
2012 Q2	$1,985,788	2	2
2012 Q3	$2,314,295	3	3
2012 Q4	$2,664,500	4	4
2013 Q1	$2,498,756	5	1
2013 Q2	$2,684,764	6	2
2013 Q3	$3,067,019	7	3
2013 Q4	$3,267,067	8	4
2014 Q1	$3,111,989	9	1
2014 Q2	$3,504,479	10	2
2014 Q3	$3,729,456	11	3
2014 Q4	$4,512,940	12	4
2015 Q1		13	1
2015 Q2		14	2
2015 Q3		15	3
2015 Q4		16	4

Create a training metric **Linear Regression Revenue Prediction Analysis**. Left-click **Tools**, select **Training Metric Wizard**, click **OK**. The following window shows up, presenting the available models we can use in MicroStrategy 10:

1. Choose **Linear Regression**, then click **Next**.
2. Set **Dependent Metric** to Revenue, and **Independent Metrics** to Quarter Index and Quarter of the Year.
3. Chose **Predicted Value** for **Predictor Type**. Choose Sum for the **Aggregation function**.

Following similar steps, we can create the training metric **Exponential Regression Revenue Prediction Analysis**. The only difference is to choose **Exponential Regression** for **Forecasting numeric values**:

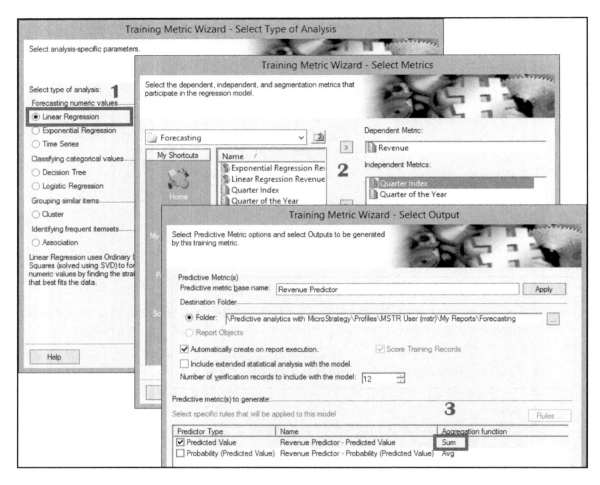

Now create a new report. Include the `Quarter` **attribute,** `Revenue`, `Quarter Index`, `Quarter of the Year`, `Linear Regression Revenue Prediction Analysis`, and `Exponential Regression Revenue Prediction Analysis` **metrics. Run the report.** Now we get the forecasted quarterly revenue for 2015, from both the linear regression model and the exponential regression model:

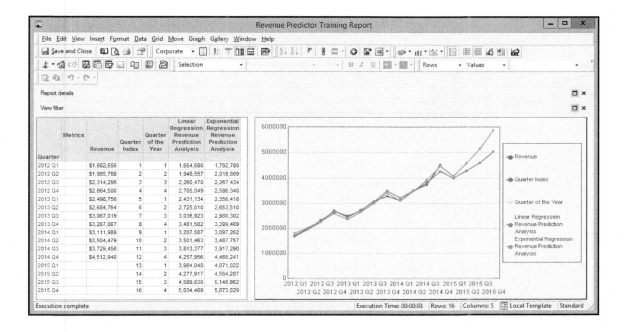

Forecasting quarterly revenues for different regions using tree regression analysis

Tree regression in MicroStrategy 10 enables us to estimate different sets of coefficients for different subsets of data, even when we specified the same model. For example, when forecasting quarterly revenues, tree regression enables us to estimate different sets of model coefficient for different regions. Here is how to do it.

Create a segmentation metric, Region:

Max(Region@DESC) {~}

Change the Level to **Report Level**, and **Region**:

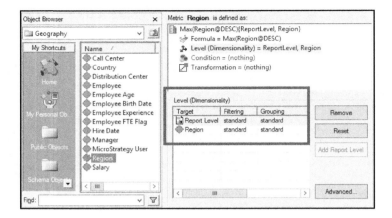

When building the training metric Tree Regression Revenue Prediction Analysis, add the Region metric as a segmentation metric, then we change from Linear Regression to Tree Regression:

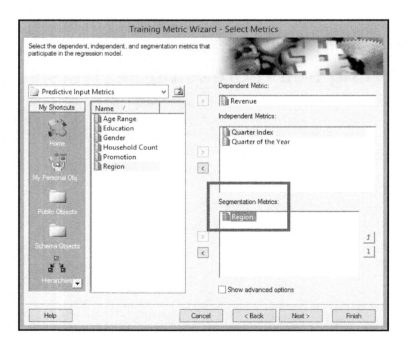

Check **Show advanced options**, change the **Type** of Quarter Index from **Default** to **Continuous**:

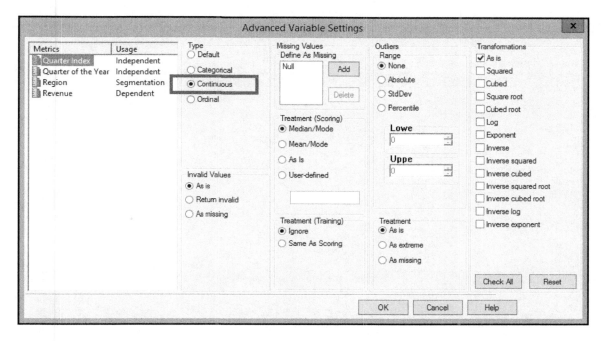

Click **OK** and follow the on-screen instructions to finish creating the Tree Regression Revenue Prediction Analysis metric. Use this metric to create a new report, and add the Region attribute as Paged By. Then we get the tree regression segmented by region report.

Tree Regression could offer better predictive results than pooled linear regression, because it offers tailored sets of coefficients for different regions:

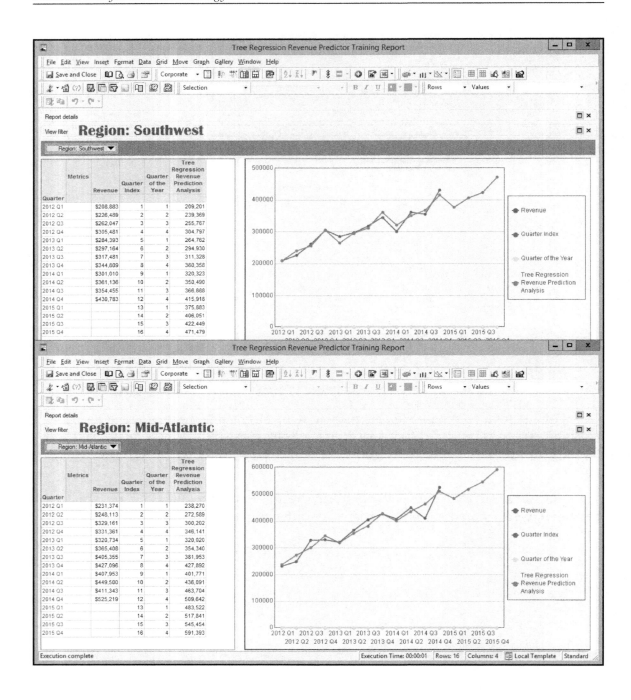

Forecasting monthly revenues using time series analysis

A time series refers to a sequence of values at regular intervals over a given period, for example, annual revenues over a decade. What makes time series special is that the observations have autocorrelation; that is, the value of *x(t)* is related to its value in the previous period, *x(t-1)*. Autocorrelation needs special econometric treatment, for example, GLS instead of OLS.

There are different approaches to time series analysis:

- **Regression**: linear and exponential regression
- **Averages**: simple, moving, centered, single double average
- **Exponential smoothing**: single, double triple Holt winter's smoothing
- **Autocorrelation model**: Box-Jenkins, auto-regression, moving average, ARIMA
- **Spectral**: discrete fourier, discrete cosine, fast Fourier, Chebyshev, polynomials

In MicroStrategy 10, exponential smoothing is used to conduct time series analysis. The single exponential smoothing can be written as:

$$x_t = Ay_t + (1 - A)x_{t-1}$$

Here, x_t is the smoothed series, y_t is the observed series, and A is the smoothing constant between and *1*.

Let's learn how to use time series analysis in MicroStrategy via an example. Let's say that monthly revenues from January 2012 to December 2014 are known; we want to forecast future monthly revenues in 2015.

Create **Month Index** using the following formula:

(Max([Month of Year]) {~} + (12 * (Max(Year) {~} – 2009)))

Create a training metric **Time Series Revenue Predictor**. Select the type of analysis as **Time Series**, select **Dependent Metric** as Revenue, **Independent Metrics** as Month Index, and the number of verification records to include with the model as 12:

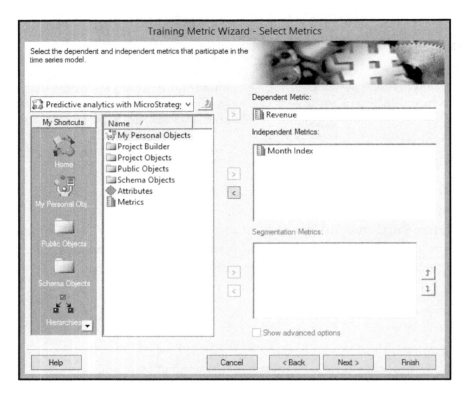

Create a new report containing a `Month` attribute, the `Revenue` metric, the `Month Index` metric, and the `Time Series Revenue Predictor Training` metric. Click **Data** and select **Report Data Options**. Change the MicroStrategy default inner join to `Outer`, to allow for viewing predictive values for the `Revenue` metric in 2014:

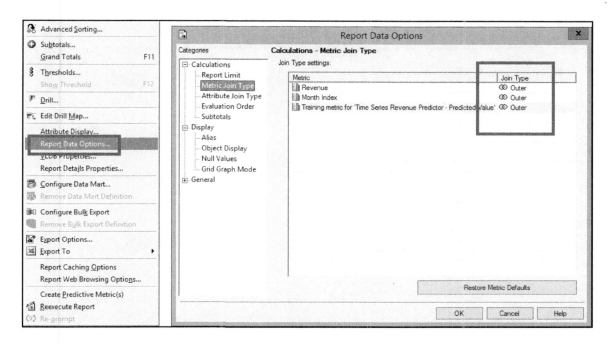

Run the report. Adjust the graph preference by clicking **Graph**, **Preference**, **Maximum number of categories**; increase this to 58 to view all the data:

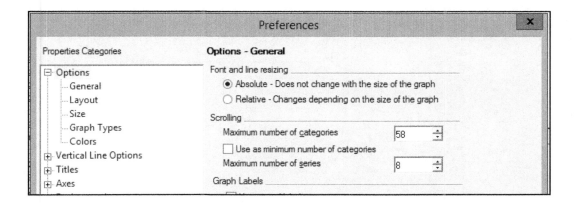

Click **OK**. Now we have our predicted monthly revenue values, along with a graph:

Telco churn analysis using classification

Classification is a data mining technique to classify data points into different groups. For example, in a hospital emergency room, a triage team classifies patients' different groups according to urgency; a bank classifies its loan applicants into high-risk or low-risk groups. There are two commonly used classification techniques: decision tree and logistic regression.

Decision tree is easy to understand, but less accurate due to its simplified model structure. Logistic regression is more accurate, but its estimation is computationally intensive.

Telco churn analysis using decision tree

A Telco corporation wants to estimate how likely it is that its customers will churn, based on customers' demographic information, usage data, and churn data.

Suppose we have the following data: average minutes during off-peak times, average minutes during peak times, dropped calls, helpdesk calls, renewals, age range, gender, household count, marital status, and income bracket:

Metric Name	Metric Definition
AvgMinOffPeak	*Sum([Phone Usage]@[Average Minutes Off-peak]){~}*
AvgMinPeak	*Sum([Phone Usage]@[Average Minutes Peak]){~}*
Dropped Calls	*Sum([Phone Usage]@[Dropped Calls]){~}*
Helpdesk calls	*Sum([Phone Usage]@[Helpdesk Calls]){~}*
Renewals	*Sum([Phone Usage]@[Renewals]){~}*
Marital Status	*Max([Marital Status]@DESC){Customer}*
Income Bracket	*Max([Income Bracket]@DESC){Customer}*
Telco Churn	*Sum([Phone Usage]@[Churn])*

Create a training metric `Telco Churn Predictor (Tree) Training Metric`, with `Telco Churn` as a target variable and other metrics as explanatory variables. In **Training Metric Wizard**, **Classifying categorical values**, choose **Decision Tree**. In **Predicted Value**, **Aggregation function**, choose `Sum`:

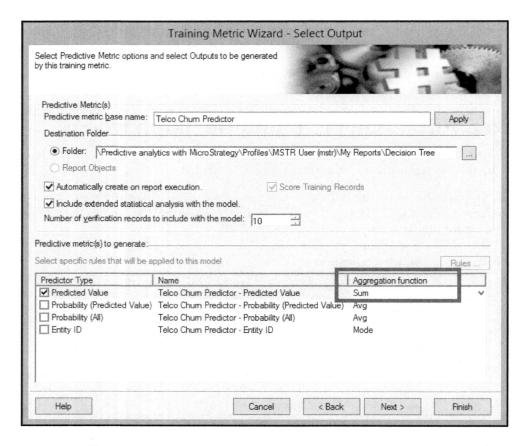

Create a report with `Telco Churn Predictor (Tree) Training Metric`, and explanatory variables:

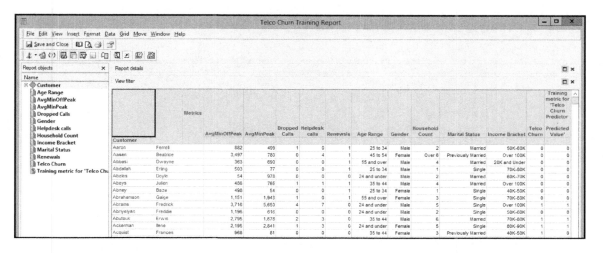

Create a new report and set a filter with a metric qualification: `Telco Churn Predictor - Predicted Value Exactly 1:`

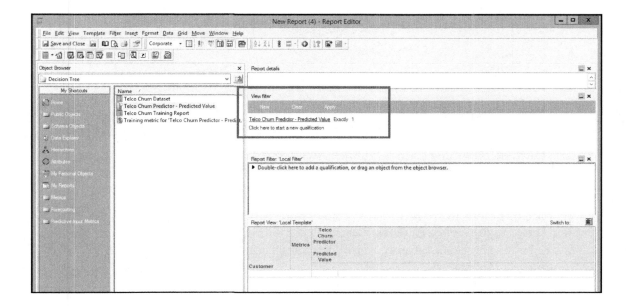

Run the report; we get a list of customers who are most likely to churn. Save it as `Telco Churn Predictor - Prediction Result (Decision Tree)`:

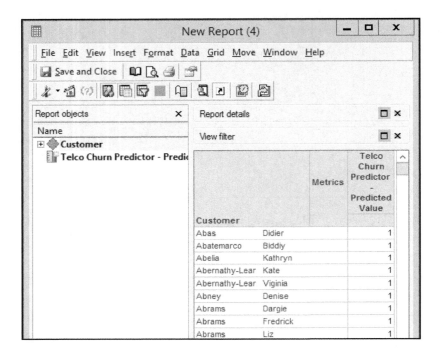

Telco churn analysis using logistic regression

We can follow steps similar to those in the previous section to do churn analysis using logistic regression. We will see at the end of this section that the model prediction accuracy improved, at the cost, however, of increased computation time.

Follow the same steps to create target variables and explanatory variables as in the previous section. The only difference is, when creating the training metric `Telco Churn Predictor (Logit) Training Metric`, and classifying categorical values, choose **Logistic Regression**:

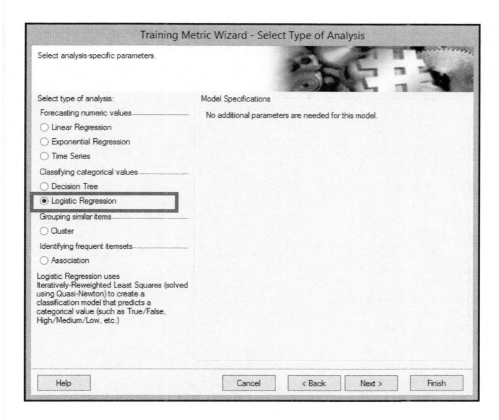

Then follow the relevant steps in the previous section to create a training report and to deploy the model. We may find that prediction accuracy is slightly improved by using logistic regression, for example, for a churned customer, `Tabitha Barker`, the logistic regression predictor made the correct prediction, but the decision tree predictor did not:

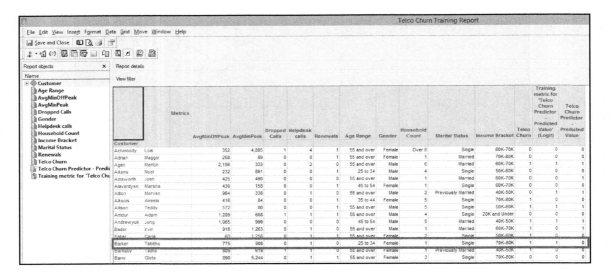

For our dataset, the prediction accuracy for logistic regression is 85.7%, compared with the 85.4% prediction accuracy for decision tree:

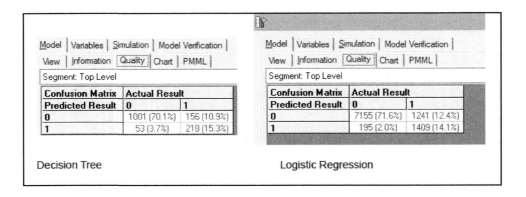

Automating the predictive mechanism

At the beginning of the chapter, we mentioned that we would discuss how to automate the predictive mechanism in MicroStrategy 10. I decided to put this section at the end because it is too simple. You may have already guessed the answer; yes, once you have built your report, automation is a piece of cake: you simply *subscribe* to your dynamic report.

For example, you can subscribe to the Telco Churn Analysis report, and tell the report to run at the beginning of every month. Then, every month, MicroStrategy will apply the predictive model to the current database, and produce a list of customers most likely to churn.

Nevertheless, the report must be *dynamic*; that is, it should not be set to use a fixed and stationary set of data and always produce identical results, instead, it should be set to allow newly available data, and produce new results when the underlying dataset refreshes.

Summary

In this chapter, we learned how to integrate R with MicroStrategy, and how to use MicroStrategy to import models developed by third-party solutions as PMML files. We also learned what data mining is, and how to use data mining techniques to do predictive analysis in MicroStrategy. Specifically, we learned how to implement learning regression, exponential regression, and tree regression to predict time series data. We also learned how to use classification techniques, such as decision tree and logistic regression, to resolve customer-churning issues.

In the next chapter, we will learn how to pack the power of MicroStrategy 10 into your iPhone and iPad. Mobile analytics could empower travelling field inspectors and managers to do their jobs as if they are in their offices with full access to their enterprise database warehouse. This power from MicroStrategy **Mobile Analytics** will help your business grow beyond existing boundaries. May the power be with you!

7

Accelerating Your Business with Mobile Analytics

Nowadays, smart phones and tablets are popular. Mobile devices enable us to do tasks traditionally only achievable by using a computer, such as checking e-mails and browsing web pages anywhere, anytime. The advantage of mobile devices is that they are more accessible; you may have access to your iPhone 24/7, but you are probably not able to access your office computer all day long. When you are away from the office traveling to another city, or doing your work in the field, and you need to access MicroStrategy, you can do so through your iPhone. Mobile Analytics enables users to harness the power of MicroStrategy from their mobile devices on the go.

In this chapter, we will discuss how to install and configure Mobile Server, how to create mobile applications that enable users to view information and provide inputs, and how to administrate mobile services. Specifically, we will cover the following topics:

- Introduction to MicroStrategy Enterprise mobile architecture
- Enterprise Mobile Server installation and configuration
- Developing mobile applications
- Mobile service deployment

Before we start

In order to make mobile services work, we will need two things: Mobile Server, and Mobile Client. In addition, several tools and interfaces are used to build and deploy apps. Developer is needed for building metrics, attributes, and filters, which are the objects inside the apps.

Web is needed for developing visual layout and organizing apps, including inserting datasets and inserting documents (apps). Of course, you can also build documents in Developer, but Web provides a more intuitive look and feel for mobile apps. Admin tools are needed for deployment and administration.

Mobile Server

Mobile Server sits on top of Intelligence Server, and provides infrastructure for Mobile Client. This is called **four-tier architecture**. For a production environment, four-tier architecture is preferred because it is more secure, since application servers (web server and Mobile Server) are separated from Intelligence Server, and there is a firewall in between:

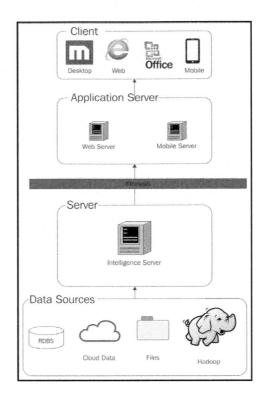

Mobile Client

You can access the MicroStrategy web interface with your cell phone, but you do not have a mouse on a cell phone, the screen is often too small, and you can't use touchscreen features; these shortcomings make it awkward to use MicroStrategy with your cell phone. Mobile application is designed to address these issues.

Dedicated mobile clients are available for iPad, iPhone and Android. Mobile clients can be delivered via an app store, enterprise deployment, or SDK. There are some out of the box functionalities that include some customization for mobile clients, but if you want rebranding app icons, app names, splash screens, notifications and action icons, copyright info, or push notification, you will need SDK.

Mobile client is the interface that enables access and interacts with the data from a mobile device. Users need to install mobile client from the corresponding app store, for example, for iPhone, users need to find and install the *MicroStrategy Mobile for iPhone* app:

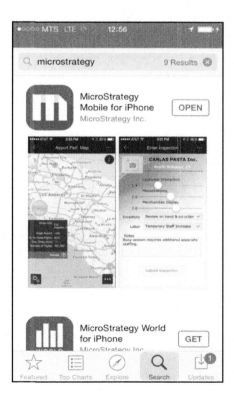

Mobile Server installation and configuration

While Mobile Client is easy to install, Mobile Server is not. Here we provide a step-by-step guide on how to install Mobile Server:

1. Download `MicroStrategyMobile.war`. Mobile Server is packed in a WAR file, just like Operation Manager or Web:

Name	Date ⌄	Type	Size	Tags
CertificateServer.war	3/16/2016 1:20 AM	WAR File	13,014 KB	
MicroStrategyMobile.war	3/16/2016 1:17 AM	WAR File	119,451 KB	

2. Copy `MicroStrategyMobile.war` from `<Microstrategy Installation folder>/Mobile/MobileServer` to `/usr/local/tomcat7/webapps`. Then restart Tomcat, by issuing the `./shutdown.sh` and `./startup.sh` commands:

```
[root@localhost bin]# ./shutdown.sh
Using CATALINA_BASE:   /usr/local/tomcat7
Using CATALINA_HOME:   /usr/local/tomcat7
Using CATALINA_TMPDIR: /usr/local/tomcat7/temp
Using JRE_HOME:        /usr
Using CLASSPATH:       /usr/local/tomcat7/bin/bootstrap.jar:/usr/local/tomcat7/bin/tomcat-juli.jar
[root@localhost bin]# ./startup.sh
Using CATALINA_BASE:   /usr/local/tomcat7
Using CATALINA_HOME:   /usr/local/tomcat7
Using CATALINA_TMPDIR: /usr/local/tomcat7/temp
Using JRE_HOME:        /usr
Using CLASSPATH:       /usr/local/tomcat7/bin/bootstrap.jar:/usr/local/tomcat7/bin/tomcat-juli.jar
Tomcat started.
```

3. Connect to the Mobile Server. Go to `http://192.168.81.134:8080/MicroStrategyMobile/servlet/mstrWebAdmin`. Use `admin/admin` as username and password, as we specified in Chapter 1, *Getting Started with MicroStrategy*. Then add the server name `localhost.localdomain` and click **connect**:

4. Configure Mobile Server. Please refer to *MicroStrategy 10 Mobile Design and Administration Guide* and `Chapter 5`, *Customization of MicroStrategy*. You can configure (1) Authentication settings for the Mobile Server application; (2) Privileges and permissions; (3) SSL encryption; (4) Client authentication with a certificate server; (5) Destination folder for the Photo Uploader widget and Signature Capture input control.

Creating a mobile application

Successfully developing a mobile application usually requires several steps before actually developing an app: (1) determine business goals; (2) storyboarding and planning; (3) creating templates; (4) creating suitable data; and finally, (5) mobile app development.

Determine business goals

In this step, mobile developers need to know the requirements. Who are the users? What kind of visualizations are needed? Are there any specific functionality requirements? How many apps need to be created? In addition, you will also need to know:

- The goals of the app and the business process
- Primary task and users
- What data is being accessed
- Assess and prioritize requested features

For example, we need to create an app that will help an organization analyze sales performance, and to help buyers with visits:

Audience	Task	Goal
Executives	Trend analysis	Company trend of sales over time
Executives Regional Managers	Product analysis	Sales performance of product: by categories and brands
Regional Managers	Customer analysis	Revenue performance by customer in region
Buyers	Supplier location	Sales visits by buyers
Buyers	Supplier analysis	Performance of supplier
Buyers	Supplier information	Contact information for the buyer

Storyboarding and planning

The second step is storyboarding and planning. The storyboard is to visualize the whole workflow based on the requirements, by providing the screens and the organization of the screens using paper, or software like Visio; storyboarding helps keep the conversation going between IT and business users.

Planning is to decide detailed objects requirements, and how to navigate in the app:

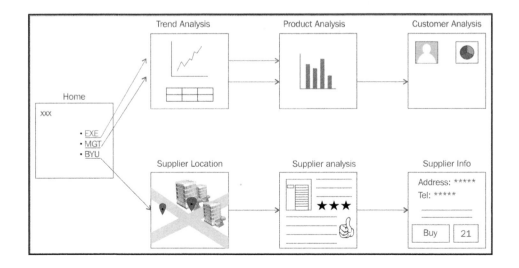

For example, after discussing the storyboard with business users, we decide to build two separate apps for different users. For executives and managers, we build *Sales Performance App*; for buyers, we build *Buyer Visit App*. Details are shown in the following image:

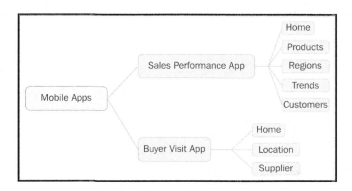

Creating an iPad Landscape template

First, we need a suitable document template. There are two ways to do this. MicroStrategy has many prebuild templates, including the iPad Landscape template. They are hidden, but you can unhide them and start using them. Alternatively, you can create the template yourself. Let us see how to unhide templates, and how to create new templates.

Unhide document templates

Certain document templates are hidden; to unhide them, follow these steps:

1. Open MicroStrategy Developer, click **Tools** | **Preference**.
2. Click **Developer** | **Browsing**, unselect **Display hidden objects**, click **OK**.
3. Now you can see hidden folders and other objects. Choose the **Object Templates** folder, choose `Document` folder; you should see some templates are hidden.

4. Right-click a hidden template, unselect **Hidden**, click **OK**:

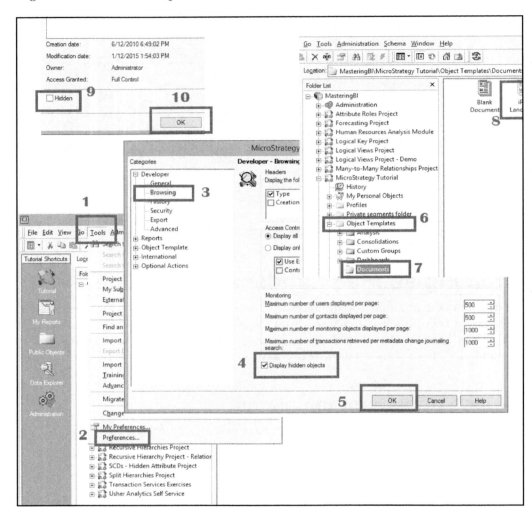

Creating templates

Before you start, you certainly need to log in to a project, and make sure you select to display **Pixels** instead of **Inches**. To do this, click **User Preference** on the top-right of the web interface, click **Preferences | General**, under **Language**, click **Advanced Options**, and choose **Pixels** for **Measurement Units**:

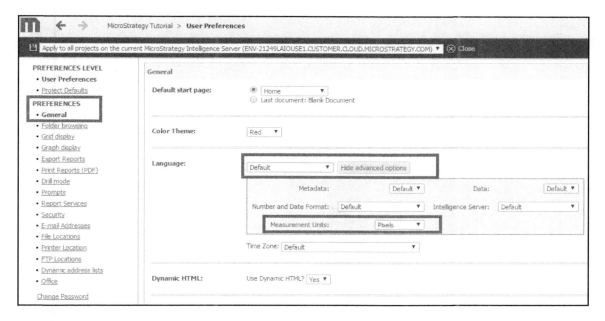

Templates are nothing more than regular documents. When you put a document into the template folder, it serves as a template. Follow these steps to create an iPad Landscape Template:

1. Click **Create Document**.
2. Click **Tools | Document Properties**.
3. Under **Layout Properties | Sections**, uncheck all except **Detailed Header**.

4. Under **Page**, input 2048 for **Width**, 1536 for **Height**, and **Landscape** for **Orientation**. Click **OK**:

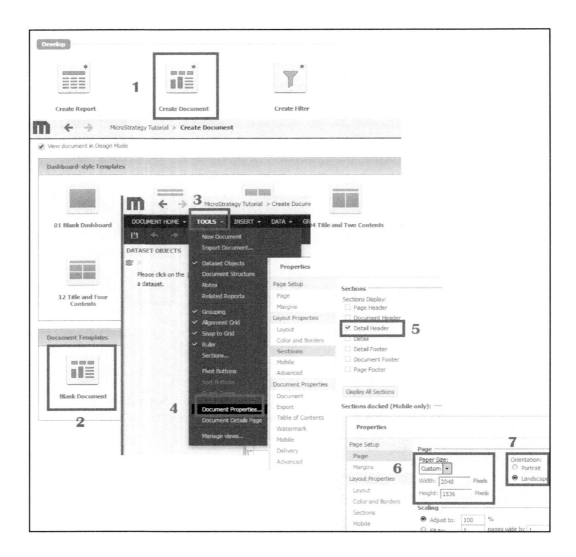

Adjust the view to make your canvas look correct:

1. Click **Tools | Manage views**.
2. Set **Resolution** to *2048* **X** *1536*, and **Orientation** to **Landscape Only**.
3. Drag the right-hand side and bottom edges of the canvas to the proper place.
4. Under **Document Home**, choose **Fit Page**. Save the document:

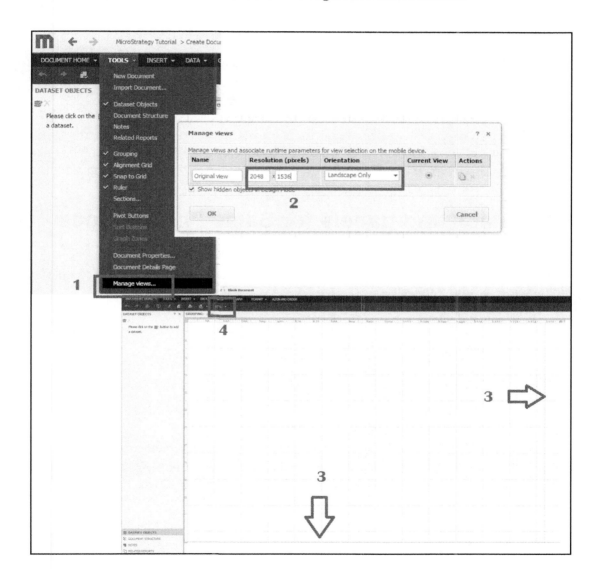

Dataset creation

Dataset creation is no different than generating ordinary reports; however, because of the limitations in processing power, network bandwidth, and in memory for mobile devices, it is a good idea to keep the datasets small.

In this chapter, we import and use the following datasets:

Panel stack and panels for Sales Performance App

In this section, we create the skeleton for the *Sales Performance App*, which is made up of the main panel stack, and panels:

1. Create a document based on the `iPad Retina Landscape` template and save it as *Sales Performance App*.
2. Click **INSERT**, click **Panel Stack**, draw a panel stack on canvas, right-click on panel stack, and click **Properties and Formatting**.
3. Set **Properties | Layout | Size**, **Width** `2048`, **Height** `1536`.
4. Click **Add Panel** and repeat five times, then rename the added panels to `Home`, `Product`, `Region`, `Trends`, and `Customer`.
5. Right-click on **Main Panel Stack** and click **Create Panel Selector**.
6. Right-click on the panel selector in **Properties and Formatting**, set the **Properties | Layout | Selector | DHTML Style** from default **Drop-down** to **Button Bar**, and click **OK**.

7. Adjust **Position**, and **Size** to proper values:

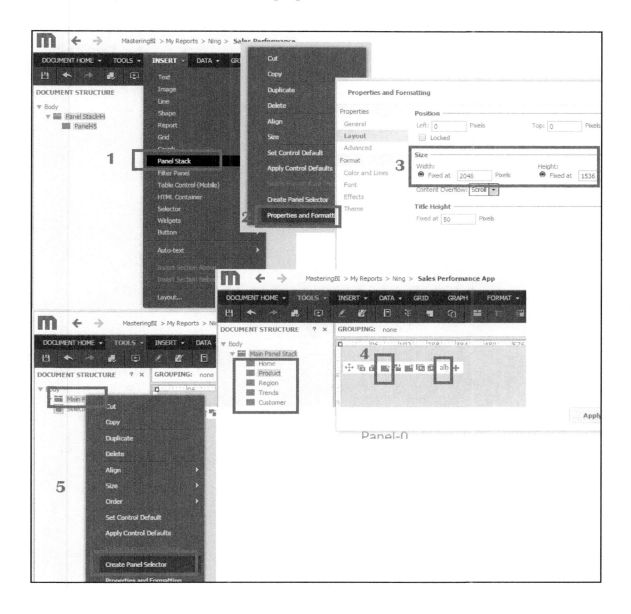

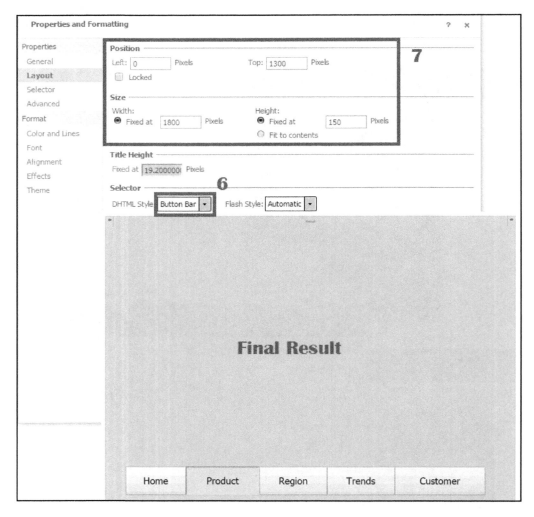

The result is a blank panel stack containing five panels and a panel selector.

Creating a Home page for Sales Performance App

We want to create a home page, a dashboard showing the sales overviews and KPIs:

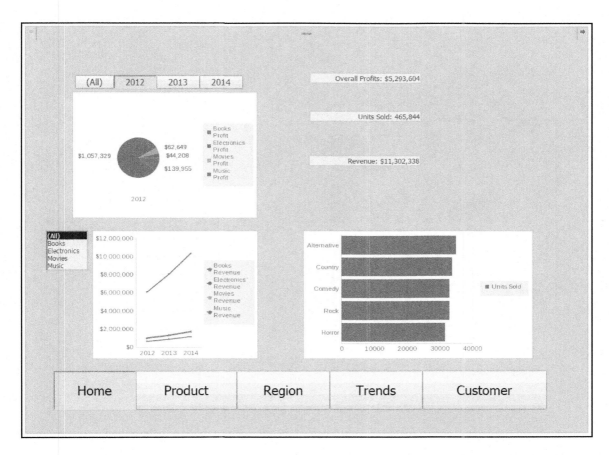

It has four parts: a profits pie chart, a time series graph of revenue, KPIs, and a bar chart for top 5 sales. We will show how to create these parts.

Creating a profit pie chart for Home

The result we want to achieve is as follows:

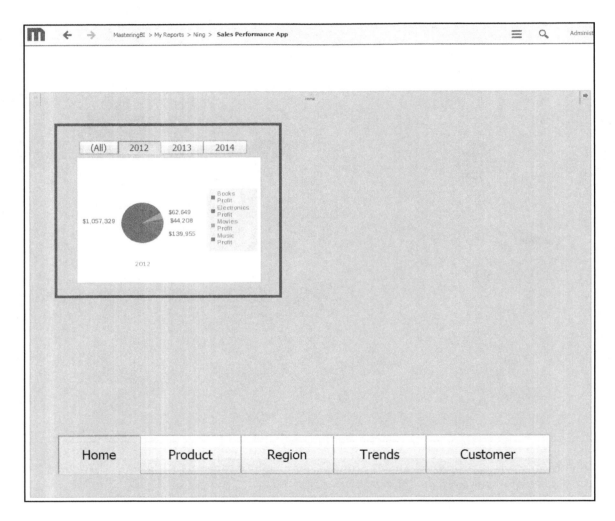

Here are the steps to create it:

1. Click **INSERT**, click **Grid**, and draw the grid on the canvas.
2. Drag **Year**, **Category**, and **Profit** into the grid.
3. Right-click on **Year** and click **Create Selector Control**.

4. Right-click on the selector control, set the **Properties | Layout | Selector | DHTML Style** to **Button Bar**, and adjust it to the proper width and height.

5. Right-click on the grid, click **View Mode | Graph View**, click on **Graph**, and change to **Pie** chart:

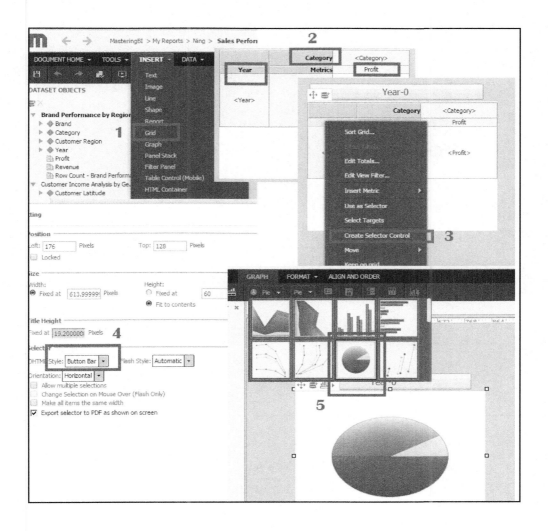

Creating a revenue time series graph for Home

The following is the result we want:

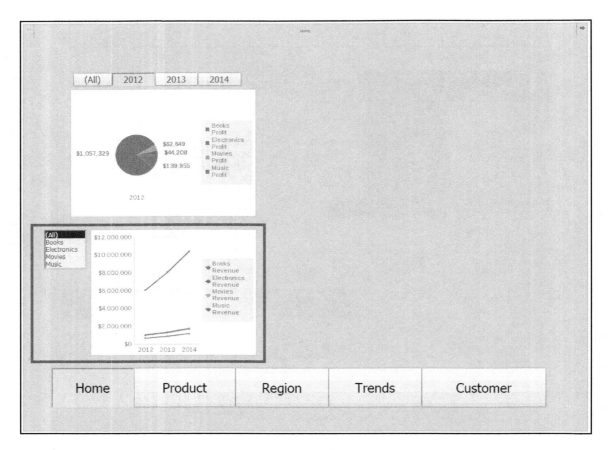

Here are the steps to create it:

1. Click **INSERT**, click **Grid**, and draw the grid on the canvas.
2. Drag **Year**, **Category**, and **Revenue** into the grid.
3. Right-click on **Category** and click **Create Selector Control**.
4. Right-click on the selector control, set the **Properties** | **Layout** | **Selector** | **DHTML Style** to **Button Bar**, and adjust it to the proper width and height.

5. Right-click on the grid, click **View Mode** | **Graph View**, click **Graph**, and change to **Pie** chart.

6. Take manual control of Property and **Formatting** | **Properties** | **Selector** | **Targets**:

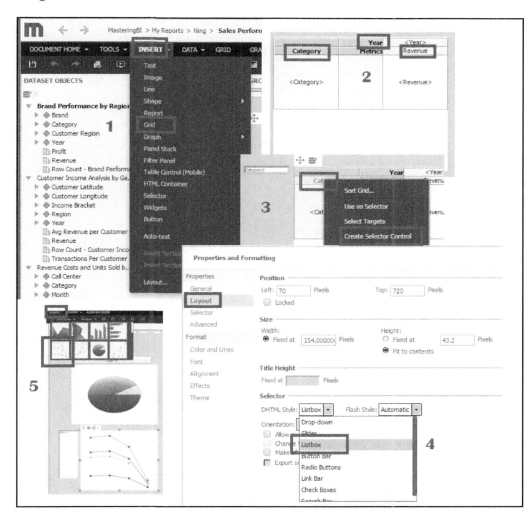

Creating KPI for Home

The following is the result we want:

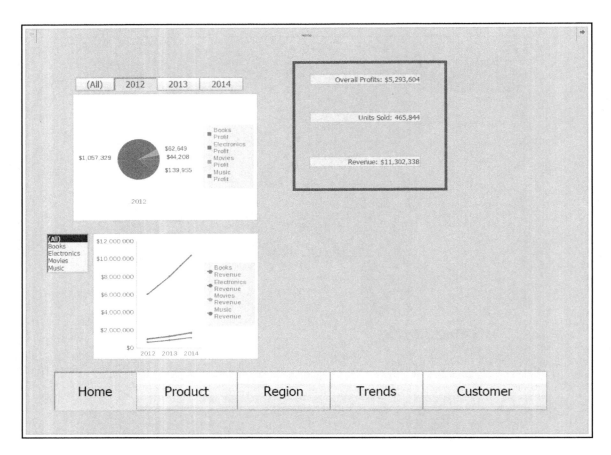

The steps to create it are as follows:

1. Drag metrics **Profits**, **Units Sold**, and **Revenue** on to the canvas.
2. Double-click the textbox and input necessary text.
3. Right-click on the textbox, click **Properties and Formatting**, and change text sizes.

Creating a top 5 units sold bar chart for Home

The result we want is as follows:

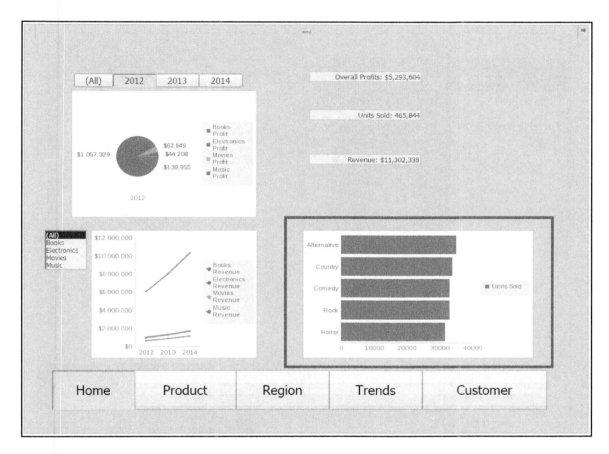

Here are the steps to create it:

1. Click **INSERT**, click **Grid**, and draw the grid on the canvas.
2. Drag **Year, Subcategory**, and **Units Sold** into the grid.
3. Change into interactive edit mode and sort by **Units Sold**.
4. Change into edit mode, right-click on **Subcategory**, and click **Edit View Filter**.

5. Click **Add New Condition**, **Units Sold**, **Highest**, and input 5 for the value.

6. Right-click on the grid, choose **View Mode** | **Graph View**, click **Graph**, and choose **Horizontal Bar**:

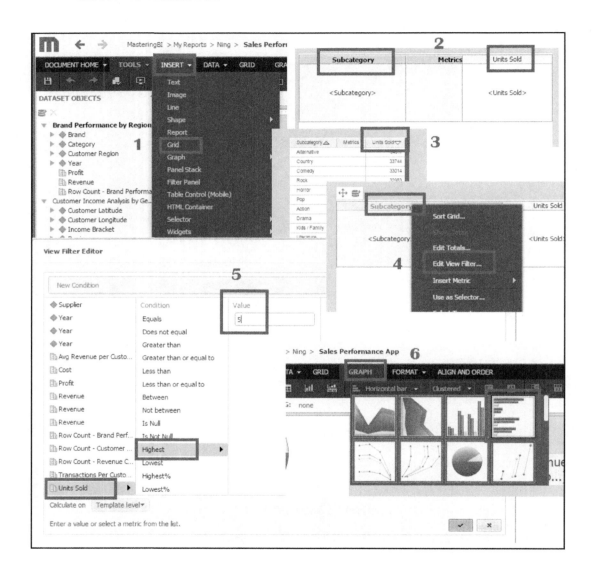

Creating a Product page for Sales Performance App

The result we want to achieve is as follows:

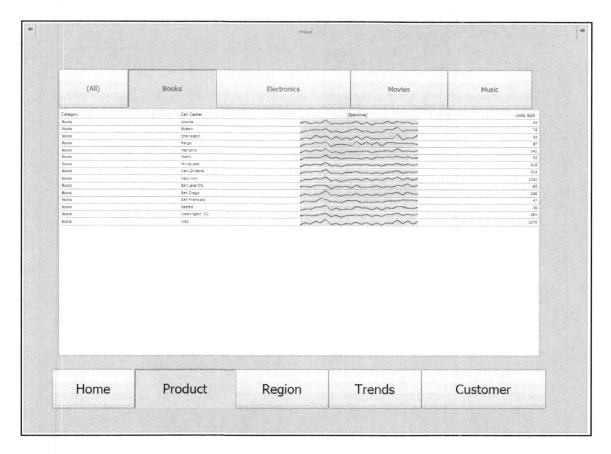

Here are the steps to create it:

1. Click **INSERT**, click **Grid**, and draw the grid on the canvas.
2. Drag **Category**, **Call Centre**, **Month**, and **Units Sold** into the grid.
3. Right-click on **Category** and click **Create Selector Control**.

4. Right-click on the grid, click **Properties and Formatting,** and click **Properties** |
    Widget | **Widget Selection** | **Widget** | **Mobile** | **Microcharts**:

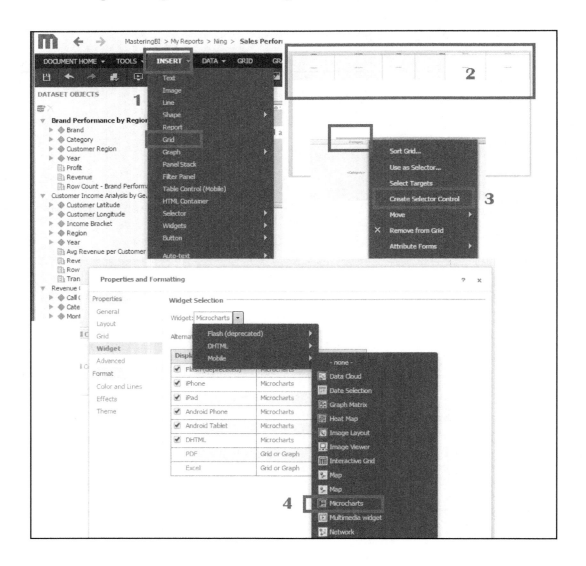

Creating a Region page for Sales Performance App

The result we want to achieve is as follows:

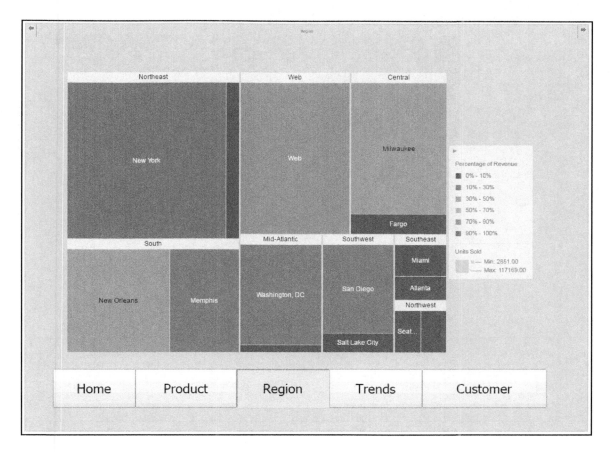

Here are the steps to create it:

1. Navigate to the **Region** panel.
2. Click **INSERT** | **Widgets** | **Mobile** | **Heat Map**.

3. Drag **Region**, **Call Centre**, **Units Sold**, and **Revenue** into the grid:

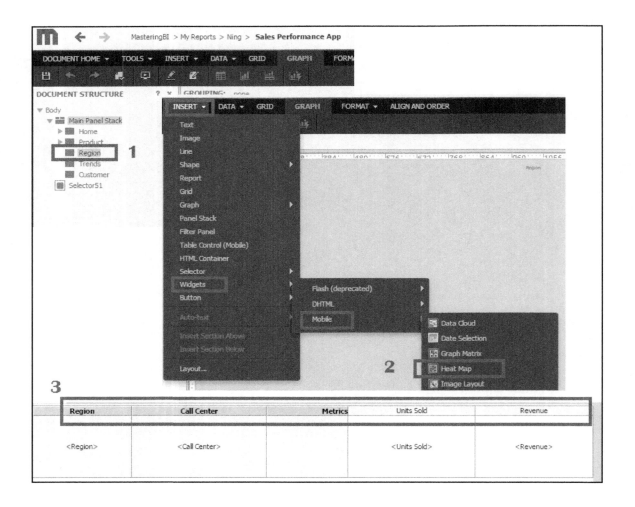

Creating a Trend page for Sales Performance App

The result we want is as follows:

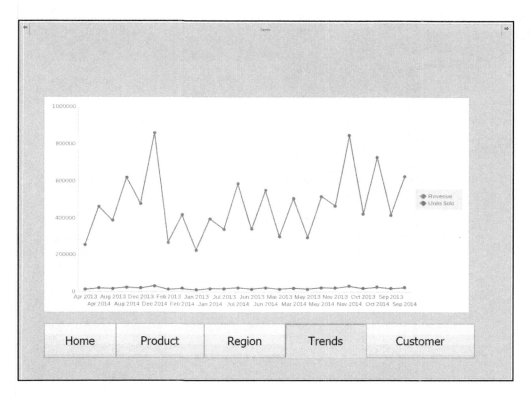

Here are the steps to create it:

1. Navigate to the **Trends** panel.
2. Click **INSERT** | **Widgets** | **Mobile** | **Time Series**.
3. Drag **Month, Metrics, Revenue**, and **Units Sold** into the grid.

4. Note that **Time Series Widgets** can only be viewed in mobile mode (we cheated on the previous result graph):

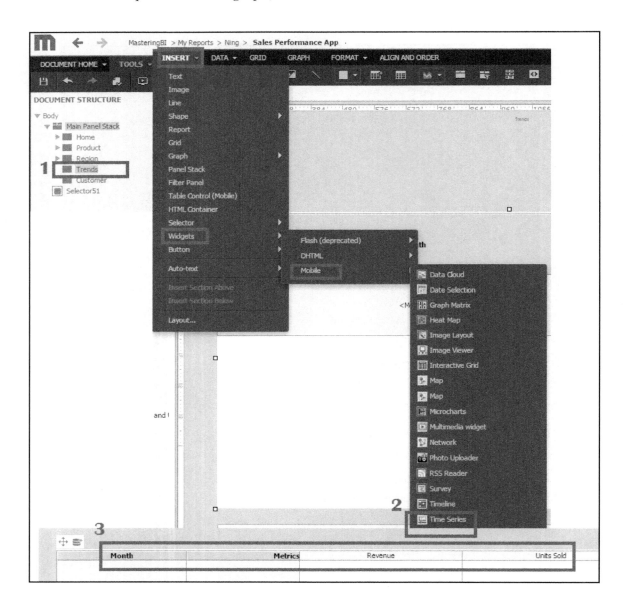

Creating a Customer page for Sales Performance App

The result we want is as follows:

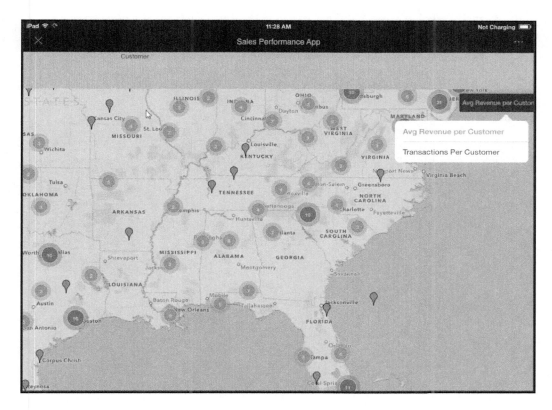

Here are the steps to create it:

1. Navigate to the **Customer** panel.
2. Click **INSERT** | **Widgets** | **Mobile** | **Map**.
3. Drag **Zip Code, Customer Latitude, Customer Longitude, Avg Revenue per Customer**, and **Transactions Per Customer** into the grid.
4. Right-click on the grid, click **Properties**, set **Select Latitude** to **Customer Latitude**, set **Select Longitude** to **Customer Longitude**, and set **Selection display attribute** to **Zip code**.

5. Note that **Map Widgets** can only be viewed in mobile mode:

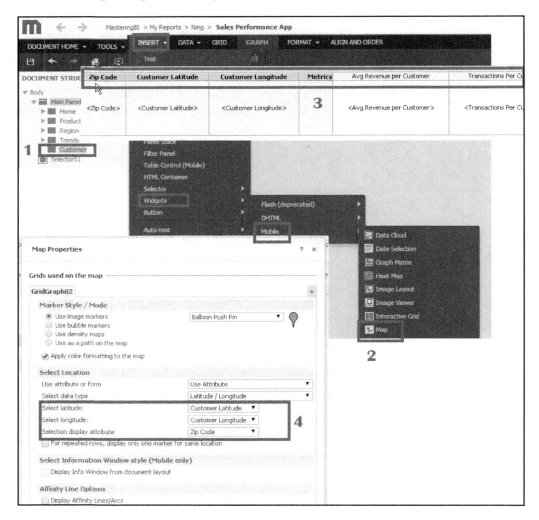

Prompts in mobile applications

Prompts in mobiles work basically the same as those in Web. Numeric value prompts display in different ways depending on the data involved, for example, date and time picker, Boolean switch, and numeric stepper. There are two prompts native to mobile:

- **Geo Location prompt**: This can work both by entering a value or choosing from an element list, for example, a list of cities
- **Barcode Reader prompt**:

Prompts can help filter out unwanted records, to target only the information of interest.

Views in mobile applications

Multiple versions of an app can be created with multiple layouts of views. A layout can have multiple views. Multiple views are useful for different screen sizes and orientation. Views do not share objects with other layouts. Views reduce design time and maintenance. Multiple views do not have to show the same data, that is, if you rotate the screen, you want to see some new content.

To add views, click **Tools** | **Document Properties** | **Advanced** | **Layout Properties** | **Mobile** | Support orientations: Portrait and Landscape.

To manage views, right-click on the object and click **Manage views**. You can create one view for portrait only, and create a second view for landscape only, by using Views Editor:

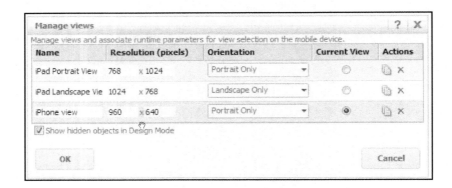

Linking

Links enable navigation to reports and documents. There are three ways to provide linking: Links Editor, Document Links, and URL API.

One thing to note is that intra-document links only work for mobiles; testing should be done on the device. External apps can be opened: mail, text messaging, phone, and so on.

Using Buyer Visit App as an example, on the home page, we have a **Location** button, which is linked to a `Buyer App - Location` document. Here is how to create it:

1. Insert a button, **Location**.
2. Right-click on the button and click **Properties and Formatting**.
3. Click **Properties** | **Button** | **Actions**.
4. Under **Links**, specify **Buyer App – Location** to run this report or document:

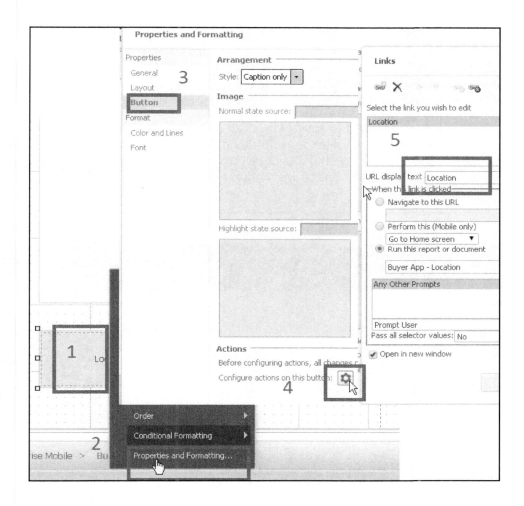

Best practices

Here are some considerations for best practices of mobile app design.

Dedicated vs unified design

If you are creating apps for iOS devices, then the dedicated design should be used for specific devices. Separate apps for each device: iPad or iPhone (creating Views can help with that: one document can handle both iPhone and iPad, with different views for one document). The cost is that it requires maintenance of multiple apps.

When creating apps for Android devices, it is better to use unified design for all possible screens. Android is designed to scale for multiple devices. Again, Views can help. The cost of maintenance is low because you have a single app providing unified design. Remember to take advantage of the **Fit page** option for automatically adapting to different screen sizes:

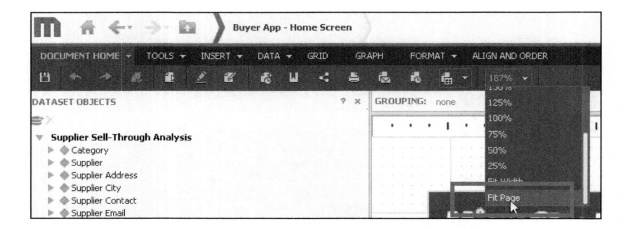

Purpose, audience, and prototype

Apps should have a specific purpose and audience in mind. Mobile functionality should be leveraged, take advantage of its location service, security, cameras, and so on. Mobile apps usually solve problems not solved by other interfaces.

Some testing can be done in a web environment, but true testing requires deployment. That is, not all functionality works on web, for example, map widget, time series widget. In addition, some UI interactions have effects not known until done.

Extending mobile capabilities

Mobile capabilities can be extended with transaction services, and Mobile SDK.

Transaction services

Transaction services allows the app to write-back to the database systems. This can enable us to send data, pictures, or barcodes, by simply pushing a **Submit** button. MicroStrategy 10 natively connects to SAP, Oracle, and SalesForce; other systems may require FFSQL.

For example, you are a restaurant inspector; you can walk into a restaurant with your phone to do your job. First, you can take a picture of the restaurant and upload it into a remote transactional database. Second, you can input scores and ratings for the restaurant.

Offline transactions are processed when connectivity resumes. If your Internet connection is lost, the data will be waiting in a transaction queue, and will try to connect when the phone is back online. Transaction Queue keeps track of transactions processed.

Mobile SDK

Mobile SDK will be discussed in another chapter.

Deployment

Deployment is simple:

1. Copy the mobile app (documents specifically for mobile devices) into a shared folder.
2. Visit the project you created with your mobile devices. The user will need to install the MicroStrategy Mobile Client if they have not already done so.
3. Click **Configure**; MicroStrategy will automatically do the configuration for you.

4. Now you should see the project and the apps in the MicroStrategy Mobile Client:

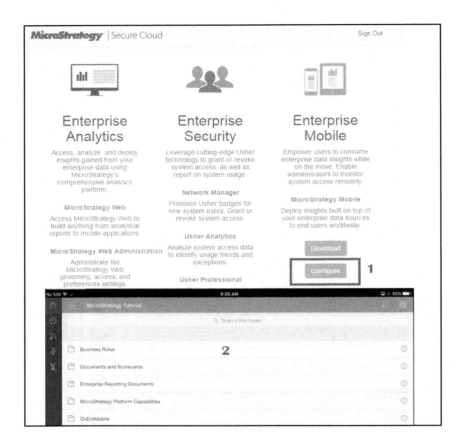

Summary

In this chapter, we discussed four topics: Mobile Server installation, how to create a mobile application with the example *Sales Performance App*, best practices for creating mobile applications, and overviews of advanced topics about extending mobile capabilities with transaction services and mobile SDK. Details of using SDK are discussed in a separate chapter.

In the next chapter, we will discuss how to use new software called MicroStrategy Desktop to explore your data, and discover business insights.

8
Data Discovery with MicroStrategy Desktop

Self-service BI is the one of the top trends in the market. The speed of business has dramatically increased. As a result, there is a high demand for quick decision making based on data. Business users want to connect to their data, immediately discover it, and extract business value from the data. They don't want to ask IT and wait a long time for their request to be processed. Moreover, they want a friendly interface that is intuitive and provides simple drag-and-drop options in order to slice and dice data. This is one of the latest trends in the analytical market. As a result, MicroStrategy have developed their own product for self-service data discovery analytics that can add value to the organization by decentralizing BI.

MicroStrategy Desktop puts the power of visual data discovery in our hands. It is designed for self-service analytics and gives us the freedom to analyze business data effortlessly with an intuitive, friendly interface. As a result, business users can easily connect a number of various data sources such as enterprise data warehouses, flat files, spreadsheets, social media data, and so on. Moreover, they can clean and transform data for better analysis.

This chapter will cover the following points:

- Connecting to various data sources
- Building ad hoc schema
- Data visualization
- Using D3 visualization
- Publishing

Meet MicroStrategy Desktop

Let's look closely at MicroStrategy Desktop. In order to download the installation files, we should go to the MicroStrategy website (`http://www.microstrategy.com/us/free-tr ial`) and choose MicroStrategy Desktop. If we don't have the license key, we can obtain a 30-day trial period. It is enough for a proof of concept project or just for playing with the tool and getting a first impression of it.

There are two versions of Desktop:

- Windows 64-bit
- Mac

This gives us the opportunity to run Desktop even on Mac OS. There are many companies that prefer to use Mac instead of classical Windows. It is gives you much more flexibility. In our case, we use the Windows environment, where we run MicroStrategy Developer.

Let's install MicroStrategy Desktop and learn it through several exercises. In order to install it, just run the installation file and it will do all the work.

These are the main features of MicroStrategy Desktop:

- Powerful Desktop analytics
- Easily connects and blends data from any source
- Cleanses and prepares data with built-in data wrangling
- Unparalleled data access
- Intuitive dashboard design
- Powerful predictive analytics
- Large data visualization library

As we mentioned before, MicroStrategy Desktop allows us to make BI decentralized. MicroStrategy Platform allows us to use both BI types, decentralized and centralized. See the following diagram in order to understand the difference between these two approaches:

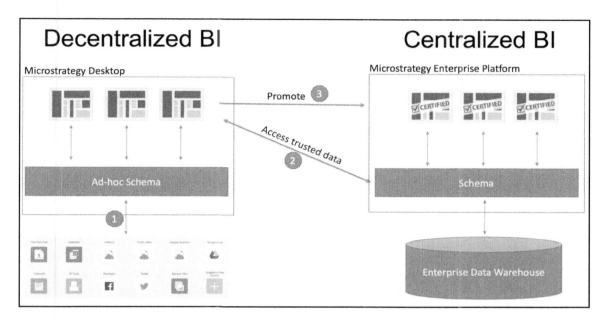

Centralized BI usually is managed by the IT department. It should be a reliable platform that offers accurate, quality data through reports and dashboards. The source of all data is the enterprise data model, mapped to the MicroStrategy schema. All attributes and metrics should be conformed and there is a small chance of getting wrong data. On the other hand, we have decentralized BI, where everyone, who has enough skills, can connect any source of data, blend it, and find business insights. In the preceding figure, three numbers demonstrate possible scenarios:

1. Connect any data source such as flat files, big data sources, NoSQL data stores, web services, transaction databases, and so on in order to quickly discover data or build dashboards.

2. In the same way, users can connect trusted schema attributes and build dashboards with clean, accurate data. In addition, they can enrich data using any data sources.

3. The final dashboard can be promoted to the enterprise platform. Before promoting any reports or dashboards, IT should review and approve it. In addition, users can just share their insights using e-mail.

Let's compare these approaches:

	Ad hoc schema	Schema	Ad hoc schema connected to the EDW
Data	Agnostic data source	SQL or MDX sources	Enrich schema data with agnostic data sources
Result	File with a localized security model	Globally-applicable set of objects that leverage the unified security model	File that hooks into the central object and security models
Value	Fast and dirty, speed to value for ad hoc analyses	Single version of the truth	Quick speed to value and ability to access the central object and security models

In addition, we want to point out the pros and cons for classical schema and ad hoc schema. Usually, developers use MicroStrategy Architect in order to build schemas. It gives fine-grained control over database concepts, schema objects, and data governance. However, it takes a long time to build complex schemas. In terms of the ad hoc schema, it dramatically increases speed of development, allows us to prototype use cases, and validate data. Unfortunately, ad hoc schemas are disconnected from the single version of truth and security models for enhanced flexibility.

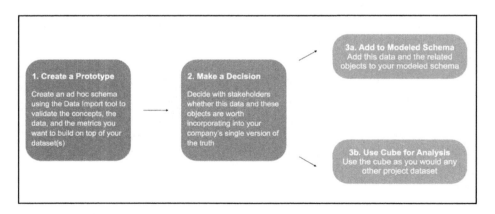

MicroStrategy allows the following workflow in order to handle all types of schema:

1. **Create a Prototype**: Build an ad hoc schema using the Data Import tool to validate the concepts, the data, and the metric you want to build on top of your datasets.

2. **Make a decision**: Decide with stakeholders whether this data and these objects are worth incorporating into your company's single version of the truth.
3. **Add to Modeled Schema** or **Use cube for Analysis**.

Before we start to work with MicroStrategy Desktop, we also want to point out the fresh magical quadrant 2016 of Gartner for BI tools:

There is a full report here: `https://www.microstrategy.com/us/go/gartner-magic-quadrant-16`.

In `Chapter 1`, *Getting Started with MicroStrategy* we looked at the Gartner BI quadrant of 2015 where Enterprise BI, such as MicroStrategy and SAP BusinessObjects, with self-service data discovery BI ,such as Tableau and Microsoft, were in one leader quadrant. However, as we see in the leaders' quadrant 2016, there are only self-service BI tools, such as Tableau and Qlik. It means that there is a shift from Enterprise BI to self-service BI. However, it is not obvious. Anyway, lots of people still use Excel spreadsheets.

In order to work with self-service BI, technical skills are still required, especially with Qlik. As a result, all BI vendors try to offer something that can help users to easily work with data. For example, SAP offers SAP Lumira and MicroStrategy offers Desktop. Most of them have something in common: their interface, which is very similar to Tableau and in fact is becoming the standard of self-service BI.

MicroStrategy Desktop interface

Let's run the Desktop application for the first time by clicking on it:

From this moment we can start to build a new dashboard using one of the following options:

- Add new data by acquiring external data from flat files, relational databases, or any other data source
- Add datasets from a server, for example, connect to an existing MicroStrategy Intelligence Server and choose grid objects
- Browse objects on the server: choose attributes, metrics, and so on, in order to build dashboards

Let's try to build our first visualization using a Microsoft spreadsheet with data:

1. Click on **Add New Data**.
2. Choose File from Disk.

> You can find all related files in an attachment to this book that you can
> download from the `www.packtpub.com` website.

3. Find `Dataset1.xls` and click **Finish**. The data will be imported. Attributes and metrics will appear in the **DASHBOARD DATASETS** toolbar.
4. In order to create a visualization, we should simply drag and drop the `Product Subcategory` attribute to the rows section and the Internet Order Quantity metric to the column section. Drag `Product Category` to rows and `Internet Order Quantity` to columns.
5. Then change the data visualization to **Heat Map**.

As a result, we can build a small chart that shows us the top product subcategory:

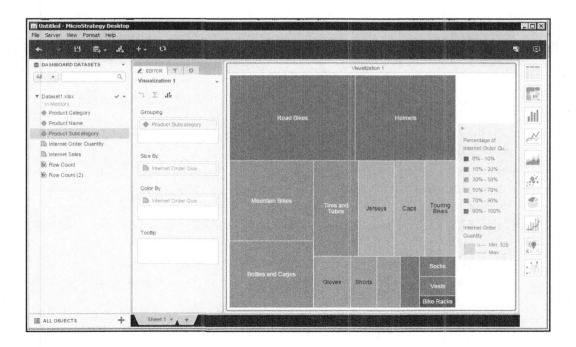

We can customize this data visualization by going to the option of **Visualization 1**; we should click on the small arrow in the top-right corner. You have to keep your cursor over the visualization to make this arrow visible:

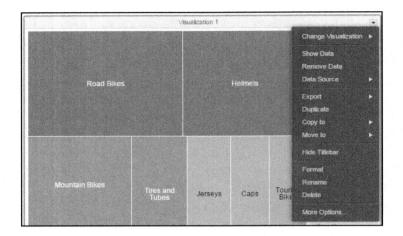

Moreover, we need to cover the main toolbar:

- **Undo**: We can take a step back in order to cancel the last change in the dashboard/report.
- **Redo**: We can take one step forward in order to apply the last change to the dashboard/report.
- **Save**: We can the save dashboard/report.
- **New Data**: We can add data from any source or MicroStrategy Intelligence Server.
- **Insert Visualization**: We can add more visualization windows and combine them into one dashboard.
- **Insert**: We can insert Text, Filters, Images, or HTML containers.
- **Refresh Dataset**: We can refresh the dashboard/report. Usually, we should do this if the source data is changed.
- **Annotation Mode**: Allows us to put annotations on the dashboards and print it or save it as an image.

- **Presentation Mode**: It is a kind of full screen in order to have a better look at the dashboard/report.

Finally, we can add more sheets to one dashboard. For example, if we want to create one dashboard covering different departments such as Sales, Marketing, and Inventory. We can create four sheets, one summary sheet, and another to detail information about every department.

Let's build a dashboard in order to see the main capabilities of MicroStrategy Desktop. Before we start to build our dashboard, we should design it. It is good practice to take a pencil and sheet of paper and draw a sketch. It can help us save time and be more productive. Another piece of advice – do not spend lot of time on sketches. Dashboard development is an iterative process. It means, we should start an early prototype dashboard and demonstrate it to our business clients.

This is a small dashboard that we will build in order to meet the functionality of MicroStrategy Desktop:

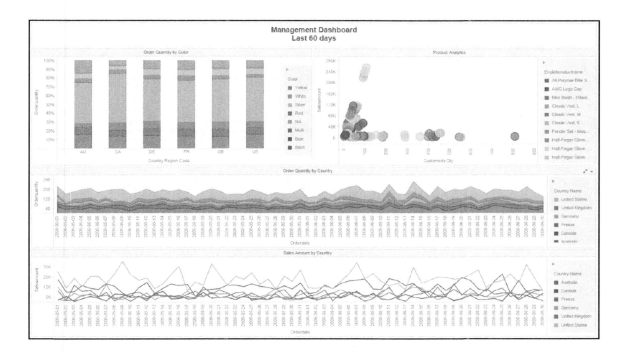

Building ad hoc schemas

MicroStrategy Desktop allows us to build ad hoc schemas in intuitive ways using a friendly interface. Ad hoc schemas help business users to achieve quicker values. The core of the ad hoc building process is Data Import, which has many features such as auto-detect attributes type, auto-create metrics, auto-identify data relations, and allows us to preview data. In addition, it allows us to combine data from multiple sources in a single dataset, create multi-form attributes, and create and edit relationships across attributes. Finally, it can be mapped to project attributes in order to inherit project security filters in MicroStrategy Enterprise.

We are going to work with relational databases and use the same source as we used in Chapter 2, *Setting Up an Analytics Semantic Layer and Public Objects* when we built schemas. There is a picture from **CA ERwin Data Modeler**, that displays physical data models. Using this model, we can easily identify what tables we need and what the joins are between tables.

CA ERwin Data Modeler is a data-modeling tool that allows us to create logical and physical data models in order to manage complex data warehouses in organizations.

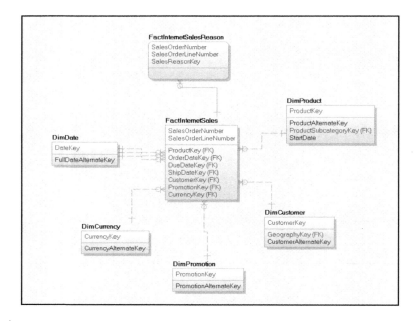

Let's connect to Oracle database and build an ad hoc schema:

1. Click **File** | **New**.
2. Choose **Database** | **Oracle 11g**. We have several options:
    - **Type a Query** – we can write an SQL query or copy it
    - **Build a Query** – with the help of a graphical interface we can create a query
    - **Pick tables** – simply choose tables that we need for analyses
      In our case we have a data model that shows us list tables.

3. Click **Add** in order to add a new data source. We can create a new DSN or use an existing one. However, keep in mind that MicroStrategy Desktop is installed on Windows and we should create an ODBC connection to Oracle if we want to use it (or we can choose DNS-less and type the host, port, login, and password):
    - **Hostname:** `localhost`
    - **Port:** `1521`
    - **SID:** `orcl`
    - **User:** `system`
    - **Password:** `MasterinBI2016`

4. Now we can choose our schema EDW and pick the required tables:

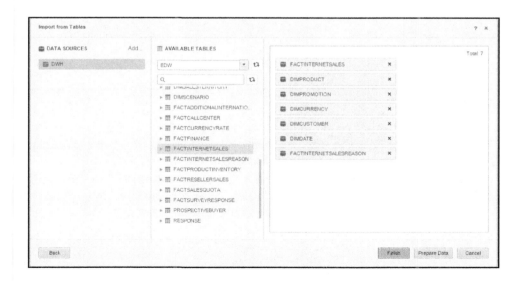

Before we finish, we should define the joins between tables, attributes, and metrics.

5. Click on **Prepare Data** and we get a **Preview** window, which helps us to prepare data. In addition, we can preview data, change data type, transform the column to measure or attribute. For all columns which we do not need for the dashboard, we can choose **Do Not Import**:

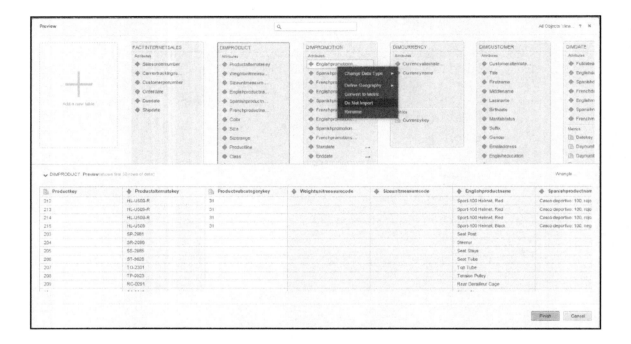

6. Let's define joins between tables. By default, all columns with numeric types become metrics. We should transform all key fields to attributes by clicking on the column and choosing **Convert to Attribute**.

7. In order to the define joins between two tables, we should drag the name of a column in one table and drop to another column in another table. As a result, an INNER JOIN will be created. These are the join conditions:

#	Join Conditions
1	`FactInternetSales.ProductKey=DimProduct.ProductKey`
2	`FactInternetSales.OrderDateKey=DimDate.DateKey`
3	`FactInternetSales.CustomerKey=DimCustomer.CustomerKey`
4	`FactInternetSales.PromotionKey=DimPromotion.PromotionKey`
5	`FactInternetSales.CurrencyKey=DimCurrency.CurrencyKey`
6	`FactInternetSales.SalesOrderNumber =FactInternetSalesReason.SalesOrderNumber`

MicroStrategy Desktop can automatically map the same columns. We should be careful and unmap all columns that do not service joins between tables.

8. Click **Finish**. We have two options: extract all data in-memory or use a live connection. When we choose the in-memory option, we can publish an in-memory cube in MicroStrategy Platform. Let's use a live connection.

Now we are ready to build a new dashboard but before we actually start to realize our dashboard, let's discuss several very important terms from the world of data analytics and dramatically increase the flexibility and power of MicroStrategy Desktop:

- **Data Blending**: A quick process of extracting data from various data sources, transforming and combining them into one dataset.
- **Data Profiling**: The process of analyzing the nature of data in existing datasets in order to find outliers or skews. In addition, it allows us to understand the distribution of data values.
- **Data Wrangling**: This allows us to map data from one format to another using the rich functionality of MicroStrategy commands.
- **Data Mashup:** Used for the integration of several datasets into one new dataset.

Let's try to understand how we can leverage these features in MicroStrategy Desktop.

Data mashup of Oracle and flat files

First of all, we need to add one more table to the existing ad hoc schema. There is an Excel spreadsheet that you can find in the attachment for this chapter – `Geography.xls`.

Let's try to mashup data with a relational database and an Excel spreadsheet:

1. Right-click on our dataset and choose **Edit Dataset...**:

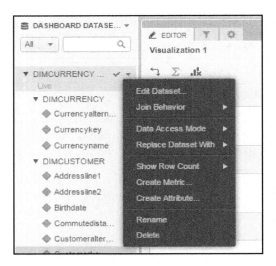

2. Click on **Add** new table and choose file from disk. Find `Geography.xls` and click **Add**. It will automatically join the fact table with `GeographyKey`.
3. Let's look at the **Preview** and we find that the field **Location** has many values separated with commas. We are lucky, because we can wrangle that data and prepare it for the dashboard.
4. Click on **Wrangle...**.
5. Choose **Location** as a field and **Split on Separate** as a function. Our separator is a comma. Click **Apply**:

6. As a result, we get six columns. Let's rename them. MicroStrategy saves all operations with data in **History Script**. We can easy rollback any of the changes:

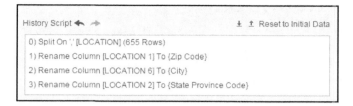

7. Let's rename the column by right-clicking on the column name:

Data profiling of geography data

We can examine our data and fix some issues. In order to examine data we should use data profiling by clicking on the column name and choosing **Text Selector**. Let's do it for **State Province Name** and **City**. There are some issues with the data:

There are two values for New York and two values for München. Let's fix it by clicking **Edit**, which appears near the value when we choose it.

We are done with data wrangling. Click **Ok**.

MicroStrategy will understand that is it geodata and will transform these attributes to geodata. There is one very useful feature – data enrichment. For example, if we have only the zip code, MicroStrategy can look up the country, state, and city for us. We don't need this because our data file already has provided all this data.

Click on **Update Dataset** and we are ready to work with our ad hoc schema.

Building a dashboard

Let's build using our ad hoc model. MicroStrategy Desktop provides us with an intuitive GUI where we can simply drag and drop attributes and metrics. In addition, we can create new derived attributes and metrics. We can start by adding text elements on top of the dashboard by clicking on **Insert** and choosing the **Text** element:

We could type any name; in our example, it is `Management Dashboard Last 60 days`. Moreover, every element on canvas such as text or a visualization has lots of settings. For text we could increase the size of the text and make it bold.

Our canvas is still empty. In order to start to building a chart we can drag and drop objects in rows, columns, or metrics or we can choose the type of chart and then drag objects.

Line charts

Let's start with a simple line chart in order to build `Sales Amount by Country`.

> In the most common case, it combines in a line a set of points corresponding to the values of the axes. For example, the daily traffic to the site in the past month. It can display multiple sets of data – for example, views statistics for the three most popular pages.

1. Drag and drop **SalesAmount** to **Vertical**, **Orderdate** to **Horizontal**, and **Country Name** to **Color By**.
2. Right-click on **Orderdate** and choose **Number Format** in order to change the date format to yyyy-mm-dd:

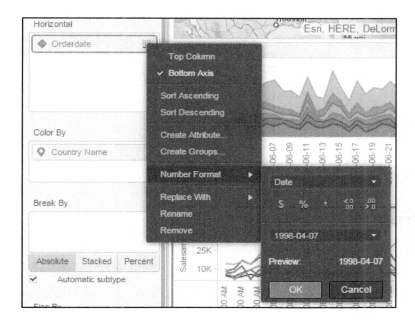

3. Click on the small icon of a funnel in order to add a date filter. We want to restrict dates in order to have only a 60-day time frame. Drag and drop **Orderdate**:

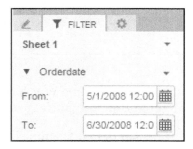

As a result, this filter will be applied to all visualizations on this sheet.

4. Click on the small arrow on top and choose **Rename** in order to rename the visualization:

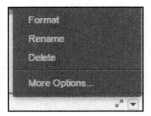

Area charts

Let's add an area chart in order to see how countries perform:

1. Choose **Area Chart Visualization**.
2. Drag and drop **Orderquantity** to **Vertical**, **Orderdate** to **Horizontal**, and **CountyName** to **Color By**.
3. Right-click on **Orderdate** and choose **Number Format** in order to change the date format to yyyy-mm-dd.
4. Check that **Break By** is **Staked**, otherwise it will be difficult to read the chart.
5. Click on the small arrow on top and choose **Rename** in order to rename the visualization.

Bar charts

Let's assume that it is very important to understand which color is the most popular for the product. For this purpose, we will build order quantity by color:

It shows one or more sets of data by comparing them with each other. There are two options in the case of multiple display sets, either in the form of several columns standing nearby, or in the form of divided portions in accordance with the values. For example, the annual profit of the three companies in the past 5 years, or their market share during the same period.

1. Choose **Bar Chart**.
2. Drag and drop **Orderquantity** to **Vertical**, **Country Region Code** to **Horizontal**,

and **Color** to **Color By**.
3. Choose **Break By Percent**.
4. Rename the visualization.

Bubble charts

We can analyze products in different dimensions. For example, we can see a correlation between the Sales Amount and Customer Quantity:

Bubble charts are useful when we want to use 2-4 dimensions. We need 2 dimensions in order to use them as axes and 1-2 to create bubbles and manage their size.

1. Choose **Bubble Chart**.
2. Drag and drop **Salesamount** to **Vertical**, **Orderquantity** to **Horizontal**, and **Englishproductname** to **Color By**.
3. Rename the visualization.

Moreover, we can use this chart as a filter for all other visualizations by clicking on the small arrow in the top-left corner and choosing **Use as a Filter**:

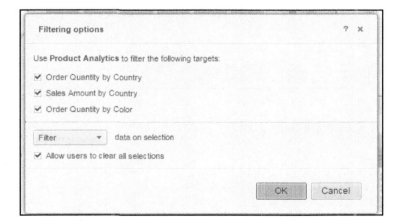

Publishing the dashboard

MicroStrategy offers us a bimodal platform. For example, Enterprise BI and self-service BI. Desktop is a product for self-service exploration as was shown at the beginning of this chapter. We built the dashboard and now we want to upload it to the MicroStrategy Platform. In order to do it, we should create a server connection to our web server. Let's do it:

1. Go to MicroStrategy Web, where the project selection page is, and copy the link:

2. In MicroStrategy Desktop go to **Files** | **Preference** and insert the server URL:

3. Then click **Test & Save Changes**.

As a result, we successfully connected to MicroStrategy Server and can now upload our dashboard onto the server in order to spread it across the organization. Be aware that before spreading a new dashboard it is a good practice to validate it with the IT department.

In addition, we can export the dashboard as a PDF or image file. Moreover, we can save the dashboard as a `.mstr` file with imported data.

Performing Pareto analysis

One good thing about data discovery tools is their agile approach to the data. We can connect any data source and easily slice and dice data. Let's try to use the Pareto principle in order to answer the question: How are sales distributed among the different products?

The Pareto principle states that, for many events, roughly 80% of results come from 20% of the causes. For example, 80% of profits come from 20% of the products offered. This type of analysis is very popular in product analytics.

In MicroStrategy Desktop, we can use shortcut metrics in order to quickly make complex calculations such as running sums or a percent of the total.

Let's build a visualization in order to see the 20% of products that bring us 80% of the money:

1. Choose **Combo Chart**.
2. Drag and drop **Salesamount** to **Vertical** and **Englishproductname** to **Horizontal**.
3. Add **Orderdate** to the filters and restrict to 60 days.
4. Right-click on **Sales amount** and choose **Descending Sort**.
5. Right-click on **Salesamount** | **ShortcutMetrics** | **Percent Running Total**.
6. Drag and drop **Metric Names** to **Color By**.
7. Change the color of **Salesamount** and **Percent Running Total**.
8. Change the shape of **Percent Running Total**.

As a result, we get this chart:

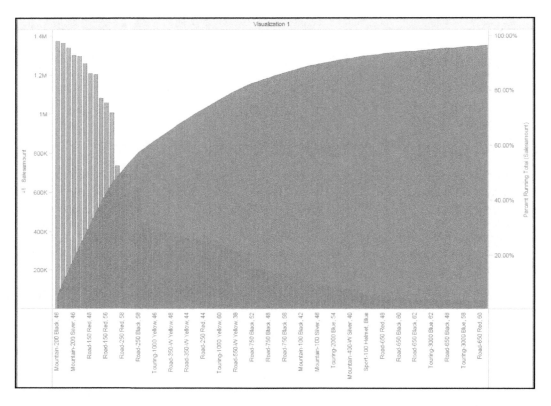

From this chart we can quickly understand our top 20% of products which bring us 80% of the revenue.

Performing cohort analysis

Another very popular analysis is cohort analysis, which is used to research the behavior of a group of people over time. In MicroStrategy Desktop, we can perform cohort analysis in order to study different groupings to understand customers' behavior, cause and effect relationships, and so on. In business, cohort analysis is very popular for exploring customer retention over time. Usually, a cohort is defined by the date of first purchase or registration; sometimes we can use demographic attributes. Using cohort analysis we can simply track customer engagement.

Our dataset has the data for first purchases. We can build cohorts by grouping people by the year and month of their first purchase and then see how they perform.

Before we start we should build some derived elements in order to get the months between the first order and all other orders:

1. The date of the first purchase has a string format. We should convert it to the data. Right-click on any attribute and choose Create Attribute.
2. Use this function in order to convert the string data to the real data format:

   ```
   ToDateTime([Datefirstpurchase@ID])
   ```

   Save this attribute as Date First Order.

3. Create a new attribute `MonthsBetween` using this syntax:

   ```
   MonthsBetween([[Date First Order]@ID], [Orderdate@ID])
   ```

4. Create a new attribute Year Month Order:

   ```
   Concat(Year(Orderdate@ID), Month(Orderdate@ID))
   ```

5. Drag and drop **Months Between** to the rows, **Year Month Order** to the columns, and **Orderquantity** to the metrics.
6. Change **Year Month Order** to descending order.

As a result, we have built a cohort table:

Cohort Analyse								
Year Month Order	20087	20086	20085	20084	20083	20082	20081	20079	20078
Months Between	Orderquantity	Orderquantity	Orderquantity	Orderquantity	Orderquantity	Orderquantity	Orderquantity	Orderquantity	Orderquantity
0	1340	2867	2975	2715	2540	2467	2560	2725	2950
1	62	42	66	51	44	45	53	123	11
2	68	64	59	94	88	85	97	19	57
3	73	64	75	76	68	83	92	63	17
4	63	83	85	78	79	90	158	26	34
5	52	91	77	89	87	120	163	28	45
6	70	89	69	92	123	115	55	45	64
7	52	54	75	166	117	23	127	36	21

We can easily visualize it. Moreover, we can use shortcut metrics in order to calculate cohorts in percentages.

Deploying D3 visualization

MicroStrategy Desktop can be easily integrated with D3 visualization. Let's add more charts to our MicroStrategy Desktop:

1. Go to `https://github.com/mstr-dev/Visualization-Plugins` and download the ZIP archive.
2. Extract it.
3. Copy all folders from the archive to `<MicroStrategy Desktop Installation Folder>/code/plugins`.
4. Restart MicroStrategy Desktop.

As a result, we get lots of new visualizations. Let's try to build a simple Sankey diagram.

There is a small dataset:

- `source,target,value`
- `Barry,Elvis,2`
- `Frodo,Elvis,2`
- `Frodo,Sarah,2`
- `Barry,Alice,2`
- `Elvis,Sarah,2`
- `Elvis,Alice,2`
- `Sarah,Alice,4`

We should copy it and insert it into the clipboard by creating a new dashboard. Moreover, we should wrangle the dataset in order to split values. In addition, we need to convert **Value** to metric. As a result, we can build this Sankey Chart:

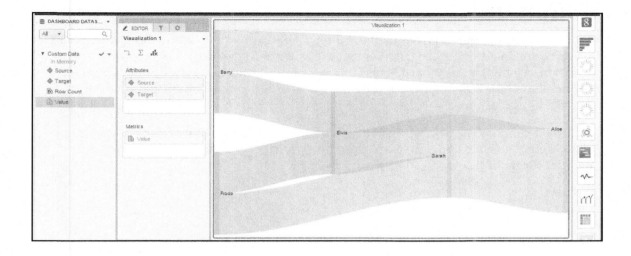

Desktop versus Tableau

Tableau is an absolute leader in Self-Service data discovery BI. However, MicroStrategy hugely invests in Desktop in order to be on the same level with Tableau. According to the magical quadrant 2016, Tableau is an absolute leader in self-service BI. According to my experience, MicroStrategy is the best in the Enterprise BI. If you are thinking about what tool to use, it will depend on the business case. If there is a requirement for a huge BI platform that should be scalable and have strong security then go for MicroStrategy. If we need quick results, agility, and flexibility then go for Tableau. And we should remember the latest trend in BI – use bimodal models. For example, we should give opportunities to users which have strong governance and a centralized BI platform with self-service data-discovery agile BI.

Summary

In this chapter, we met MicroStrategy Desktop. We learned how to download and install this software. In addition, we talked about the modern BI market and its requirements. Moreover, we built a dashboard, learned how to build cohorts and performed Pareto analysis. Finally, we deployed D3 visualization in order to enrich the capabilities of MicroStrategy Desktop.

In the next chapter, we will learn about MicroStrategy Mobile Analytics. You will meet MicroStrategy Mobile app and learn about best practices of design and development analytics for mobile devices.

9
MicroStrategy System Administration

BI solutions provide reports, dashboards, and ad hoc queries for the whole organization. Usually, MicroStrategy implementation is huge and it requires many administration tasks such as installation, update, and configuration of MicroStrategy servers. In addition, the administrator ensures the high availability of systems as well as performance. Moreover, they should manage security, monitor the project's environment, and manage the project's life cycle. Finally, they are responsible for troubleshooting.

MicroStrategy provides rich functionality for managing and monitoring the whole system and makes the life of an administrator easier with automatization of routine administrator tasks. Usually, developers are responsible for deploying and running BI solutions. As a result, it is important for BI developers to understand the architecture of BI tools and know how to manage them.

In this chapter, we will learn about:

- Managing MicroStrategy platform
- Monitoring MicroStrategy
- Deploying Operations Manager and Enterprise Manager
- MicroStrategy products and tools
- Change Journal

Managing MicroStrategy platform

In Chapter 1, *Getting Started with MicroStrategy* we covered the installation process of MicroStrategy and MicroStrategy Web. Let's look at how we can manage MicroStrategy Intelligence Server. In order to see the status of Intelligence Server or to start, stop, or restart it, we should use MicroStrategy Service Manager. There are several options available to run MicroStrategy:

- MicroStrategy Service
- Command Manager
- Service Manager

In order to run MicroStrategy, we could go to the home folder and run Service Manager.

These are the main commands for MicroStrategy tools:

- `./mstrcmdmgrw`: MicroStrategy Command Manager
- `./mstrcfgwiz`: MicroStrategy Configuration Wizard
- `./mstrconnectwiz`: MicroStrategy Connectivity Configuration Wizard
- `./mstrdbquerytool`: MicroStrategy DB Query Tool
- `./mstrdiag`: MicroStrategy Diagnostics and Performance Logging
- `./mstrsuppappcfgwiz`: MicroStrategy Health Center Configuration Wizard
- `./mstrsuppappgui`: MicroStrategy Health Center Center Console
- `./mstrlicmgr`: MicroStrategy License Manager
- `./mstrodbcadx`: MicroStrategy ODBC Administrator
- `./mstrsvcmgr`: MicroStrategy Service Manager

In order to run commands on a Linux environment, we should go to the home folder and run the name of the command:

```
# cd /mstr10/microstrategy_home/bin
# ./mstrsvcmgr
```

> In case we use putty to communicate with a Linux machine, we should run the Xming application in order to get a GUI: https://en.wikipedia.org/wiki/Xming.

MicroStrategy Service Manager will appear as shown in the following screenshot:

We can start, stop, and restart Intelligence Server as well as manage other services:

- MicroStrategy Listener
- MicroStrategy Enterprise Manager data load (collect statistics and load to Enterprise Manager)

In order to manage MicroStrategy Web we should access the MicroStrategy Web Administrator page using the browser. Go to `http://192.168.81.134:8080/MicroStrategy/servlet/mstrWebAdmin`.

This page allows us to:

- Connect to Intelligence Server and configure connection properties (for example, we must mark that Intelligence Server automatically connects to MicroStrategy server)
- Configure security
- Deploy custom widgets
- Download MicroStrategy Office distributive

Another important configuration is setting project defaults in order to set different options for all users, such as font, grid options, and so on.

Monitoring MicroStrategy

In order to monitor MicroStrategy Intelligence Server, we have two options:

- MicroStrategy monitors
- Operations Manager

Let's start with MicroStrategy monitors. We should open MicroStrategy Developer, where we can find Project monitors:

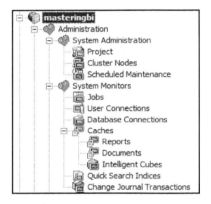

These monitors are very useful and can give a quick overview of what is going on with our MicroStrategy server. For example, one of the most useful is **User Connections**, which helps to understand who is logged on now. In addition, if we have enough rights, we can kill the session of a particular user. Another one is **Jobs** – this shows us reports that are executing or in a queue waiting to execute. On our small training server, there isn't lots of information, but if you have a production MicroStrategy, you can get lots of insights from these monitors.

One of the main new features of MicroStrategy 10 is MicroStrategy Operations Manager, which is a web-based tool for administrative tasks. It allows us to monitor all environments in one place. For example, Operations Manager allows us to:

- View system heartbeats
- Monitor system resources
- Set alerts
- View dashboards with the main KPIs of system performance
- Administer multiple environments

There is detailed guide available about Operations Manager at `https://community.micr` `ostrategy.com/mxret26282/attachments/mxret26282/351/13236/1/OperationsM` `anager.pdf`.

Let's set up Operations Manager for our server. In order to run Operations Manager, we should:

1. Deploy WAR files on our web server
2. Set up Master Health Agent on this machine
3. Install JRE version 1.7+

In `Chapter 1`, *Getting Started with MicroStrategy* we deployed both WAR files for Operations Manager and Web. However, if we try to access Operations Manager now via its link, we get a message that we need JRE version 1.7 and higher. Let's check what Java version we have on the Linux machine:

```
# java -version
java version "1.6.0_38"
```

It's not the required Java version. Let's try to upgrade it:

```
# cd /opt/
# wget --no-cookies --no-check-certificate --header "Cookie:
gpw_e24=http%3A%2F%2Fwww.oracle.com%2F;
oraclelicense=accept-securebackup-cookie"
"http://download.oracle.com/otn-pub/java/jdk/8u77-b03/
jdk-8u77-linux-x64.tar.gz"
# tar xzf jdk-8u77-linux-x64.tar.gz
# cd /opt/jdk1.8.0_77/
# alternatives --install /usr/bin/java java /opt/jdk1.8.0_77/bin/java
# alternatives --config java
```

Choose a new version of Java:

```
# java -version
java version "1.8.0_77"
```

The next step is to restart Tomcat in order to use new Java.

Now, when we go to the link, we can see that Operations Manager is working. In order to create a new environment, we should install MicroStrategy Master Health Agent on the same machine where we have Tomcat. Let's do it:

```
# cd /mstr10/microstrategy_home/bin
# ./mstrcfgwiz
```

In the Configuration Wizard:

1. Choose **Health Center**.
2. Choose **Set up a Master Health Agent**.
3. Click **Configure daemon** and all others leave as default.
4. Create a Health Center Repository by creating System Access Code and specifying the `Repository` folder.
5. Finish the wizard steps by choosing the appropriate information.

As a result, we set up Master Health Agent. Now we can go to Operations Manager and create a new environment:

1. Go to `http://192.168.81.134:8080/MicroStrategyOM/servlet/mstrOM` from your Windows machine.
2. **Connect to Master Health Agent** using the port number and password that you used when you set up Master Health Agent:

Now we are using Master Health Agent for Intelligence Server and Operations Manager because we deployed Tomcat (MicroStrategy Web, Operations Manager) and Intelligence Server on one physical machine. However, in the production environment, we should split the web server from the MicroStrategy server. In this case, we should install Master Health Agent on the machine where we deploy Operations Manager and Health Agent on the machine where we deploy Intelligence Server. There is a very good explanation of how to do it in Linux or Windows at `https://community.microstrategy.com/t5/Server/TN`

```
32554-How-to-Configure-a-MicroStrategy-Health-Center-system/ta-p/18341
3.
```

1. The next stop is to create a new environment by adding Intelligence Server and web server information. Click on **Create Environment** and **Add**:
   - **Environment Name**: `MasteringBI`
   - **Intelligence Server Name**: `localhost.localdomain`
   - **Port**: `34952`

2. Click on **Test Connection** and enter `Administrator` as a login. Then add the web server information:
   - **Web Server Name**: `localhost.localdomain`
   - **Application Path**: `MicroStrategy`
   - **Port**: `8080`
   - **Server Type**: `JSP`

As a result, we add our environment to the Operations Manager. Now we are able to monitor performance and create alerts. Moreover, we can add other environments, for example, if we have a MicroStrategy cluster or just want to have one place for monitoring multiple environments such as Test, Development, and so on. In addition, we can connect Enterprise Manager to the Operations Manager.

Deploying Enterprise Manager and collecting statistics

MicroStrategy Enterprise Manager is just a project on top of MicroStrategy server that includes its own schema and lots of reports in order to monitor and analyze Intelligence Server statistics. Let's install Enterprise Manager:

1. We should create a new database for Enterprise Manager. Now we should choose Oracle. MicroStrategy Enterprise Manager doesn't support PostgreSQL. Let's create a new Oracle schema using SQL Developer:

```
CREATE USER MSTREM IDENTIFIED BY HAPPY2016 default tablespace USERS;
GRANT UNLIMITED TABLESPACE TO MSTREM;
GRANT ALL PRIVILEGES to MSTREM;
```

2. Now we need to reconfigure Intelligence Server by adding an Enterprise Manager repository based on the MSTREM database that we just created. Enter all the information that we entered in `Chapter 1`, *Getting Started with MicroStrategy* and during the statistics configuration step, we should create a new DSN for the Enterprise Manager repository:

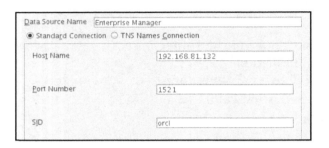

3. Then we should choose this **DSN** (**Enterprise Manager**) and mark all rectangles:

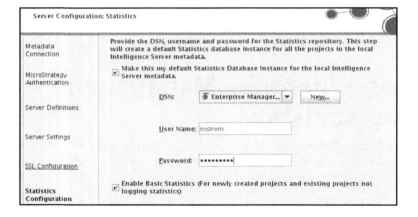

4. Click **Next** and Configuration Wizard will create tables in Oracle database. After this, we should click **Finish** and Configuration Wizard will do the rest of the work.

5. The next step is deploying the Enterpise Manager project via Configuration Wizard. Click **Create Enterprise Manager Project** and choose our DSN from the previous step. As a result, we can open MicroStrategy Developer and find a new project – Enterprise Manager.

We can go to SQL Developer after some time to see how it is going. For example, let's look at one of the tables with statistics:

```
SELECT * from
MSTREM.STG_IS_SESSION_STATS;
```

We should see data in this table. In MicroStrategy, we collect statistics in one table and then load them to another table. Running this script, we can see when MicroStrategy last loaded the data to the Enterprise Manager tables:

```
SELECT
max(is_win_end),max(is_proc_begin),max(is_proc_end)
FROM EM_IS_LAST_UPDATE;
```

This script didn't return us a new date for the data load.

Enterprise Manager is comprised of three major parts: Statistics, Enterprise Manager Warehouse, and the Enterprise Manager Project. Activity within MicroStrategy is logged into the Statistics tables (these tables typically end in _STATS; for example, IS_SESSION_STATS records user session data) by the Intelligence Server. A majority of the out-of-the-box reports available in the Enterprise Manager project are sourced from Enterprise Manager Warehouse tables (these tables typically end with _FACT). In order for the reports to reflect the current data, a data load needs to be performed to move the data from Statistics tables into the Enterprise Manager tables.

MicroStrategy provides best practices for configuring Enterprise Manager at https://com munity.microstrategy.com/t5/Server/TN273206-Best-practices-for-configur ation-of-MicroStrategy/ta-p/273206.

If the data load is not working, we should use MicroStrategy Command Manager in order to create a schedule for the load. Let's look at Command Manager and understand why it is important to use it. Command Manager gives us the opportunity of different admin tasks using script language or procedures such as:

- Modifying Intelligence Server and project settings
- Managing intelligent cubes
- Creating triggers for fire events and running schedule reports
- Managing security
- Managing administrative objects

There is detailed information about Command Manager available in the Administrator System Guide.

Let's create a script that will set up a data load to the Enterprise Manager project:

1. Open **Command Manager**.

2. Connect to Enterprise Manager using the following Command Manager outline:

   ```
   CONNECT TO ENTERPRISE MANAGER "LOCALHOST.LOCALDOMAIN" IN
   PORT 9999;
   ```

   > We should open port 9999 on Linux by modifying iptables as we did in Chapter 1, *Getting Started with MicroStrategy*.

3. Once you have connected to Enterprise Manager, you have to create an environment (this step only needs to be done once). You can accomplish this by using the following Command Manager outline:

   ```
   START MONITORING SERVER " LOCALHOST.LOCALDOMAIN" IN PORT34952 USING
   USERNAME "ADMINISTRATOR" PASSWORD "" FOR ENTERPRISEMANAGER
   "MSTR101.TEST.MICROSTRATEGY.COM" IN PORT 9999;
   ```

4. Once you have the environment configured, you can then use the following Command Manager outline to create a data load:

   ```
   CREATE DATA LOAD "DATALOAD" FOR ENVIRONMENT " LOCALHOST.LOCALDOMAIN"
   AND PROJECT "MASTERINGBI", ENVIRONMENT " LOCALHOST.LOCALDOMAIN» DO
   ACTION UPDATEWAREHOUSE CLOSESESSIONS UPDATEOBJECTDELETIONS BEGIN DATE
   "10/22/2015 22:00:00 +0000" TO "10/25/2025 22:00:00 +0000" FREQUENCY
   WEEKLY ON SATURDAY SUNDAY FROM 02:00:00 TO 06:00:00 EVERY 2 HOURS
   ENABLED IN ENTERPRISE MANAGER " LOCALHOST.LOCALDOMAIN" IN PORT 9999;
   ```

5. Once you have the data load created, please run the following Command Manager outline to ensure that the data load was created successfully. The output should display all the parameters for your data load:

   ```
   LIST ALL DATA LOADS IN ENTERPRISE MANAGER " LOCALHOST.LOCALDOMAIN"
   IN PORT 9999;
   ```

6. Once the data load has been verified, you can run the following command to trigger a manual data load:

   ```
   EXECUTE DATA LOAD "DATALOAD" IN ENTERPRISE MANAGER
   " LOCALHOST.LOCALDOMAIN" IN
   PORT 9999;
   ```

The following screenshot shows the Command Manager interface:

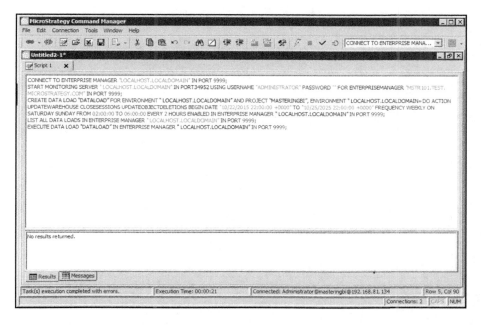

As a result, we will see data in Enterprise Manager tables as well as in Enterprise Manager reports. Moreover, we can connect Operations Manager to Enterprise Manager.

In order to start collecting statistics about the projects, we should set up a statistics database on Database Instance if there isn't one yet and set collection statistics for every project by going to the settings in MicroStrategy Developer:

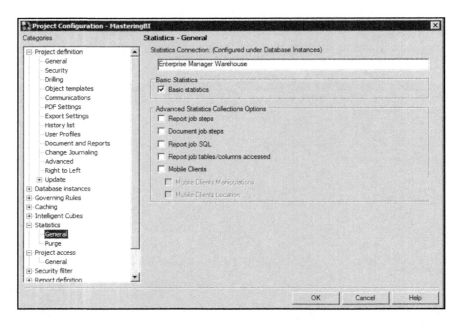

Before we go to another part of the chapter, it is good to learn one more use case of using Command Manager – creating procedures that will disable the schedules. Let's imagine that we copy metadata and run it on another machine. We will meet one issue – all schedules will continue to work and business users will get their reports twice. We can write procedures that will return us a list of schedules and update the start date:

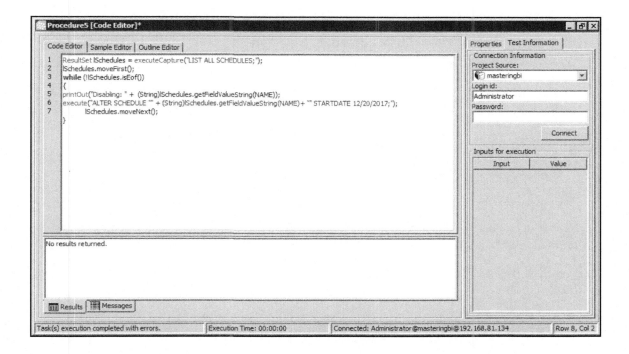

Project life cycle with Object Manager

Let's talk a little bit about usual BI projects. Usually, we use several environments, such as development, test, and production. It gives us flexibility and we can make sure that no one will destroy production. We can build new staff on development then test it on test and then promote to the production. In MicroStrategy, we should use Object Manager. Object Manager tracks the version ID of every object in MicroStrategy. Be aware that if you apply changes on both environments, then the version ID of objects will be different. That's why it is important to not make any changes on production, because it will be difficult to maintain consistency of the project across various environments.

Another feature of Object Manager is that it searches all dependents, such as schema objects, public objects, and so on. We can select from metadata tables all the information about relationships between objects:

```
SELECT * FROM DSSMDOBJDEPN;
```

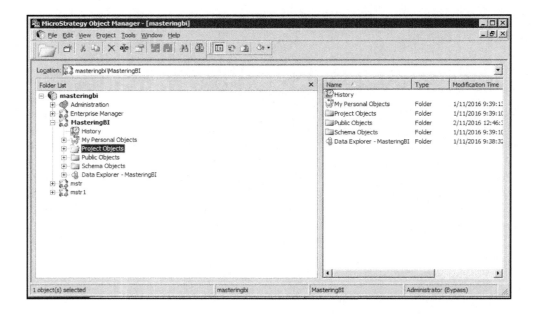

```
mstrmd=# select * from dssmdobjdepn limit 10;
          project_id          |          object_id           |          depn_prjid          |          depn_objid          | object_type | depnobj_type
------------------------------+------------------------------+------------------------------+------------------------------+-------------+-------------
 38A062302D4411D28E71006008960167 | C0CF1CCA4959D739BCCE07822A6FBB86 | 38A062302D4411D28E71006008960167 | 1033238C45C86FB79EFA40A977316969 |          31 |           30
 F2EF6A1C11E5B8DD00000080EF558B47 | 494A9B8B4886909EE25D64AB69DA7AA7 | F2EF6A1C11E5B8DD00000080EF558B47 | 45C11FA478E745FEA08D781CEA190FE5 |          12 |           21
 F2EF6A1C11E5B8DD00000080EF558B47 | 494A9B8B4886909EE25D64AB69DA7AA7 | F2EF6A1C11E5B8DD00000080EF558B47 | B41D0DE311E5BD8A07490080EF85C064 |          12 |           26
 F2EF6A1C11E5B8DD00000080EF558B47 | 494A9B8B4886909EE25D64AB69DA7AA7 | F2EF6A1C11E5B8DD00000080EF558B47 | AE32140E4AB7B148ABA2FC9CB03DAC70 |          12 |           15
 F2EF6A1C11E5B8DD00000080EF558B47 | E111581D4EED7E9E7C409298A6D9F5BC | F2EF6A1C11E5B8DD00000080EF558B47 | B41E1DAE11E5BD8A07580080EF85C064 |          12 |           26
 F2EF6A1C11E5B8DD00000080EF558B47 | E111581D4EED7E9E7C409298A6D9F5BC | F2EF6A1C11E5B8DD00000080EF558B47 | 9C3FA2054129B5738A9D99BB3392D594 |          12 |           15
 F2EF6A1C11E5B8DD00000080EF558B47 | E111581D4EED7E9E7C409298A6D9F5BC | F2EF6A1C11E5B8DD00000080EF558B47 | 45C11FA478E745FEA08D781CEA190FE5 |          12 |           21
 F2EF6A1C11E5B8DD00000080EF558B47 | 0F6661F04C763D1C6B54A8A366EBD1D3 | F2EF6A1C11E5B8DD00000080EF558B47 | 45C11FA478E745FEA08D781CEA190FE5 |          12 |           21
 F2EF6A1C11E5B8DD00000080EF558B47 | 0F6661F04C763D1C6B54A8A366EBD1D3 | F2EF6A1C11E5B8DD00000080EF558B47 | B41E0A6D11E5BD8A075B0080EF85C064 |          12 |           26
 F2EF6A1C11E5B8DD00000080EF558B47 | 0F6661F04C763D1C6B54A8A366EBD1D3 | F2EF6A1C11E5B8DD00000080EF558B47 | F56C3F584E5055FCC1BBC8A6230DE1E9 |          12 |           15
(10 rows)
```

There is a very good presentation about Object Migration Management at `http://www.sli deshare.net/BryanBrandow/world-2010-migration-process`.

Let's look at the interface of Object Manager by running it from the MicroStrategy Products folder:

There is red widget that allows us to compare projects in different environments and then promote only the changes. We have two options to promote changes:

- Directly to the project
- Via a package

Very often during direct migration, we can break something, for example, MicroStrategy schemas. Therefore, it is better to use packages. In cases where we use a package, we can always roll back.

Usually, Object Manager is used for migrating part of projects. However, if we need to migrate an entire project, we should use the Project Merge wizard.

Integrity Manager overview

Another useful MicroStrategy Product is Integrity Manager. Integrity Manager allows us to quickly compare reports or documents from two various environments and identify any issues. The following diagram demonstrates the workflow of Integrity Manager:

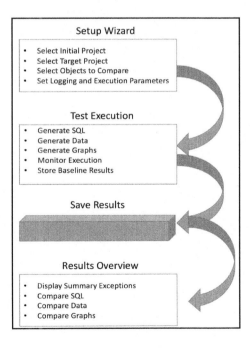

One of the most popular cases for Integrity Manager is to compare two projects after a MicroStrategy upgrade. We should have one project in an old environment and another one in a new. By comparing two projects, we can identify problems related to SQL generation, PDF creation, or any data issues. Moreover, using Integrity Manager, we can run lots of reports at the same time and look at the behavior of Intelligence Server using Operations Manager, for example.

System Manager overview

The role of MicroStrategy administrator isn't easy. There are lots of ongoing processes that should be monitored and if we have multiple environments with thousands of users then it becomes more challenging. MicroStrategy allows us to use System Manager that can atomize many processes. For example, we can build a workflow that will restart MicroStrategy Intelligence Server under specific circumstances and send us a notification. Another example is we can set thresholds and clean caches when needed. In other words, we can transform any manual process into a workflow using a user-friendly interface.

This is an example of a workflow:

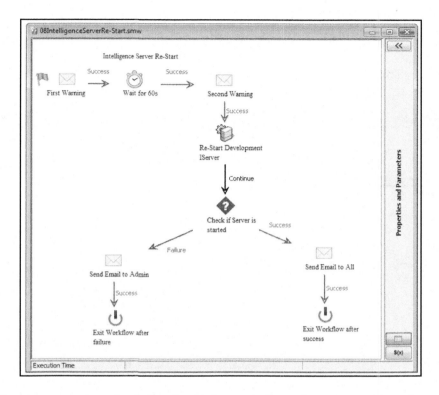

This workflow executes its schedule when it is needed or when it is triggered.

There is a good presentation about using System Manager at `https://www.microstrateg
y.com/Strategy/media/downloads/training-events/microstrategy-world/2014
-vegas/MSTRWorld2014_T2_S7_Automating-Your-BI-Administration.pdf`.

Activating Change Journal

Usually, MicroStrategy has complex environments. There are many people working and making changes. It is good practice to track all changes using Change Journal in order to detect irregular activity among MicroStrategy developers. It stores data in MicroStrategy metadata. Change Journal exists at the following levels:

- **Project**: Track modifications of applications and schema objects
- **Server**: Track modifications of configuration objects

Let's activate Change Journal for our MicroStrategy server and MasteringBI project:

1. Right-click on **Project Source** and choose **Configure MicroStrategy Intelligence Server**.

2. Go to **Statistics**:

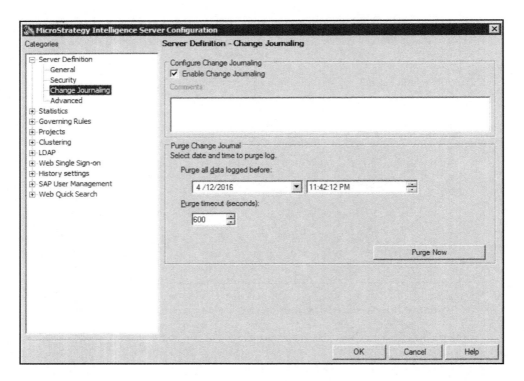

There is statistic collection enabled by default.

3. Right-click on MasteringBI project and choose **Project Configuration** and choose **Statistics**:

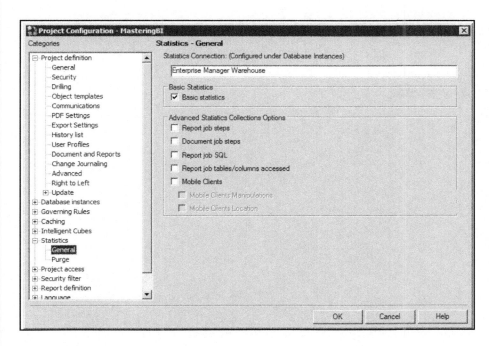

It is also enabled by default.

4. In order to see changes, we can click on **Properties** and choose **Change journal**:

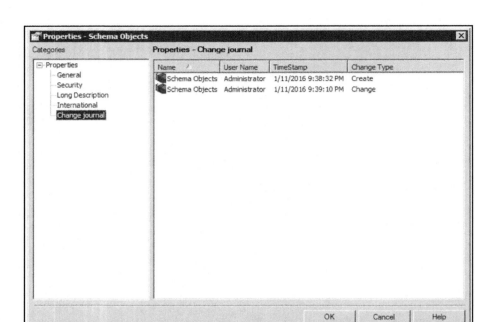

In addition, we can have a quick look at any change and learn more about it.

Summary

In this chapter, we learned about MicroStrategy administration and some of the most useful tools that can make the life of a MicroStrategy administrator much easier. We looked at Service Manager, set up Enterprise Manager, and initialized collection of statistics using Command Manager. We learnt about Object Manager as well as Operations Manager. In addition, we met System Manager and Change Journal.

In the next chapter, we will build security models using MicroStrategy best practices.

10
Design and Implementation of the Security Model

Usually, big companies choose enterprise BI solutions in order to meet all their requirements. One of the main requirements is providing security for thousands of users, because, usually, organizations have lots of various sensitive data, such as finance, marketing, inventory, and so on. For example, salary information is private information, and we should be sure that only HR people have access to this data. Another example is security rules based on geography. If a company has many branches, we should add security rules in order that every branch can see only their own information. Moreover, BI tools offer us rich functionality for creating, publishing, and sharing reports. We should be careful with types of access, because inexperienced users can change the dashboard, or even break it.

Despite the fact that there are plenty of BI tools on the market, they all use the same idea for building security models. In this chapter, we will learn about MicroStrategy security functionality and, using our example, will design and implement a security model.

This chapter will cover the following themes:

- Project source security
- Project level security
- Users and groups
- Privileges and security roles
- Object permissions and Access Control List
- Creating a security model

MicroStrategy security overview

MicroStrategy offers us a very powerful and flexible mechanism of security. It gives us the power to manage our environment on a very granular level. The complexity of security depends on business requirements and our fantasy, that is, we can design and implement any security model in order to meet business requirements and we can choose several ways to do it. Before we start to create our own security model, we should be familiar with the main terms of MicroStrategy security functionality.

MicroStrategy allows us several options to manage security at the project source level:

- Users
- Groups
- Privileges
- Security roles

The following diagram demonstrates an overview of MicroStrategy security functionality:

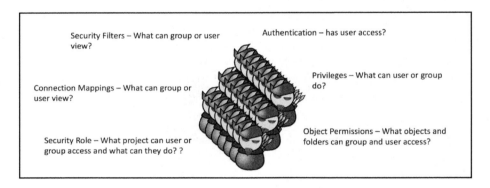

Let's look at security functionality more closely.

Users and groups

Usually, we create a username for every individual using their name and surname. We create a username and password. It is good practice to use one template of username. For example, if my name is Dmitry Anoshin, then my username is `danoshin`. Moreover, we can set up a connection with the LDAP server of the organization in order to import users from the LDAP directory. We can even import groups from LDAP and maintenance group and users in LDAP. Besides that, we can import users and groups from file or Windows.

In order to group users, we use groups. For example, we can create groups according to organization structure, and assign privileges and object access to many users at once. In other words, they make our life easier.

There are two main groups in MicroStrategy:

- **Everyone** – All users are members of this group
- **MicroStrategy Groups** – These are entry points for accessing the system

We can access and manage groups and users using **User Manager** by clicking on **Administration** under **Project Source**:

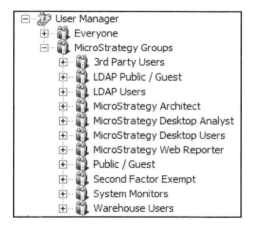

By default, MicroStrategy has only two users:

- Administrator
- Guest

We can create a new user by choosing any group and clicking **New** | **User**. We will do this later in the chapter, as well as creating new groups.

Privileges and security roles

MicroStrategy security roles serves us in order that we can grant to a user or group a set of privileges so that they can access reports, create schema objects, or administer MicroStrategy.

Let's look at security roles and privileges more closely by clicking the right-hand button on any group, for example, MicroStrategy Web Reporter, and choosing **Edit** | **Project Access**:

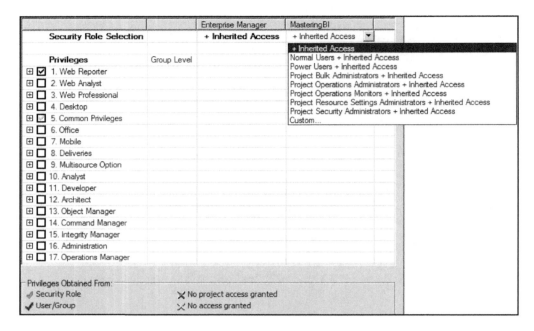

In this window, we can see what privileges members of the **Web Reporter** group have by expanding **Web Reporter**:

It is clear that users from this group have basic access through MicroStrategy Web. According to the legend, blue marks mean privileges obtained from the user/group and green marks mean they are obtained from security roles.

There are several predefinedsecurity roles available by default:

- **Normal Users** – This group doesn't have any privileges and is assigned to the **Everyone** group
- **Power User** – This group has many advanced privileges and is good for advanced developers or administrators
- **Project Administrator** – There are several administrator groups with specific privileges for various administration tasks

On the preceding screen, we saw that security roles use **Inherited Access**. Let's look at what this means:

- **+ Inherited Access** – Access according the security role that is assigned to the **Everyone** group. By default, it is **Normal Users**. Moreover, if a user belongs to a specific group, it will inherit its privileges as well.
- **Role + Inherited Access** – This means that we have the access of the security role assigned to the **Everyone** group and any other.
- **Custom Security Role** – We can modify security roles and create new ones.

Row-level security

MicroStrategy allows us to manage data access in the data source by **security filters** and **connection mappings**.

Security filters are filter objects that can restrict data access to a user or group by adding an additional condition in a WHERE statement. However, for Freeform reports, it doesn't work. In order to create a security filter and assign it on a project, we should right-click on **Group** or **User** | **Edit** | **Security Filter**.

We should choose the project name and click **View**. In order to create a new filter, we should click **New** and create a new filter definition using existing objects. We will do it later in this chapter:

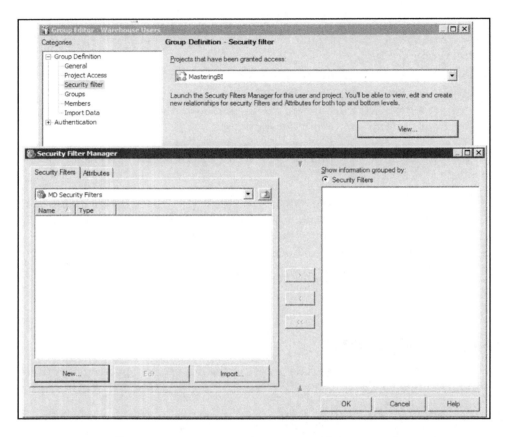

Connection mappings allow mapping users or groups with various data source connections. It gives **opportunity** to use an existing security model from the data source. For example, when a user has database access, we can use his username to connect him with the database through MicroStrategy. Let's look at the following workflow, where we have a group of normal users and one VIP user:

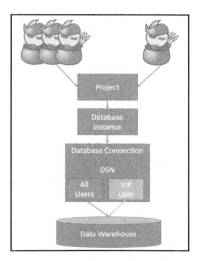

In order to assign a connection for a group or user, we should right-click on **Project Name** | **Project Configuration** | **Database Instances** | **Connection Mappings**. Moreover, we can use connection mapping to map different databases in one project.

MicroStrategy objects permission

We can define user access to folders and objects by managing permissions. Each object in MicroStrategy has an **Access Control List**, which specifies permissions that users or groups have on a specific object. There are several types of Access Control List permissions existing in MicroStrategy:

- **Browse** – See the folders
- **Read** – View the object definition
- **Write** – Modify the object definition
- **Delete** – Delete the object
- **Control** – Modify and take control of the object
- **Use** – Use the object
- **Execute** – Execute grids and documents

The following table demonstrates object access permissions:

	View	Modify	Full Control	Denied All	Default	Custom
Browse	Grant	Grant	Grant	Deny	Default	
Read	Grant	Grant	Grant	Deny	Default	
Write	Default	Grant	Grant	Deny	Default	
Delete	Default	Grant	Grant	Deny	Default	
Control	Default	Default	Grant	Deny	Default	
Use	Grant	Grant	Grant	Deny	Default	
Execute	Grant	Grant	Grant	Deny	Default	

In order to see the default permissions, we should right-click on **Folder** | **Properties** | **Security**. For example, here are the default permissions of the **Reports** folder (shared reports in Web):

User	Object	Children
Administrator	Full Control	Default
Everyone	Custom	View
Public / Guest	Custom	View

Custom means that users are granted browse and read permissions. In other words, all users who are part of the **Everyone** group can see objects in the `Reports` folder and execute them, but they cannot modify or delete them. Moreover, on the screen there are Access Control List of an object `Reports` folder:

- **User** – Which users or groups have access to the object
- **Object** – Object permissions for the user or group
- **Children** – Object permissions for the folders that belong to a parent folder

Security design

Usually, before starting doing anything hands-on, we should collect requirements from the whole organization in order to build a matrix of user access. Moreover, we should specify what kind of permissions are granted to particular groups and users. The easiest and most transparent way is to design security according to organizational structure, that is, each department has one folder with its name in shared folders. In addition, we can create a name folder under the department folder. We recommend denying delete access in order to save content.

Let's imagine that we have just started to implement BI and the first users come from the following departments:

- Business Intelligence
- Sales
- Product
- Finance

Let's create these folders in **Public Objects | Shared Folders**.

After several meetings from departments, we came up with the following matrix:

			BI	Sales		Product	Finance
				Order by Country	Sales by Country	Cost by Product Name	Revenue and Sales by Year
		Raw Level Access	N/A	Order by Country	Sales by Country	Cost by Product Name	Revenue and Sales by Year
Groups	BI		x	x	x	x	x
	Sales	Australia		x	x		
		Canada		x	x		
		US		x	x		
		Europe		x	x		
	Product					x	
	Finance						x

Apply Raw Acees

Raw Level Access means that we should show **Sales** metrics of their region only. In addition, we can define privileges for groups or users. Let's assume that BI users have access to MicroStrategy Developer only and all businesses have only web access.

Before we start, we should create the following simple reports in the department folders:

- Sales department
    - Orders by Country
        - **Attributes**: Country Region Name
        - **Metrics**: Internet Order Quantity, Reseller Order Quantity

- Sales by Country is free from SQL report with the following statement:

```
select  a12.COUNTRYREGIONname  COUNTRYREGIONCODE,
  a12.CITY  CITY,
  sum(a11.SALESAMOUNT)  WJXBFS1
from  EDW.FACTINTERNETSALES    a11
  join  EDW.DIMGEOGRAPHY  a12
    on  (a11.SALESTERRITORYKEY
=a12.SALESTERRITORYKEY)
group by  a12.COUNTRYREGIONCODE,
  a12.CITY
```

There is a screen of report definition:

- Product
    - Cost by Product Name
        - **Attributes**: Product Name
        - **Metrics**: Total Cost

- Finance
    - Revenue and Sales by Year
        - **Attributes**: Calendar Year
        - **Metrics**: Amount, Amount Revenue, Internet Profit, Internet Sales, Reseller Profit

When we finish creating all reports, we can start to manage security in order to satisfy user access requirements.

Security model deployment

We are ready to start building a security model. We have folders and reports. Moreover, we have a list of users. Let's create users:

1. Click on **Administration**
2. Click on **User Manager**
3. Choose **Everyone** and create new users:
    - bi_developer, bi_architect
    - sales_australia, sales_europe, sales_canada, sales_us
    - product_analyst
    - finance_analyst

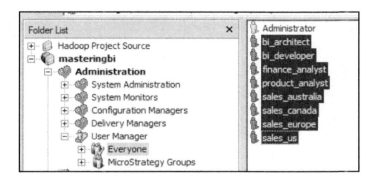

All new users belong to the **Everyone** group, in other words, they have the **Normal Users** security role. In other words, they haven't any access. If you want to try to connect using a new user, you will get this message:

> **The Web Server encountered an unknown runtime error.**
>
> (The following privilege is required to access the resource you requested: WebUser.Please contact the Microstrategy Intelligence Server Administrator to verify that the required privilege is granted.)

The next step is to create groups in order to divide users by their departments. Usually, we should start from groups and then we can create a new user inside of a group. Sometimes a user can belong to several groups. Let's create groups for business departments. According to user access requirements, we will create a Sales group under the MicroStrategy Web Reporter group and **Product** and **Finance** groups will be created under the **MicroStrategy Web Professional** group.

In order to understand what privileges have been granted to a particular group in MicroStrategy, we could click on group and choose **Edit** | **Project Access**. As a result, we will see a list of privileges. Let's create the groups and add users to them:

1. Go to **Administration** | **User Manager** | **MicroStrategy Groups** | **MicroStrategy Web Reporter** | **MicroStrategy Web Analyst** | **MicroStrategy Web Professional**.
2. Create new group **Finance** users and add member `finance_analyst`:

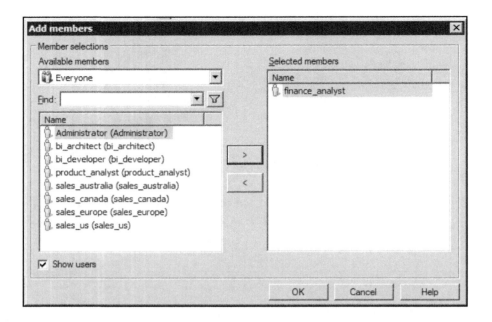

3. Create new group **Product** users and add member `product_analyst`.
4. Go to **Administration** | **User Manager** | **MicroStrategy Groups** | **MicroStrategy Web Reporter**.
5. Create new group **Sales** users.
6. Go to **Members** and add all **Sales** users.
7. Add `bi_architect` and `bi_developer` users to MicroStrategy Desktop Designers group in order to get access to Developer and Architect.

As a result, all our users have access to the MasteringBI and Enterprise Manager projects, all folders and reports. Moreover, BI users have access to MicroStrategy Developer and Architect. In order to finish security, we should change the security of objects, in order to show folders and reports according to user access recommendations as well as restrict data access to the sales team according to their geographical location. In addition, we should hide the Enterprise Manager project from business users.

All our users are members of the **Everyone** group, and as a result they have the **Normal Users** security role that allows them to see all projects.

In order to hide a project, we should right-click on the project name | **Project Configuration** | **Project Access** and delete everyone from **Selected members**:

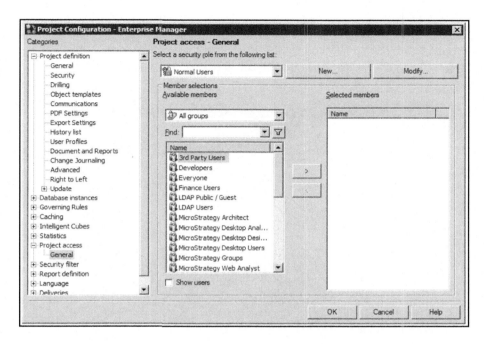

As a result, we hide the project from all users, even BI users. In order to return the Enterprise Manager project to BI users, we should create a new security role, for example, BI developers, and assign to it all privileges. As a result, we can choose our new role and select members – users or groups. Now we can check in MicroStrategy Web that business users can see only the MasteringBI project, and BI users can see the MasteringBI and Enterprise Manager projects.

The next step is to set up security for the object in order to make department folders visible only for their users. Only BI users are able to see all folders. Therefore, we will change security only for business users.

We have two strategies:

- Deny access to everything and grant access to specific folders
- Grant access to everything and deny access to specific folders

In our case, it is better to deny everything in the **Shared Reports** folder and then add access for a specific group to a specific folder. Let's update access on the **Shared Reports** folder in order to show it for BI users with content, and hide content from business users:

1. Go to project **MasteringBI** | **Public Objects**.
2. Right-click on **Reports** (shared reports in Web) and choose **Properties**.
3. Go to security in order to change the settings, as in the following screenshot:

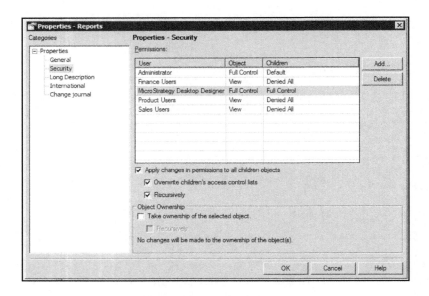

We deleted the **Everyone** group and **Guest**, but added groups with our users. For BI developers, we made **Full Control** access, and for business users, we chose **Denied All** in order to hide all folders and later to give access only to specific folders. Moreover, we applied changes to all children. We marked the sub options in order to apply changes for all objects in all folders. If we check the result of this change, we figure out that users can see folders but can't see reports. This isn't the desired result. However, we can quickly adjust it. For example, in order to leave the **Finance** folder for finance users we should perform the following steps:

1. Right-click on the folder and click **Properties**.
2. Choose **Security**.
3. Delete all business users groups except the **Finance** group.
4. Choose **View Permissions for Object and Children**.
5. Mark **Overwrite children's access control lists** and click **OK**.

6. Repeat these steps for **Products** and **Sales** folders respectively.

As a result, we provided the required security access to our MicroStrategy platform. This was one of the examples of how to build security using flexible security functionality. In addition, we should take into consideration that users should have view access on public objects such as filters, consolidations, and so on, as well as schema objects. The last thing that we should implement is raw security in order to separate access for sales managers according to their location.

Let's create security filters for our sales managers. We created one user per region, but it is better to create one subgroup per region in order to apply a security filter to this group.

Let's create a security filter for users `sales_canada`:

1. Go to the **Everyone** group and **Edit** user `sales_canada`.
2. Choose **Security Filter**.
3. Specify project **MasteringBI** and click **View**. As a result, **Security Filter Manager** will appear.
4. Click **New** in order to open **Security Filter**.
5. Create a new filter definition by using **Country Region Name** attribute equals `Canada` and save this filter. Moreover, it is possible to add multiple filters and build complex filters.
6. Click on > in order to apply this filter as shown in the following screenshot:

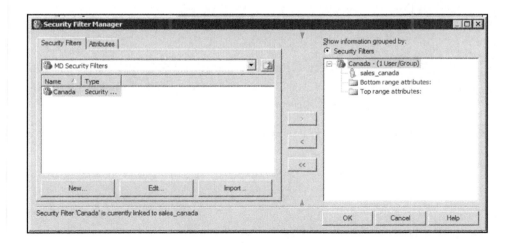

7. Repeat these steps for the rest of the finance users.

In order to check how a security filter works, we should log in as a `sales_canada` user and run an **Orders by Country** report:

If we are able to check the SQL definition, we will see an additional condition under WHERE.

Despite the fact that the security filter will be applied globally for all reports that will be run by this user, it has one exception – the **Freeform SQL (FFSQL)** report. In addition, the report should have attributes that are used in security filters. In the **Finance** folder we have one more report – **Sales by Country**, that is, a FFSQL report. Let's add a security filter to this report by modifying the SQL definition:

1. Edit the report Sales by Country.
2. Click **Data** | **Freeform SQL Definition**.
3. Add the following condition:

   WHERE a12.englishcountryregionname is not null

   We should add this condition because the security filter will be applied as an additional condition only for users who have this right. As a result, we can leave just the security filter, because if the security filter isn't applied, the report will return an error message.

4. Click **Edit** | **Insert Security Filter**. The **Security Filter Dialog** will appear.
5. Choose Country Region Name in **Object Browser** and click on it. Choose ID as the form and type as the following string:

   and a12.englishcountryregionname

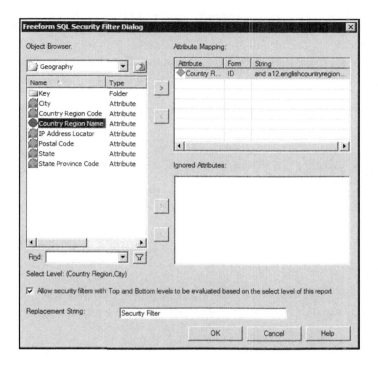

As a result, we will apply a security filter for the report:

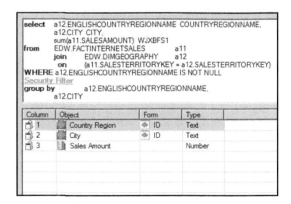

If we run the report in Web, we will get only **Canada** as a result.

Building an advanced security model

Sometimes we can get very sophisticated requirements about security and it will be impossible to create security using the default MicroStrategy security functionality. In this case, we can use MicroStrategy Object [User Login] – System Prompt. It returns a user login during the SQL generation of report. It gives us capabilities to hardcode security and build additional filters for the report. For example, this definition will filter country for the specific users:

```
ApplySimple("Case when #0 IN ('lsmith','bcassidy','nzhou','mdiploma') Then
'Canada' Else '%' End",? [User Login])
OR
ApplySimple("Case when #0 IN ('lsmith','bcassidy','nzhou','mdiploma') Then
'Australia' Else '%' End",? [User Login])
```

Another way to do it is to build a table in the data warehouse and set up all security and access there in order to join this table with the report using user login. In this case, it costs **Extract, Transform, and Load (ETL)** efforts.

The last option is the most powerful – use MicroStrategy Usher. There is a lot of information about Usher here: https://microstrategyhelp.atlassian.net/wiki/display/USHER/Installing+and+configuring+MicroStrategy+Usher.

Summary

In this chapter, we learned about MicroStrategy security functionality and we looked at security principles such as users, groups, permissions, security filters, and many others. In addition, we transformed the requirements of security in a working security model that is easy to maintain and scale. Moreover, we learned about security filters for FFSQL reports. Finally, we had a quick look at advanced security for MicroStrategy.

In the next chapter, we will learn about the integration of MicroStrategy and Hadoop. Moreover, we will talk about the value of big data on the market.

11
Big Data Analytics with MicroStrategy

Data with no analysis has no value, and similarly, for analysis we need data. Therefore, the two terms, data and analytics, go together and form big data, Business Intelligence analytics. There are several factors that drive **Business Intelligence (BI)**, and a few of these are:

- **Speed**: Every organization wants to eliminate delays in getting processed information such as reports and dashboards in order to make early and quick business decisions.
- **Intelligence data**: This means use of lots of data and information for predictive and proactive analysis. This data can be of different data types and from multiple sources.
- **Effectiveness**: This helps manage costs by increasing productivity for a business.

Big data is a solution to many of the BI needs. Hadoop has become synonymous with big data; it is an open source software framework for processing large amounts of data and for distributive storage across large clusters of computers. Therefore, we can say there are several big data capabilities that bring Hadoop closer to BI, such as the following:

- High retention of data
- Additional data sources, structured or unstructured
- Resilience to failure, that is, great fault tolerance
- Reduction of the data transfer between data sources

So, in this chapter we will cover the following topics:

- An overview of big data technologies
- Hadoop and Splunk architecture
- Connecting Hadoop and Splunk to MicroStrategy

Hadoop and MicroStrategy

First off, lets look at Hadoop.

Hadoop architecture

The Hadoop framework consists of two main layers:

- **Hadoop Distributed File System (HDFS)**
- **Execution engine (MapReduce)**

HDFS is a distributed file system that allows storage of a large volume of data across all the machines in a Hadoop cluster.

MapReduce is a programming model that is used to process the large volume of data that is stored in HDFS. It divides large tasks into smaller tasks and finally joins the smaller tasks together to provide a single result.

The following is the high-level architectural design of the Hadoop architecture:

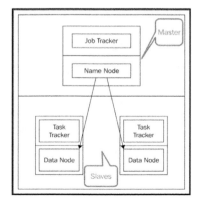

MicroStrategy Analytics Platform over Hadoop

The following diagram shows how MicroStrategy and Hadoop are tied together:

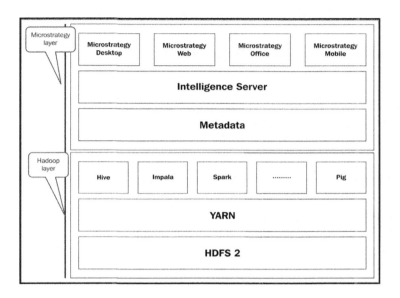

Hadoop and MicroStrategy use cases

MicroStrategy is an analytics tool that uses data from Hadoop to perform analysis. There are several use cases that are difficult to implement by using a data warehouse.

Sample use cases are as follows:

- Analysis of social media posts, pictures, videos, or information for customer retention, marketing, and so on
- Analysis of sensor data for pricing auto insurance or health insurance
- Analysis of web applications or mobile data logs from digital marketing for new product design and customer service
- Genomic, DNA sequence analysis based on data from multiple sequencing technologies

- Traffic analytics, that is, predictive congestion analysis and alternate route detection based on road segment geolocation data
- Weather analytics is a use case of big data that could even be used for pricing catastrophic insurance

Example of log file analysis in a Hadoop system

Here:

- **Log files** capture network or server operational data. In our example web server, logs are being collected and sent to HDFS.
- **Flume** streams logs into Hadoop.
- **HDFS**, as discussed previously, is a storage file system.
- **Pig** is a platform that parses these log files into a structured format using various user-defined functions.
- **Hive** defines schemata for this structured data, which is later stored in the Hive metastore.
- **MicroStrategy** is a visualization tool that provides connectivity to the Hive server.

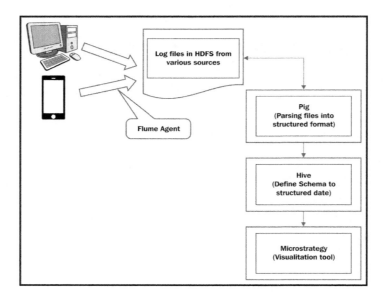

Configuring Hortonworks and MicroStrategy

Before we start the installation and integration of Hadoop with MicroStrategy, we need to set up a Hadoop environment. For this chapter we will be using our existing MicroStrategy environment and a virtual machine with a Hortonworks Hadoop distribution.

Steps:

1. Download a virtual box or VMware virtual machine from either of these links:
   - `https://www.virtualbox.org/wiki/Downloads`
   - `https://my.vmware.com/en/web/vmware/downloads`

2. Download the Hortonworks sandbox from the following URL:
   - `http://hortonworks.com/products/sandbox/`

3. Open the `.ovf` file with VMware by accepting the default settings and clicking **Import**:

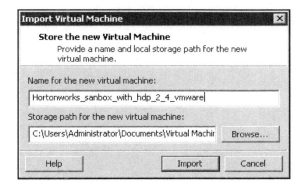

4. This will build up a Hortonworks VMware virtual machine

5. Before starting the Hortonworks appliance, change the network card settings by adding a new network card, as shown in the following screenshot:

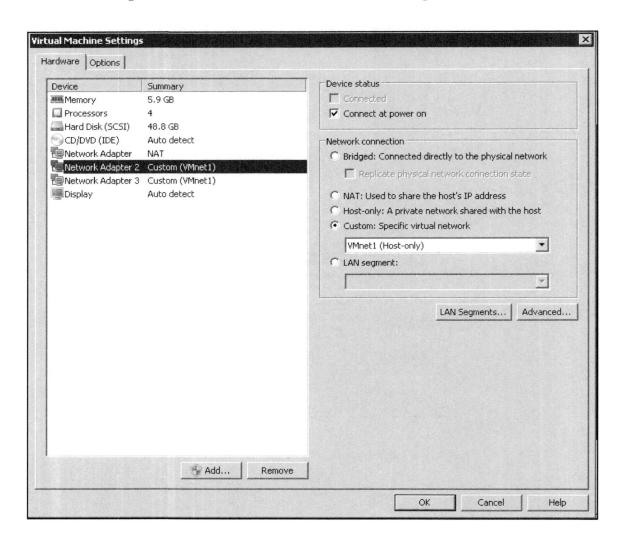

6. Now we need to add this virtual machine to the same domain as our MicroStrategy. For that, do the following:

    1. Click **Edit** | **Virtual Network Editor** | select the network card that was added in the previous step

    2. Click **DHCP Settings** on the following screen:

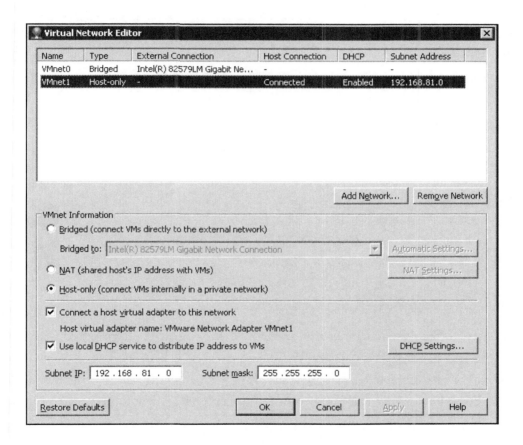

3. Enter the starting and ending network address based on the MicroStrategy machine's network address and click **OK**.

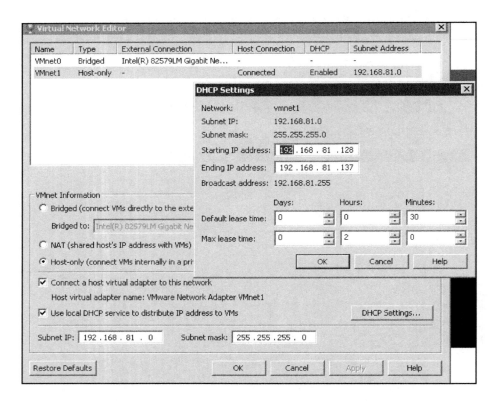

4. Start the machine; after some time, the user will be presented with a URL to access the web interface.

7. In our case, the URL is: `http://192.168.81.130:8080`

8. Enter the username and password on this screen. The default username and password is `maria_dev/maria_dev`

9. Upon entering the username and password, the sample screen looks like the following screenshot:

 Note: To validate whether the IP address has been changed successfully, open the terminal window by pressing *Alt + F5*, in the case of Linux. In the terminal type the `ifconfig` command. The result should include the IP address that we changed previously in the DHCP settings.

Connecting Hortonworks with MicroStrategy

There are two ways to connect Hortonworks to MicroStrategy:

- **Using an ODBC connector**, which is an application programming interface for accessing a Hadoop system.
- **Using a Native connector**, also known as a MicroStrategy Hadoop gateway, which is a data processing engine included in MicroStrategy 10. It natively taps into HDFS and generates the schema on read, allowing faster parallel data transfer from Hadoop:

For this book we will be using an ODBC connector. To read more about setting up via a Native connector, the user can refer to the following URL:

```
https://community.microstrategy.com/t5/Server/TN248914-Overview-and-ins
tallation-of-the-MicroStrategy-10/ta-p/248914
```

Setting up an ODBC connector

1. Open the MicroStrategy machine and download the 64-bit Hortonworks ODBC driver – Hortonworks ODBC Driver for Apache Hive (v2.1.2) – from the following link:

   ```
   http://hortonworks.com/downloads/#addons
   ```

2. Install the driver by double-clicking the download file.
3. Once it's installed, go to **Start** | **All program** | **Administrative tools** | **Data Sources (ODBC)** to open the ODBC data source administrator.
4. Click on **System DSN** and click on the **Add** button.

5. Select the Hortonworks Hive ODBC driver and enter DSN setup:

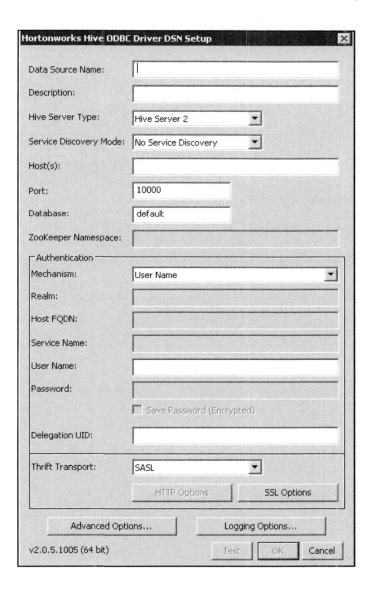

6. Fill the form with the following information:
   - **Data Source Name**: sample Hortonworks Hive DSN
   - **Host**: `192.168.81.129`
   - **Port**: `10000`
   - **Database**: `default`
   - **Mechanism**: `User Name`
   - **User Name**: `maria_dev`

Setting up a MicroStrategy environment

1. Open the MicroStrategy Desktop application.

2. Click on **File** | **Add data**.

3. Select **Hadoop** | **Hortonworks Hive** from the following screen:

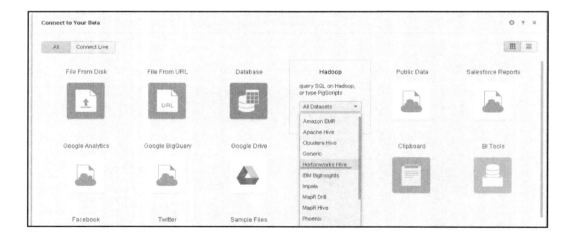

4. Select **Build a query** and then **Next**.
5. Click **Add** on the import from tables screen.
6. Select the data source. The user can either choose DSN-less data source or a DSN data source.
7. In our case we will select a DSN data source. Select the appropriate information and click **OK**.

8. Now, clicking on Hadoop under **DATA SOURCES** will populate all the tables available in Hive under **AVAILABLE TABLES**:

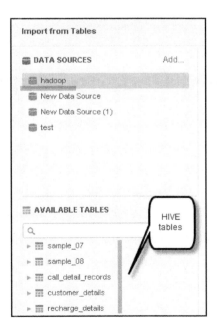

9. We can confirm this by checking the tables available in the Hive interface:

Design your first Hadoop dashboard

Download any sample big data files or extract logs from systems using Flume and so on. For the purpose of the book we will be downloading the dataset from the following URL:

```
http://www.seanlahman.com/?s=lahman591-csv.zip
```

Extract the ZIP file.

Upload the data file to HDFS by following these steps:

1. Navigate to the HDFS files directory from the Hortonworks web interface.

2. Navigate to /usr/maria_dev and click on the **Upload** button.

3. Click on the **Browse** button, navigate to the location where we extracted the downloaded ZIP file, and select the batting.csv file.

4. Now, open a Hive view by clicking on the **Hive View** button.

5. In this view, create a table to hold the data by executing the following command:

```
create table intermediate_batting (col_value STRING);
```

6. Upon execution of the query, we can view the intermediate_batting table under default databases.

7. Execute the following command to load the batting.csv data file into the intermediate_batting table:

```
Load data inpath '/user/maria_dev/Batting.csv' overwrite into table
intermediate_batting;
```

8. Create a table called batting using the following command:

```
create table batting (player_id STRING, year INT, runs INT);
```

Extract data from the intermediate_batting table to the batting table using the following commands:

```
insert overwrite table batting
SELECT
   regexp_extract(col_value, '^(?:([^,]*),?){1}', 1) player_id,
   regexp_extract(col_value, '^(?:([^,]*),?){2}', 1) year,
   regexp_extract(col_value, '^(?:([^,]*),?){9}', 1) run
from intermediate_batting;
```

Now, that we have the table in Hadoop we can start creating a MicroStrategy report based on this as:

1. Select the table from the list of available tables.
2. Double click on table selected and click **Finish** (this step also let user prepare their data).

This gives you two data access options, as follows:

- **Connect Live** allows users to select data directly from the data source
- **Import as an in-memory dataset** allows users to access data based on the stored results.

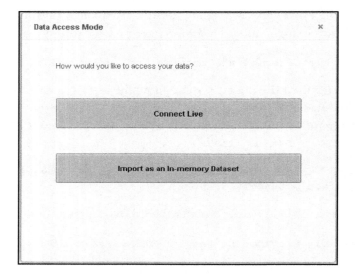

Select **Connect Live** and create a dashboard based on the data imported.

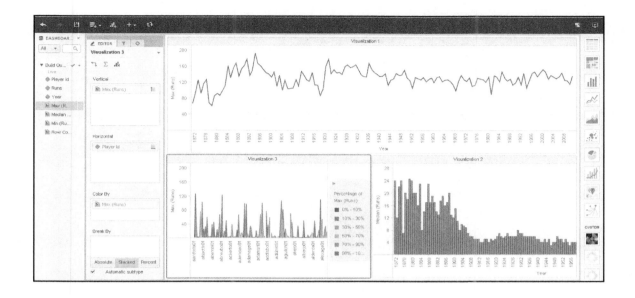

Data wrangling

With MicroStrategy 10, users have the ability to prepare data. In the previous section, when we were creating a dashboard using data from Hadoop, we were presented with the step of data preparation, or **data wrangling**, which allows business users to explore the data to improve its quality before it is imported to MicroStrategy. Example of data preparation include:

- Removing white spaces
- Concatenating columns
- Deleting cells with null values

The following screenshot presents data wrangling:

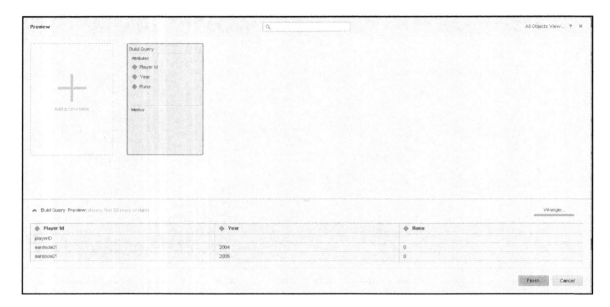

So, even if the user is exporting data from any source, they can still prepare it without ETL and data modeling.

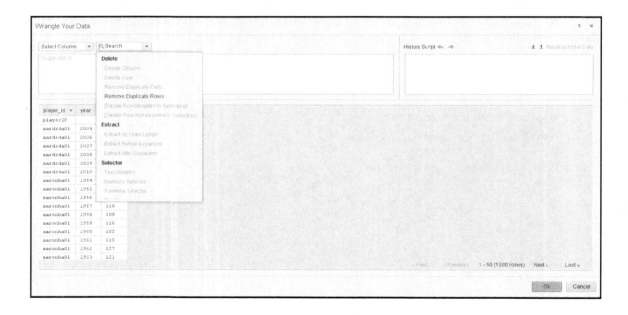

So, let's say we have data loaded from a source to store coordinates in one column, but we want to have two separate columns to store this data. We can do it using data wrangling.

The following screenshot shows data loaded from source:

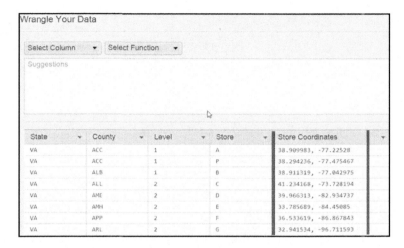

Use the data wrangle functionality to prepare data for reporting:

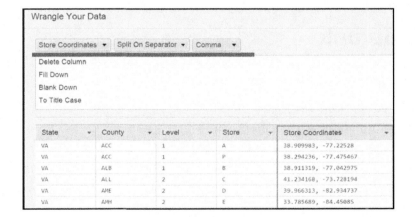

Output columns will be displayed as follows:

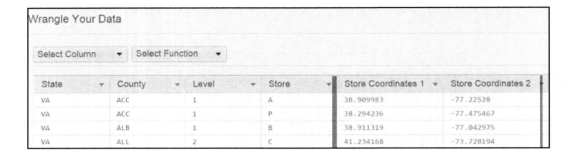

Splunk and MicroStrategy

MicroStrategy 10 has announced a new connection to Splunk. I suppose that Splunk is not very popular in the world of BI. Most people who have heard about Splunk think that it is just a platform for processing logs. This is both true and false. Splunk was derived from the world of spelunking, because searching for root causes in logs is a kind of spelunking without light, and Splunk solves this problem by indexing machine data from a tremendous number of data sources, starting from applications, hardware, sensors, and so on.

What is Splunk

Splunk's goal is making machine data accessible, usable, and valuable for everyone, and turning machine data into business value. It can:

- Collect data from anywhere
- Search and analyze everything
- Gain real-time Operational Intelligence

In the BI world, everyone knows what a **data warehouse** (**DWH**) is. The following screenshot compares the Splunk approach with the DWH approach:

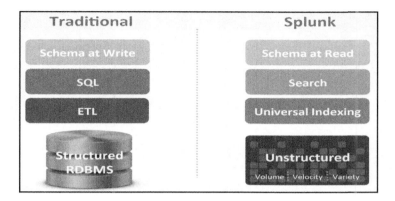

For Splunk, it doesn't matter what the format of the data is, because it creates schemas at read. For sure, Splunk is more suited for work with unstructured data. We can highlight the following use cases:

- Application delivery
- IT operations
- Security, compliance, and fraud
- Business analytics
- Digital intelligence
- Industrial data and Internet of Things

All these use cases have one thing in common – a large volume of unstructured data.

Splunk architecture

Splunkconsists of several elements:

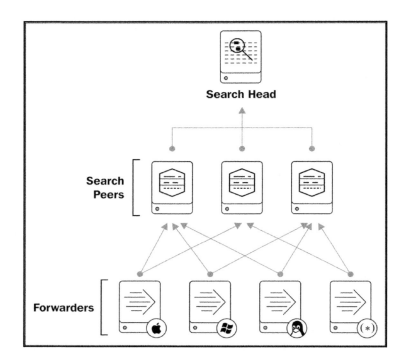

- **Search Head** – sends search requests to the indexer for processing and displaying results.
- **Search Peers** – instance of the indexer that performs indexing and searching. According to the Splunk documentation, one indexer can index 1700 GB per day. But in reality it is around 250 GB.
- **Forwarders** – remote instances of Splunk that can only send data to the indexers.

Splunk can be horizontally scaled in all layers. The core of Splunk is a MapReduce algorithm. There is a good document about it at the following URL:

```
https://www.splunk.com/web_assets/pdfs/secure/Splunk_and_MapReduce.pdf
```

Splunk and MicroStrategy use cases

Splunk complements traditional BI and DWH, as shown in the following diagram:

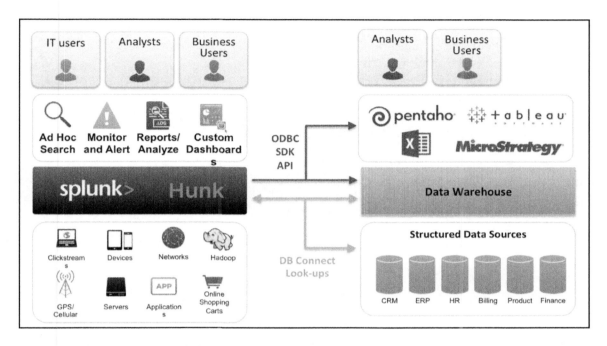

Usually, we use a DWH to analyse our transactional data from structured data sources, but there is lots of unstructured data that is valuable to us. Using Splunk, we can extract value from machine data and blend it with existing DWHs and business data. For example, we can run an online store. In the backend we have the order processing system that is fulfilling our DWH. We know lots about orders, prices, shipping, and so on. Using Splunk, in the same way we can see how our web servers, applications, and mobile apps are performing. And if we see a drop in sales or outages we can simply drill down to the data and find the root cause. It's called **Operation Intelligence**.

Deploying Splunk

Let's download and install Splunk in order to learn how we can use it as a data source for MicroStrategy:

1. Go to
   `https://www.splunk.com/en_us/download/splunk-enterprise.html`.

2. Download Splunk for Windows.

3. Install Splunk.

4. Go to `http://localhost:8000/`.

   Use the default credentials: `admin/changeme`.

5. Click on **Adding Data to the Splunk**.

6. We will analyze access combine logs. Unpack the archive for this chapter with 3 log files. In order to separate data we will create a new index by clicking on **Settings** | **Indexes** | **New**. Give a name to the index, for example, Web.

7. Now we should create new data inputs, in order to load data into the new index. Click on **Settings** | **Data Inputs** | **Files and Directories**. Choose the folder as a source.

Set Input Settings

As a result, Splunk ingested the data. One of the good things about Splunk that it compresses data up to 40-50%. It is very good for license usage.

After indexing data, we could start to search by clicking on **Search Data**. On the following screenshot there is a search window with a default query to our new dataset:

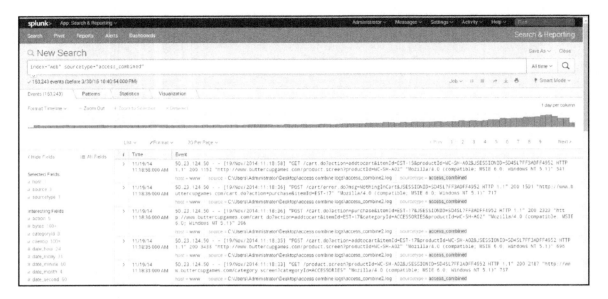

Splunk allows us to write queries using **Splunk search language**. It is a very powerful language. In addition, in Splunk we can build reports and dashboards. It is a kind of powerful analytics platform. Let's create reports in Splunk in order to use them as datasets (tables) in MicroStrategy:

We can create reports using SPL or we can just extract all fields:

```
index = "web" | table *
```

We prefer to build, report, and then add them as data sources to the dashboard:

- The most popular Internet browsers:

```
index = web | eval browser=useragent | replace *Firefox* with
Firefox,
*Chrome* with Chrome, *MSIE* with "Internet Explorer",
*Version*Safari*
with Safari, *Opera* with Opera in browser | top limit=5 useother=t
browser
```

- Purchases and views by product category:

```
index = web | chart count AS views,
count(eval(action="purchase")) AS
purchases by categoryId | rename views as "Views", purchases AS
"Purchases", categoryId AS "Category"
```

- Transaction duration

```
index = web action=purchase | transaction clientip maxspan=10m |
chart count by duration span=log2
```

When we create a report, it asks about security permission:

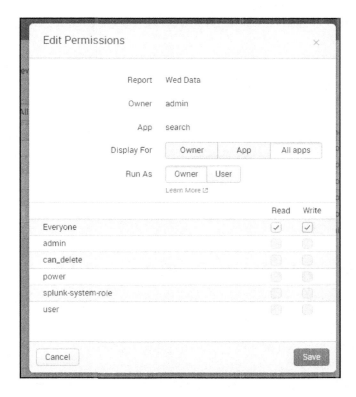

We should give permissions to everyone so that MicroStrategy doesn't have any problems connecting to Splunk.

Installing the Splunk ODBC driver

MicroStrategy uses the Splunk ODBC driver to connect Splunk. Let's download and install it:

1. Go to `https://splunkbase.splunk.com/app/1606/` and download the last version of the Splunk ODBC driver.
2. Install the `SplunkODBC64` driver. During installation, we can input data for the ODBC driver:

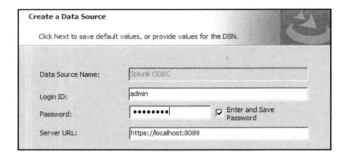

Creating reports from Splunk

Now we are ready to build reports using MicroStrategy Desktop and Splunk. Let's do it:

1. Go to MicroStrategy Desktop, click **Add Data**, and choose **Splunk**
2. Create a connection using the existing DNS based on Splunk ODBC:

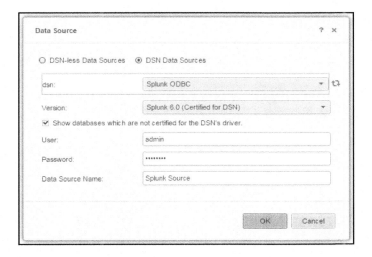

3. Choose one of the tables (Splunk reports):

4. Add other tables as new data sources.

Now we can build a dashboard using data from Splunk by dragging and dropping attributes and metrics:

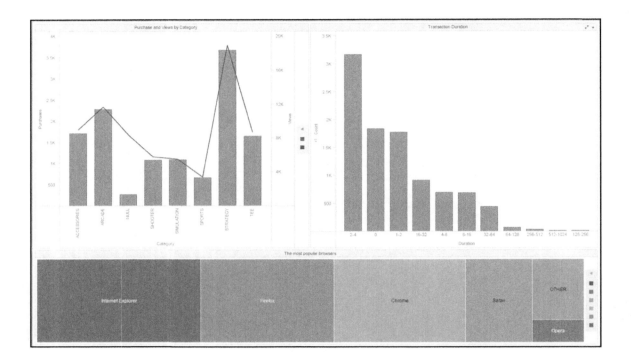

Summary

In this chapter, we learned about big data and its usage in analytics. We discussed Hadoop, Splunk, different architectures, and the integration of these tools with MicroStrategy. In the next chapter, we will be focusing on identifying and resolving the errors by analysing log files such as DSS log files. Apart from that, we will be covering different MicroStrategy tools such as diagnostic, performance logging, and health center tools, which help enable and disable traces for the purpose of troubleshooting and diagnosing problems.

12
MicroStrategy Troubleshooting

MicroStrategy is a complex product with many layers. There is a lot of space for errors and issues such as problems with performance, data, SQL generations, or even stable work of Intelligence Server.

Mastering BI is not only building reports and dashboards, and administering a BI platform, but it is also searching for solutions to any of the problems that any BI developer can meet. It is important to understand the various components of BI tools and know the different ways to troubleshoot. Sometimes, an issue can be outside BI tools. For example, in order to find the root cause of metrics, we should able to dive in to the **data warehouse (DWH)** and data integration.

MicroStrategy makes a tremendous effort to provide tools and logs for the fast identification of issues. In this chapter, we will discover different ways of troubleshooting MicroStrategy:

- MicroStrategy Community
- MicroStrategy Health Center
- MicroStrategy logs
- The MicroStrategy Diagnostics and Performance Logging tool
- Exploring problems with security and data discrepancy

Meeting the MicroStrategy Community

MicroStrategy offers their customers a big community that you can visit through this URL: `https://community.microstrategy.com/`. MicroStrategy developers share their experience, provide best practices, and troubleshoot issues around the world:

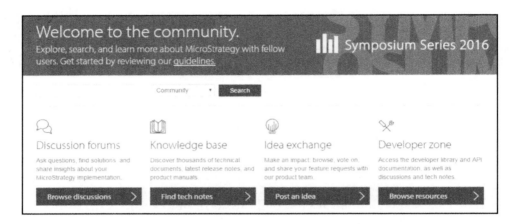

This is the best place to start searching for solutions to your MicroStrategy problem. For sure, Google is our best friend, but it will forward us to this page in 90% of cases.

Setting up MicroStrategy Health Center

One of the main troubleshooting tools is MicroStrategy Health Center. It exists in order to help identify and fix issues with the MicroStrategy platform. In addition, it can send e-mails to the system administrator.

We already created Master Health Agent in order to set up Operations Manager. In Configuration Manager, we have two options: to create a **Master Health Agent** (**MHA**) or a **Health Agent** (**HA**). An MHA serves as a hub and collects information from HAs across networks. In other words, we can deploy HAs on every MicroStrategy Client, Intelligence Server, web server and Mobile Server in order to collect information about MicroStrategy components and hardware.

Let's look at the Health Center interface.

Go to the Linux server and open the terminal:

```
# cd /mstr10/microstrategy_home/HealthCenterInstance/bin
# ./mstrsuppappgui
```

Enter the hostname, port, and password that was created in the Configuration Wizard:

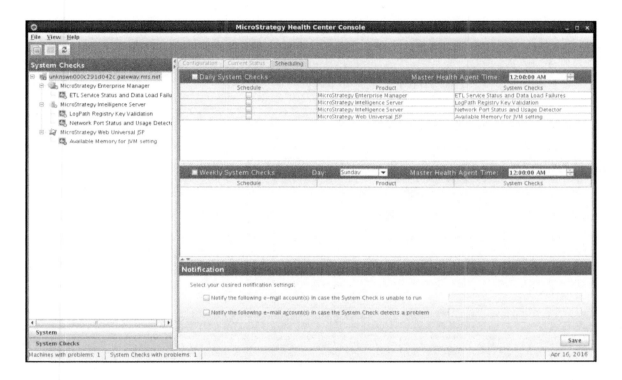

 You may notice that the name of the host has been changed. During the writing of the book, our VM with MicroStrategy crashed and we had to restore it from a VMware snapshot. It is very important to have backups of production MicroStrategy metadata as well as the operating system with the MicroStrategy Server installation.

We can build our topology by adding all the machines that are related to MicroStrategy implementation. There is detailed information about Health Center configuration on Linux at the following link: https://community.microstrategy.com/t5/Server/TN39868-How-to-configure-MicroStrategy-Health-Center-in-a-UNIX/ta-p/189920.

Discovering MicroStrategy logs

MicroStrategy components generate tons of logs about low-level activity such as memory use, service information, errors, and so on. One of the most valuable logs is `DSSErrors.log`. If MicroStrategy has any problems, it is good practice to start from this log and look at the information. You can find it using this command:

```
# cd /root/mstr10/microstrategy_logs
```

If we open the log file, we can see rows of data and search information about particular issues:

For example, let's imagine that the MicroStrategy server was shut down. In order to understand why it happened, we should open DSSErrors.log and look to see what the problem is. It will be in the last couple of rows.

How the DSSErrors file works

There are two files, as shown in the following screenshot:

The default size of DSSErrors.log is 2048 KB. When it becomes more than 2048 KB, MicroStrategy renames it DSSErrors.log.bak and creates a new DSSErrors.log file.

It is possible to change the destination of the DSSErrors.log file. Here are links that give a detailed overview of how to do it:

- https://community.microstrategy.com/t5/Server/TN13943-How-to-change-the-log-destination-for-the-DSSErrors-log/ta-p/174444
- https://community.microstrategy.com/t5/Architect/TN13940-How-to-change-the-log-destination-for-the-DSSErrors-log/ta-p/174442

Overview of the MicroStrategy Diagnostics and Performance Logging tool

In some cases, there is not enough existing functionality to troubleshoot the issue. In this case we should use the MicroStrategy **Diagnostics and Performance Logging (DAPL)** tool. It allows us to enable trace. Let's open the DAPL tool using the CLI:

```
# cd /mstr10/microstrategy_home/HealthCenterInstance/bin
# ./mstrdiag
```

As a result, we get the DAPL tool interface:

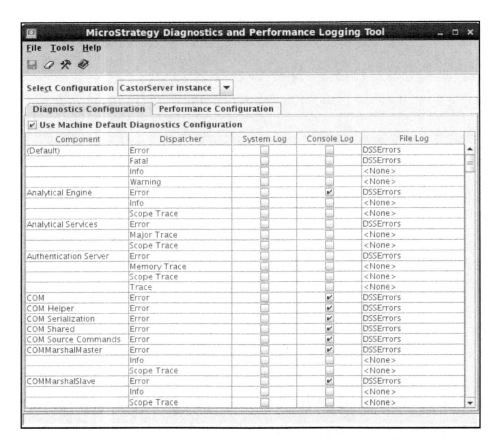

There is lots of information and settings here. Let's try to better understand what's going on.

First of all, there are two configurations available:

- **Diagnostics Configuration** – allows us to choose the diagnostics message we want to write in the log
- **Performance Configuration** – allows us to fine-tune performance logging

In the preceding screenshot, we have the **Diagnostics Configuration** tab. It has two available configurations:

- **CastorServer** – information related to server-specific features
- **Machine Default** – information related to the machine on which the current user is working

We never used **Machine Default**, that's why it is good to go with **CastorServer**. Three log destinations are available:

- **System log** – in Linux we can find the system log in `/var/log/messages` or `/var/adm/messages`.
- **Console log** – send the log to the default system debugging output. In Linux it is redirected to the `stderr` device.
- **File log** – we can set any filename and destination.

In addition, we should know the other components of the DAPL tool:

- **Component** – a MicroStrategy component that will write logs
- **Dispatcher** – level of system activity

Let's imagine that we have a problem with subscriptions. We want to trace the scheduler by creating a new log file. We should find **Distribution Service** and enable a **SchedulerTrace** by choosing **<New>** as the file log:

It is important to restart the Intelligence Server after any changes in the DAPL tool.

As a result, we will get a new **SchedulerTrace** log file with information about schedules.

Let's look at **Performance Configuration**:

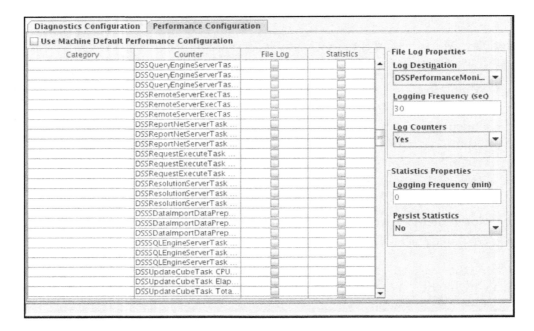

In terms of performance, we can measure different counters, such as how much time it takes for the CPU to run MicroStrategy functions or run reports.

Contacting MicroStrategy Support

Usually, organizations pay for MicroStrategy Support and it gives opportunity to submit cases to MicroStrategy and ask help from their support consultants. We try to use support quite often in order to save time and get detailed answers that can help fix issues and improve things. Moreover, it is a part of a learning curve. In order to submit a case, we should follow these steps:

1. Go to `https://resource.microstrategy.com/support/` and log in using your MicroStrategy account:

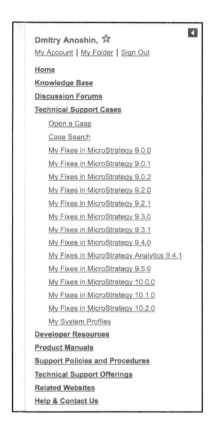

2. Click **Open a Case** and submit all information. It is very important to provide detailed information with screenshots and steps in order to give the full picture of your problem.

Exploring problems with security

One very common issue in MicroStrategy is problems with access. In Chapter 10, *Design and Implementation of the Security Model*, we learned about the security model of MicroStrategy. Sometimes, when we create a new schema object or public object, it can lack security. For example, the user could complain that they have problems with access. The best way to do it is to add a test user to the same groups as the complaining user and then try to add writes. We should read error messages; they can give us the direction to search for the problem and help us find out what we should update.

Discovering data discrepancy issues

One of the main purposes of BI is creating reporting for the decision-making process. But what if the report produces the wrong data? We should find the reason and fix it. In order to do this, the best way is to copy the SQL statement in the SQL client and start to troubleshoot it.

Using VLDB settings, we can change the behavior of SQL generation in order to better understand the flow of data and easily troubleshoot it. For example, we can use sub-queries instead of temporary tables, and so on.

In addition, it is important to have the right numbers in order to know what to expect from numbers.

For example, we have the following report:

Color	Sales Reason	Metrics	Reseller Order Quantity
Black	Demo Event		70,025
	Magazine Advertisement		70,025
	Manufacturer		70,025
	On Promotion		70,025
	Other		70,025
	Price		70,025
	Quality		70,025
	Review		70,025
	Sponsorship		70,025
	Television Advertisement		70,025
Blue	Demo Event		19,689
	Magazine Advertisement		19,689
	Manufacturer		19,689
	On Promotion		19,689
	Other		19,689
	Price		19,689
	Quality		19,689
	Review		19,689
	Sponsorship		19,689
	Television Advertisement		19,689

It is obvious that Order Quantity isn't aggregated. In order to understand why, we should look at SQL:

```
select        a12.SALESREASONNAME   SALESREASONNAME,
       a13.COLOR   COLOR,
       sum(a11.ORDERQUANTITY)   WJXBFS1
from   EDW.FACTRESELLERSALES    a11
       cross join   EDW.DIMSALESREASON       a12
       join   EDW.DIMPRODUCT      a13
         on   (a11.PRODUCTKEY = a13.PRODUCTKEY)
group by     a12.SALESREASONNAME,
       a13.COLOR
```

Now it is clear. Report produce cross join. We can ask the DWH architect or look at the data model in order to fix the MicroStrategy schema.

It was a simple case, but we can get a number that will be only 1-2% different from the real value. In this case, it isn't enough just look at SQL; we should go deeper and research all transformations in the DWH and ETL. Sometimes, the problem can even be in the source files.

Summary

In this chapter, we looked at the process of MicroStrategy troubleshooting using existing functionality and tools such as Health Center and the DAPL tool. Moreover, we looked at DSSErrors.log and learned how we can trace low-level system activity. Finally, we looked at some issues that can be faced while working with the BI tool.

Index

Printed in Great Britain
by Amazon

82672098R00228